TURNER FAMILY STORIES

FROM ENSLAVEMENT IN VIRGINIA TO FREEDOM IN VERMONT

Comics by Marek Bennett,
Francis Bordeleau, Joel Christian Gill,
Lillie Harris, & Ezra Veitch

Edited by Jane C. Beck
and Andy Kolovos

Cover art by Robyn Smith

 Vermont Folklife Center

Turner Family Stories: From Enslavement in Virginia to Freedom in Vermont

Edited by Jane Beck and Andy Kolovos

Vermont Folklife Center
88 Main Street
Middlebury, VT 05753
www.vermontfolklifecenter.org

Foreword "A Day with Daisy Turner" © 2021 Gretchen Holbrook Gerzina
Preface © 2021 Jane C. Beck
Introduction "Turner Family Stories: Laboring for Freedom" © 2021 Julian Chambliss
"Grafton, Vermont 1985" © 2021 Ezra Veitch
"The Adventures of Alec Turner" © 2021 Marek Bennett
"Alec Turner: Strongest Man in Town" © 2021 Joel Christian Gill
"Daisy's Premonition" © 2021 Lillie Harris
"I Am Vindicated" © 2021 Francis Bordeleau

Book design by Eureka! Comics

Publication of this book supported by grants from the National Endowment for the Arts, the Vermont Arts Council and the Windham Foundation.

ISBN: 978-0-916718-01-5 pbk.
LCCN: 2021938304

Contents

FOREWORD
A DAY WITH DAISY TURNER

Gretchen Holbrook Gerzina

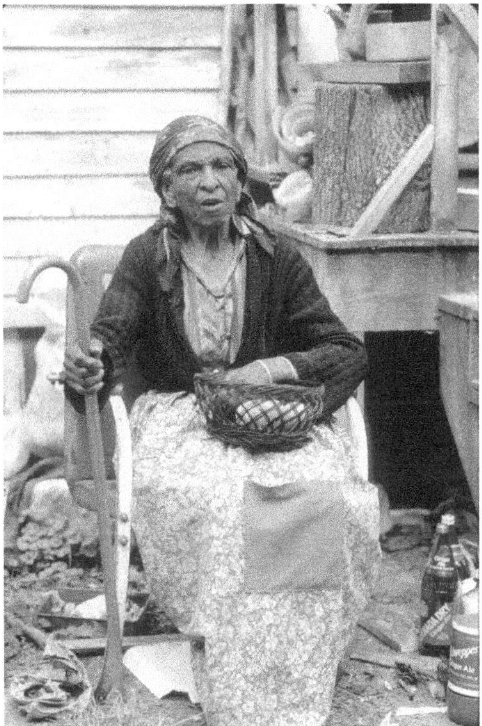

In late spring or early summer of 1970, my Marlboro College friend Albie Holland and I were taken by our professor, Val Chambers, to Grafton, Vermont to visit Daisy Turner and her sister. We'd never heard of the Turners, and were initially skeptical about the purpose of the visit. It turned out to be an extraordinary afternoon.

Decades later I would move back to southern Vermont and write the book *Mr. and Mrs. Prince*, about two formerly enslaved people who settled in my town, Guilford, Vermont, in the 1770s. The Princes entered the history books with their extraordinary and unrelenting fight to preserve their property and family against those who did not want them there. They had supporters—and the law—behind them, but it wasn't easy. Abijah Prince, a veteran of the French and Indian Wars, used the law to engineer his freedom and to take to court those who short-changed him or abused their children. Lucy Terry Prince was a poet who could recite from the Bible. Like Daisy Turner, Lucy was a storyteller.

Two hundred years separated Lucy and Daisy, but there is something remarkable about these two determined, resilient African American women, both captivating speakers, each with her own important story, each from an enslaved family that originated elsewhere, and eventually made their way to New England. Their stories change the way that we need to think about American history and race in general, but also about New England and Vermont in particular.

The first thing that Daisy told us, after we were introduced, was that she needed us to go to the nearby store to pick up something for lunch (I remember hot dogs being on the list). Before Albie and I headed out, Daisy had a warning: "They don't like us in the store," she said. "They don't want us here." And it was true; we paid under the suspicious and distinctly unfriendly eye of the owner and didn't linger.

That afternoon many of the stories you're about to read unfolded. Daisy's sister, Zebbie, was mostly silent, standing tall and nodding from time to time, a photograph of her younger self standing with a long rifle, in view behind her. "All of my sisters but her married local white men," Daisy said. "Our family was here before most people now in this town. We helped make this place, and our parents had us understand that it was ours. Our father built our house. We went to school and had friends and stayed." She showed us photographs and was herself a living history that I'd never imagined.

During her long life, Daisy made sure that everyone understood that the Turners not only belonged there, but unlike many contemporary Grafton families, had been there first. Jane Beck and the Vermont Folklife Center are keeping this extraordinary history alive. It is a story that needs to be retold and passed on.

Gretchen Holbrook Gerzina, the author of *Mr. and Mrs. Prince: How an Extraordinary Eighteenth-Century Family Moved Out of Slavery and into Legend*, is the Paul Murray Kendall Chair in Biography and Professor of English at the University of Massachusetts, Amherst.

PREFACE

Jane C. Beck

It was Margaret MacArthur, song collector, singer and fine musician who first suggested I visit Daisy Turner, daughter of a formerly enslaved couple who had settled in Grafton, Vermont. Margaret had heard she was a fine storyteller and singer. I was intrigued and wanted to meet her. I tried finding someone who might introduce me to her, but quickly discovered a real reluctance to do so. Daisy Turner was reputedly suspicious, cantankerous, and owned a shotgun she was not afraid to use. As a result, I decided it was best to write her a letter explaining why I was interested in talking with her. I would follow up with a phone call.

I was nervous as I first dialed her number, afraid she would turn me down. I knew she was 100 and realized she might be in poor health. The phone rang and rang, but nobody answered. I hung up, worried and discouraged, hoping the next day would bring better results. This time after three rings, I was greeted by a reverberating "Hello!" Could this be a one hundred year old woman? "Miss Turner?" "Yes!" I started in on my desire to meet her. She listened for a few seconds, and then taking charge, boomed over the phone, "Are you a prejudiced woman?" Startled, I stammered out, "I don't think so." "Well, come any time." "How 'bout next Wednesday?" I was thrilled as we agreed on our meeting.

I drove down to Grafton on a warm September day, and as I pulled into Daisy's yard I heard raised voices shouting at one another. A man stood a short distance away, while an elderly woman sat on her steps. The argument was fierce, and I found myself thinking I should leave. Just then the man raised his fist, jumped into his car, slammed the door and took off. Now what? What an inopportune time to meet someone.

I took a deep breath and walked over and introduced myself. It was a rocky beginning. I tried to explain my interest in meeting her. She thought I was a writer and told me I should write about her court cases. I tried to explain that rather than a writer, I was someone who recorded Vermonters' life experiences in their own words, stories that might otherwise not be heard. Would she be willing to tell me a little about her life. I had heard she had an interesting story to tell. As the focus turned to Daisy and her family, she quieted, abandoning her tirades as she settled into storytelling mode. For well over two hours I was held spellbound, not quite grasping the scope of what she was relating. She was in Africa, New Orleans, to a Virginia plantation where her grandfather and father were enslaved, there was the Civil War. She was in the moment and drew me in, her rich timbered voice rising and falling as she poured out her stories, performing them, her cane and hands mimicking a task, her face pantomiming a reaction. What was she telling me? Could this have any basis in fact? I tried to take notes as she mentioned place names, events, Civil War battles, attempting to get my bearings. She wouldn't allow me to record her, but I knew I had to return. And return I did, almost weekly over a two year period, and then a bit more sporadically until her death in 1988.

As the weeks turned into months, trust and a warm friendship grew between us. She asked me to call her Aunt Daisy, and allowed me to record her, even to video tape her. I was also subject to her tirades when our conversation edged toward certain subjects. I realized these were anchored in what she experienced as deep injustices: her father's inability to obtain a Civil War pension, and land disputes over Turner property. Any discussion of these usually ended in her becoming angry and working herself into such a state that her heart began to pound and I found it imperative to change the subject.

As I listened to her stories I was astounded by the scope of her family saga, spanning two centuries and four generations. I knew of no other family story that described the journey so completely, from the coast of what today is Benin and Nigeria, through two generations of enslavement on a Virginian plantation, to escape, the Civil War and eventual settlement on a Vermont hill farm. I began to try to document various parts of her narrative, recognizing that memory could be notoriously unreliable, and was astounded by how many elements of the Turner family story could be confirmed.

Daisy adored her father Alec; for forty years she had listened to his stories. Every night after dinner he would sit down and tell his children about incidents from his life. Daisy learned these word for word. Both her father and grandfather were brought up in the tradition of the West African griot, the keeper of a community's history, its significant stories, and ritual songs. Following in her father's footsteps, Daisy became the griot for her generation. Her narrative was made up of a series of touchstone stories: pivotal events and defining moments of her great grandmother, her grandfather, her father and herself. Abraham Lincoln was beloved by Alec, and he often shared that he had "heard the hooves of Booth's horse" as he rode away from the dastardly event of Lincoln's assassination. Alec became known as the strongest man in Grafton by carrying a barrel of flour up Turner Hill. Daisy believed she had psychic abilities, and she told me many times that Joseph Boinay was the only man she had really loved. These are only a few of the touchstone stories included in her narrative, a well-polished heirloom she believed it was essential to preserve. Thanks to her storytelling gifts, she has.

Now, thanks to these six talented cartoonists, touchstones of that narrative are retold in a visual medium that welcomes new "listeners" to be held in the storyteller's spell.

Folklorist **Jane Beck** founded the Vermont Folklife Center in 1983, the same year she began interviewing Daisy Turner. She is author of *Daisy Turner's Kin: An African American Family Saga* and is Founding Director of the Folklife Center's Board of Trustees.

INTRODUCTION
TURNER FAMILY STORIES: LABORING FOR FREEDOM

Julian Chambliss

The history of graphic narratives in the United States offers a window on the challenge of race and national experience. From the beginning, comics have been a space where Black people have been subjects of a white gaze, fitting into a visual landscape defined by white fears and anxieties about Blackness. In the modern era, contemporary comic culture in the United States has broadened, reflecting the social evolution around race and Black comic creators' impact. Turner Family Stories reflect this complex history and the role comics can play in our civic culture today.

This may seem a bold statement, but the long history of race in the United States and the place of comics in that story looms large in this volume. As Ian Gordon explained in Comic Strips and Consumer Culture, 1890-1945 comics were a "humor-based response to the problems of representation" in a rapidly changing 19th-century United States.[1]

The caricatures in early comics were rooted in racial anxiety, often linked to politics and social policy. Creators such as Richard F. Outcault made a fortune capitalizing on an emerging consumer culture that used stereotypes to entertain white readers.[2]

1 Ian Gordon, Comic Strips and Consumer Culture, 1890-1945 (Smithsonian Institution Press, 2002), 6.

2 Alan Havig, "Richard F. Outcault's "Poor Lil' Mose": Variations on the Black Stereotype in American Comic Art," Journal of American Culture 11, no. 1 (1988): 33, https://doi.org/10.1111/j.1542-734X.1988.1101_33.x.

Early cartoonists took racist assumptions about Black people rooted in slavery and normalized them as Jim Crow segregation stripped away the promise of citizenship offered by Reconstruction. Based on the antebellum minstrel image we can trace back to the 18th century, the comic image of Black people crafted after the Reconstruction became a cornerstone of consumer culture. The Black Sambo's public appeal rested on the affirmation found in seeing Blacks as foolish and ignorant, further justifying white supremacy. The Sambo thrived in popular consumer culture well into the 20th century. In the wake of George Floyd's death and Black Lives Matter protests in the summer of 2020, Quaker Foods finally acted to abandon the Aunt Jemima logo, admitting it was based "on a racial stereotype."[3]

POOR LIL' MOSE AND HIS HATCHET
POOR LIL MOSE
Geo. Washington's ole daddy was different fum my pa,
I reckon dad's de strangest man yo' mostly ever saw
When George went out an tuck his axe an smashed de cherry tree;
You knows de story, all by heart, I reckon, well as me.
I tried it on my daddy in a nuther kin' ob way,
Ef I lives ter be a hundred yeahs, I wont fergit dat day.
My pa had got a lot ob wood, for work, fum Cunnel Small,
An he dumped it by de wood shed, but it was n't cut at all.
So I tuck my saw an hatchet - an ter show wot I cud do,
I started in on dat yar wood an cut a cord er two.
I piled it all up nice an neat, it tuck me mos' all day,
An waited roun' fer daddy, jes' ter see wot he 'ud say.
Nex' mawnin daddy called me out, an says, look heah, Mose Pryor,
Doan say yo' did n't cut dat wood, yo' knows yo' is a —
An I says yas deah father, I kin-not tell a lie,
I done it wif my hatchet, an I looked him in de eye.
I'll never tell de truth agin, cause I knows better now,
I never b'lieved dat foolish hatchet story any how.
Pa grabbed me by de collar an he used me mighty rough,
An he handed me a spankin' wich wus certain'y enough
He said dat choppin' fire wood wus his mos' favorite fad.
Now wot wud Washington have done ef he'd had sich a dad?
R. F. Outcault
YES FATHER I CANNOT TELL A LIE
HOW DARE YOU HIT DAT CHILE
I WANTED TO CUT DAT WOOD MYSELF

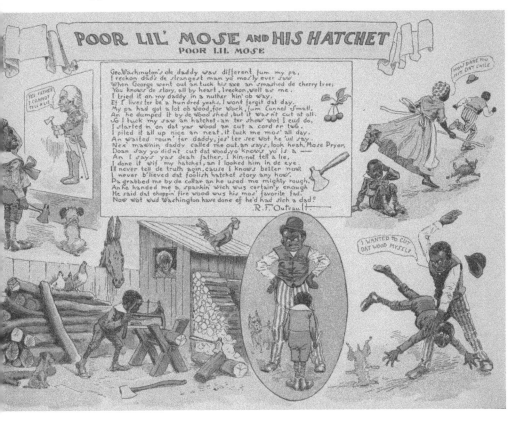

Comic cartoons from the New York Herald of 1901-02

3 Adam Gabbatt, "Aunt Jemima Brand to Change Name and Logo Due to Racial Stereotyping," The Guardian, June 17, 2020, http://www.theguardian.com/us-news/2020/jun/17/aunt-jemima-products-change-name-image-racial-stereotype.

The contested nature of the Black image in comic and consumer culture makes those instances of an authentic and historically grounded narrative of the Black experience crucially important. The rise of the civil rights movement made the comics strips in African American newspapers one of the first opportunities for Black America to see their history and worldview in comic form. Newspapers, including the Amsterdam News, Pittsburgh Courier, and Chicago Defender, published work such as Ollie Harrington's Dark Laughter comic strip, which offered cutting political commentary about race in America. Tom Feelings' Tommy Traveler in the World of Black History offered readers history of Black accomplishment ignored by the white culture. Both comics are examples of robust post-World War II Black culture seeking economic and social opportunity and pushing back against racist action and imagery in popular culture. Boycotts and protests were the tools for much of this activism, but the widespread appeal of comic books in this era prompted white publishers to offer some progressive depictions.

As expectation and activism around civil rights expanded, major comic book publishers used real-life African American lives as the basis for comic stories. Fawcett Comics produced a Joe Louis comic in 1950 and six issues of a Jackie Robinson comic between 1949 and 1952. Robinson's efforts to desegregate baseball and Louis' success as the heavyweight champion who defeated Max Schmeling, and by extension the myth of Aryan superiority at the heart of Nazi Germany, made these easy figures for white America to celebrate. Perhaps the most consequential non-fiction comic of this period was Martin Luther King and the Montgomery Story, written by Alfred Hassler and Benton Resnik and illustrated by Sy Barry and published by the Fellowship of Reconciliation to spotlight King's civil rights activism. Widely read within the Black community, the publication provided countless Black Americans an understanding of King's philosophy. Today, a new generation knows of this publication because the late Representative John Lewis, himself inspired by this comic, created his own award-winning autobiographical graphic novel series called March (2013-2016).[4] The success of that series highlights a contemporary comic culture that has evolved. Today

4 Vann R. Newkirk II, "What John Lewis Knows About the Cycle of Racism in the United States," The Atlantic, July 21, 2016, https://www.theatlantic.com/politics/archive/2016/07/john-lewis-march-book-three-politics/492191/

we have a greater variety of content dealing with questions of culture and identity than ever before, and more Black creators can tell stories of everyday Black life.

The volume you hold is less an oddity and more of a promise long linked to comics and race. Originating with the memory and legacies of Daisy Turner's family, this collection of graphic stories captures the substance of Black history from a crucial period of the American experience. Turner's stories give us a snapshot of the post-Reconstruction United States. The challenges Black Americans faced and the contributions they made have been deliberately obscured and erased by white supremacy. In Turner's stories, we can see the aspirations that defined Black America's sociopolitical outlook come into focus. Famously, Frederick Douglass reflected on the fate of African Americans in 1862 as emancipation loomed; he answered the question of what should be done with the slaves by saying, "do nothing with them; mind your business, and let them mind theirs. Your doing with them is their greatest misfortune." Yet he made it clear that the future he foresaw for African Americans was one building vibrant lives; he wrote, "As colored men, we only ask to be allowed to do with ourselves, subject only to the same great laws for the welfare of human society which apply to other men..." Douglass's concern for African Americans was not that they would be unable to make their way. Instead, he understood the system that enslaved would not easily let freedmen live free of the prejudices that it created. For Douglass, allowing Blacks to pursue education and work was the key, as he explains, if you see the former slave, "at work with a spade, a rake, a hoe, a pickaxe, or a bill—let him alone... If you see him on his way to school, with spelling book, geography and arithmetic in his hands—let him alone."[5] Today we still struggle to understand the complications African Americans need to overcome to achieve these fundamental goals.

Turner Family Stories sheds light on this struggle through the lens of one American family. In many ways, it is a truer narrative of the American experience because it is grounded in those oral traditions so central to the resilience that defines the Black experience. The talented graphic storytellers assembled here bring to life these stories of labor and citizenship entrusted to Daisy Turner. Their differing style and interpretive flare

---

5 Frederick Douglass, "What Shall Be Done with the Slaves If Emancipated?," Frederick Douglass Project, accessed January 14, 2021, https://rbscp.lib.rochester.edu/4386.

create a unique experience for the reader. In doing so, they accomplish something not easily achieved, they recover some small part of the hidden narrative of our collective past. These stories matter now more than ever as we continue to struggle with the implication of protecting citizenship for all and dedicating ourselves to the collective labor to safeguard the promise of liberty.

Julian Chambliss is a professor of English at Michigan State University. With a joint appointment in the Department of History, and as core faculty in Consortium for Critical Diversity in a Digital Age Research, he teaches courses exploring Critical Making, comics, and culture in the United States. Chambliss explains, "My work is framed around a central question: What does it mean to be a scholar in the twentieth-first century? Informed by a community engagement framework that emphasizes the Classroom as Platform, I pursue a public humanity practice that supports student learning and community action."

GRAFTON, VERMONT 1985

By Ezra Veitch

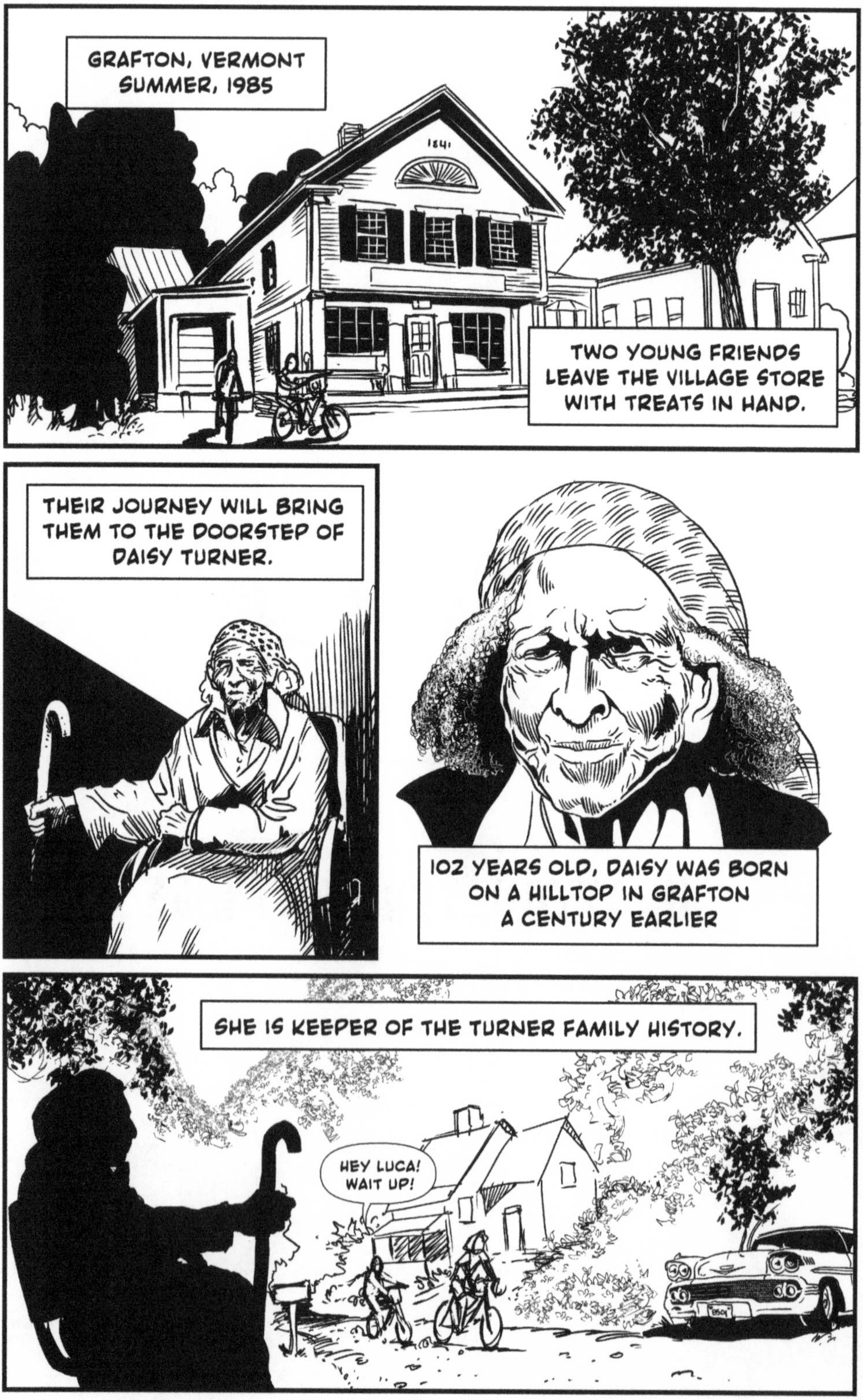
GRAFTON, VERMONT
SUMMER, 1985
1841
TWO YOUNG FRIENDS LEAVE THE VILLAGE STORE WITH TREATS IN HAND.
THEIR JOURNEY WILL BRING THEM TO THE DOORSTEP OF DAISY TURNER.
102 YEARS OLD, DAISY WAS BORN ON A HILLTOP IN GRAFTON A CENTURY EARLIER
SHE IS KEEPER OF THE TURNER FAMILY HISTORY.
HEY LUCA! WAIT UP!

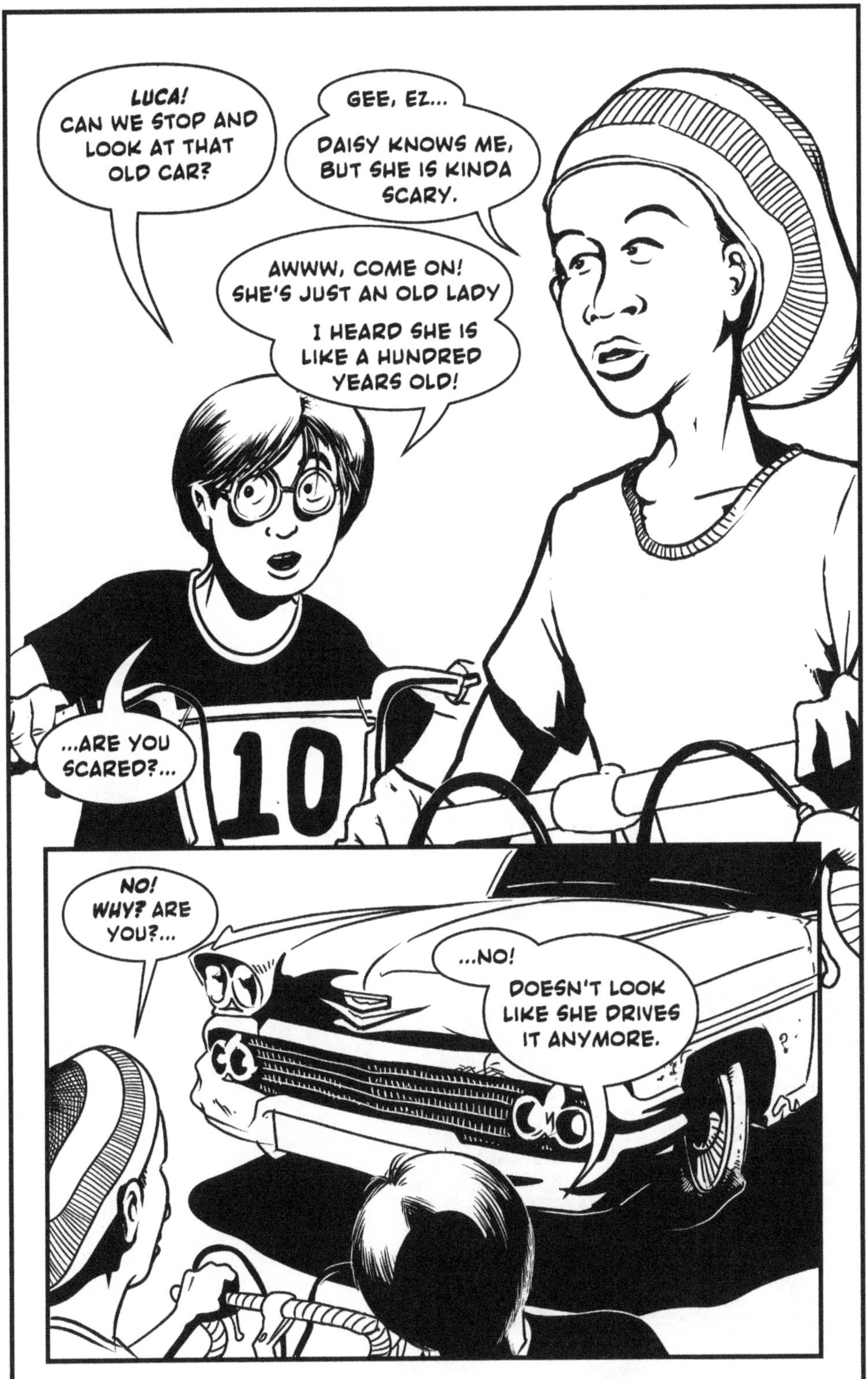
LUCA!
CAN WE STOP AND LOOK AT THAT OLD CAR?
GEE, EZ...
DAISY KNOWS ME, BUT SHE IS KINDA SCARY.
AWWW, COME ON!
SHE'S JUST AN OLD LADY
I HEARD SHE IS LIKE A HUNDRED YEARS OLD!
...ARE YOU SCARED?...
10
NO!
WHY? ARE YOU?...
...NO!
DOESN'T LOOK LIKE SHE DRIVES IT ANYMORE.

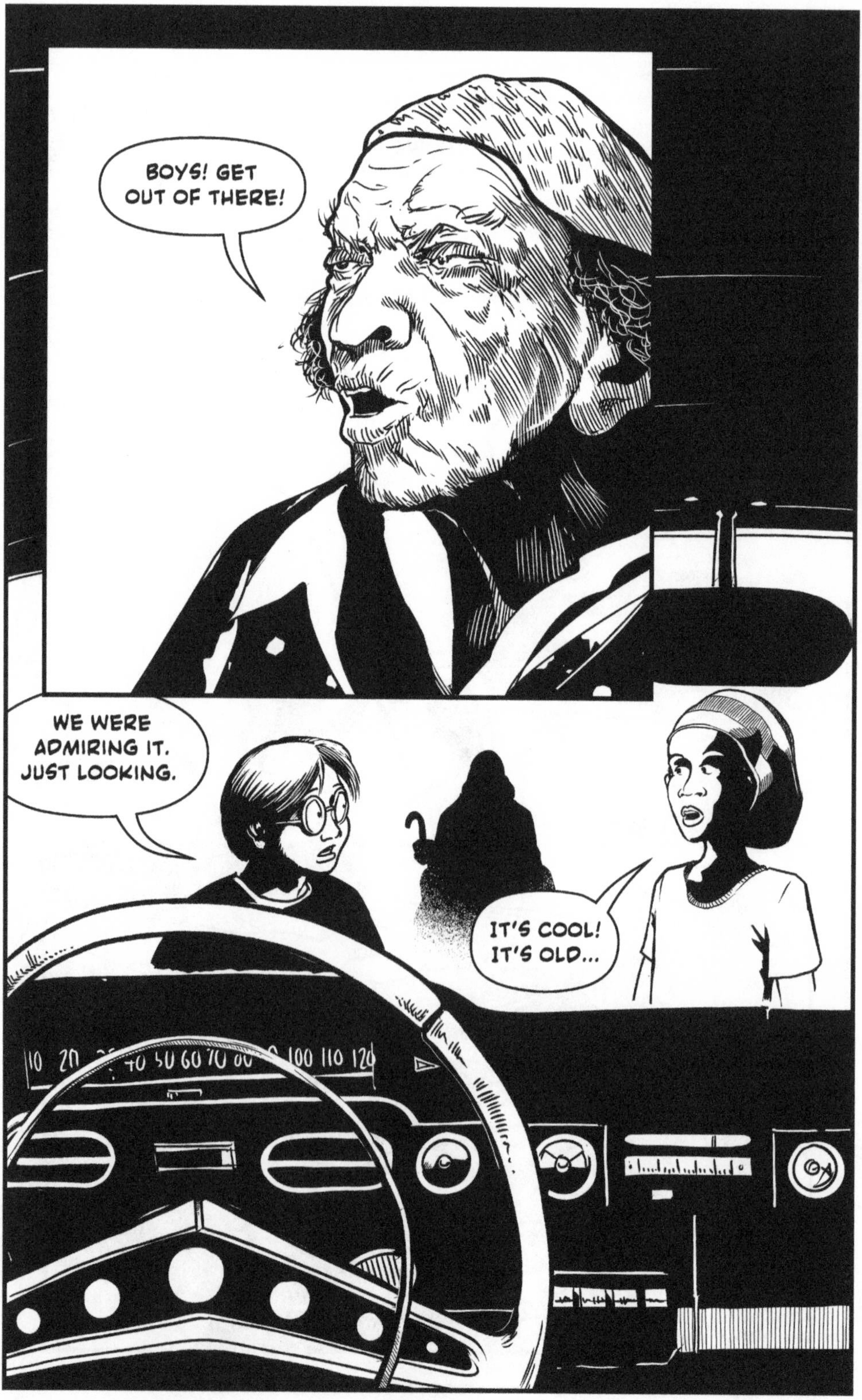
BOYS! GET OUT OF THERE!
WE WERE ADMIRING IT. JUST LOOKING.
IT'S COOL! IT'S OLD...

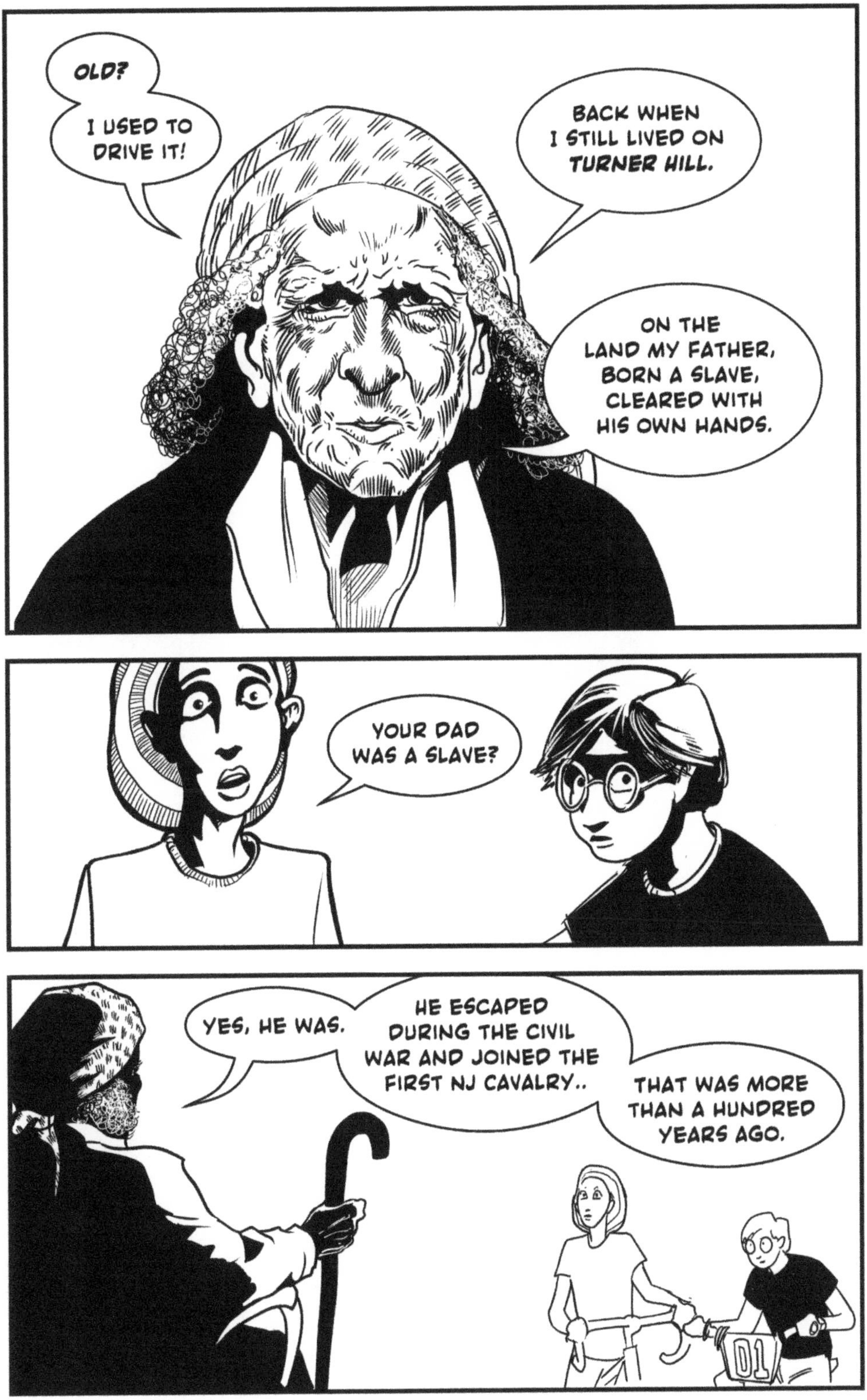
OLD?
I USED TO DRIVE IT!
BACK WHEN I STILL LIVED ON TURNER HILL.
ON THE LAND MY FATHER, BORN A SLAVE, CLEARED WITH HIS OWN HANDS.
YOUR DAD WAS A SLAVE?
YES, HE WAS.
HE ESCAPED DURING THE CIVIL WAR AND JOINED THE FIRST NJ CAVALRY..
THAT WAS MORE THAN A HUNDRED YEARS AGO.
01

THE ADVENTURES OF ALEC TURNER

By Marek Bennett

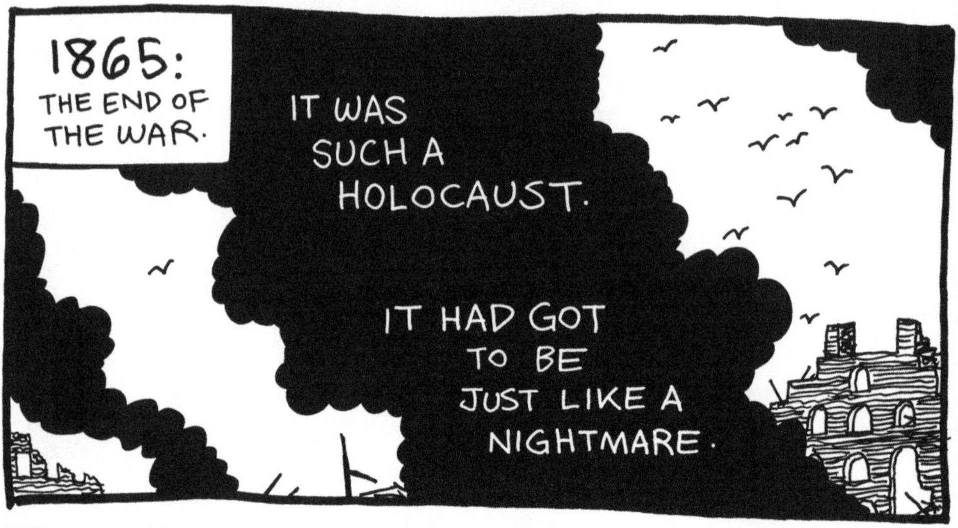
1865: THE END OF THE WAR.
IT WAS SUCH A HOLOCAUST.
IT HAD GOT TO BE JUST LIKE A NIGHTMARE.

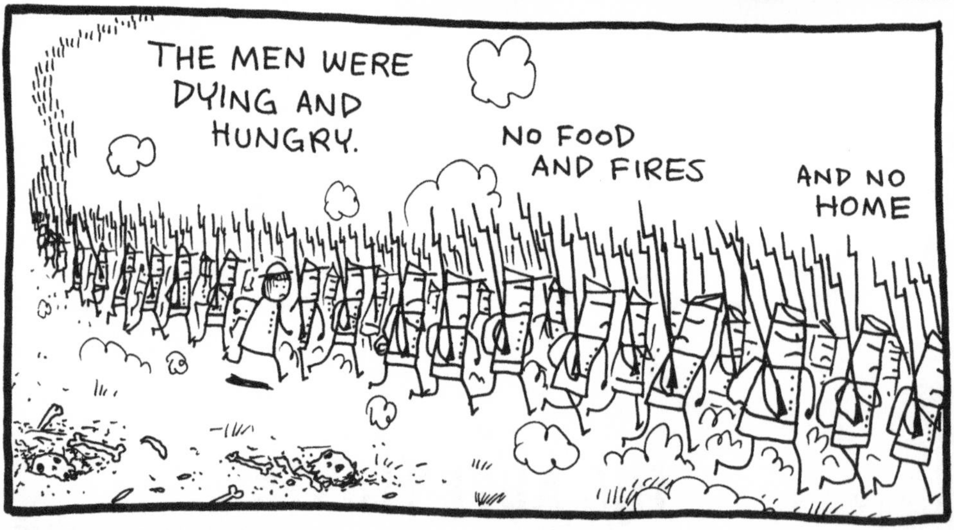
THE MEN WERE DYING AND HUNGRY.
NO FOOD AND FIRES
AND NO HOME

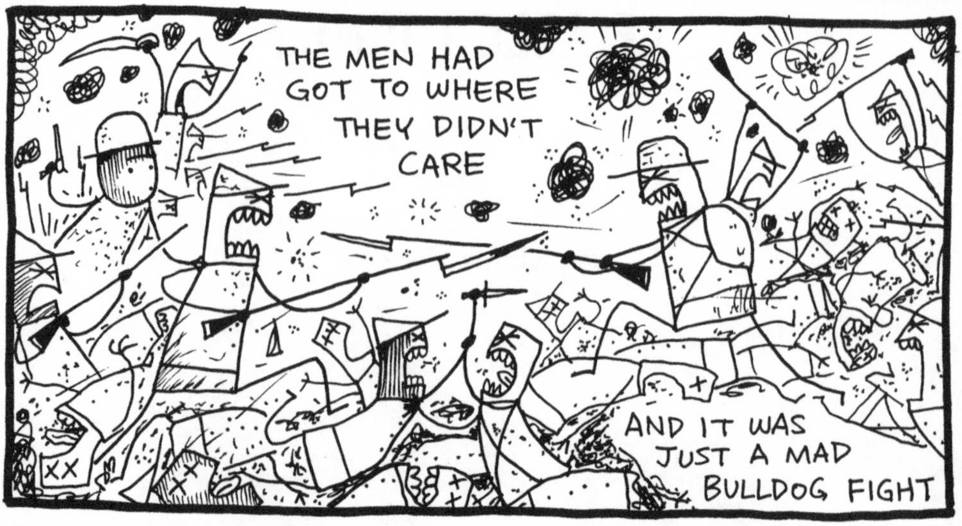
THE MEN HAD GOT TO WHERE THEY DIDN'T CARE
AND IT WAS JUST A MAD BULLDOG FIGHT

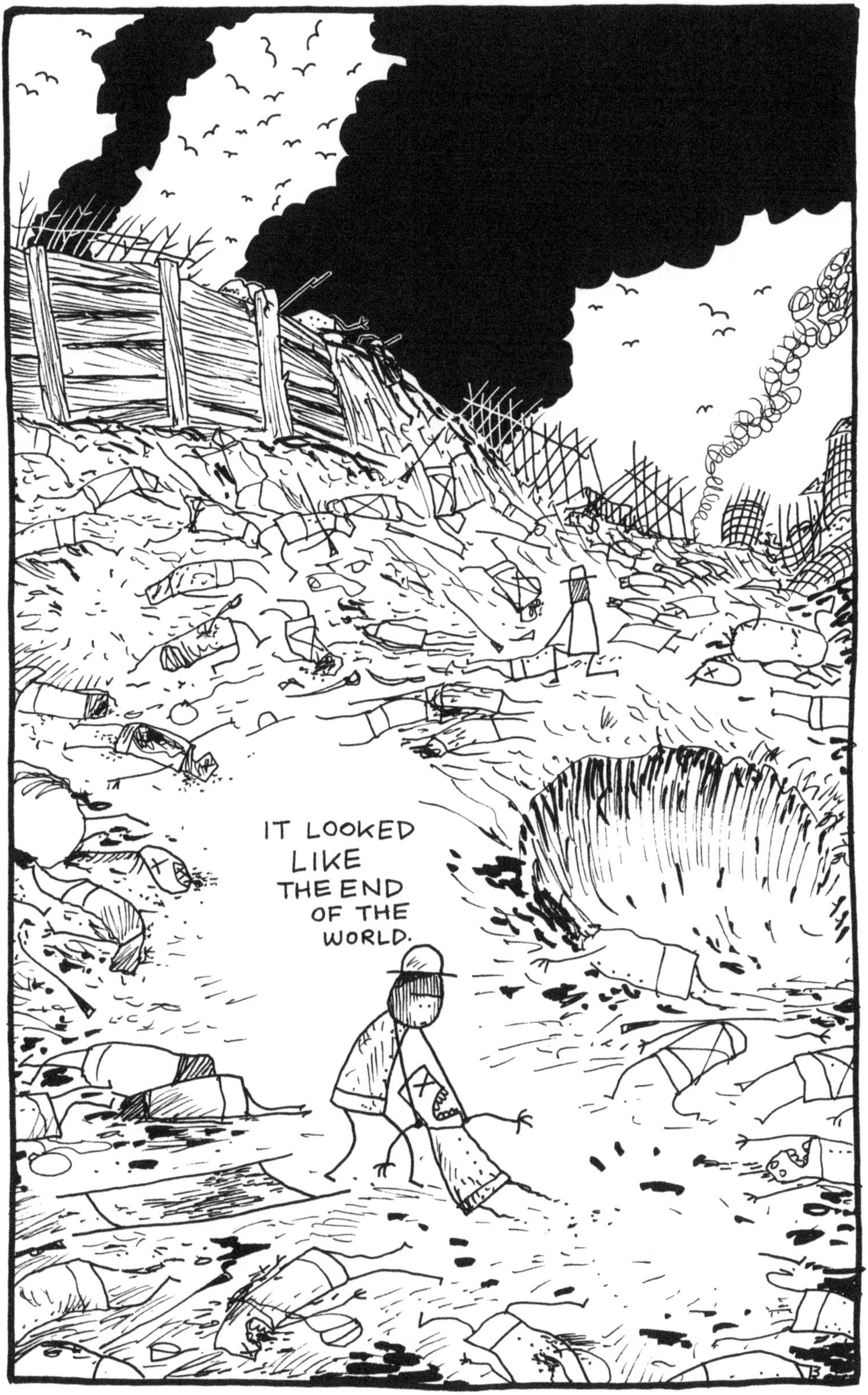
IT LOOKED LIKE THE END OF THE WORLD.

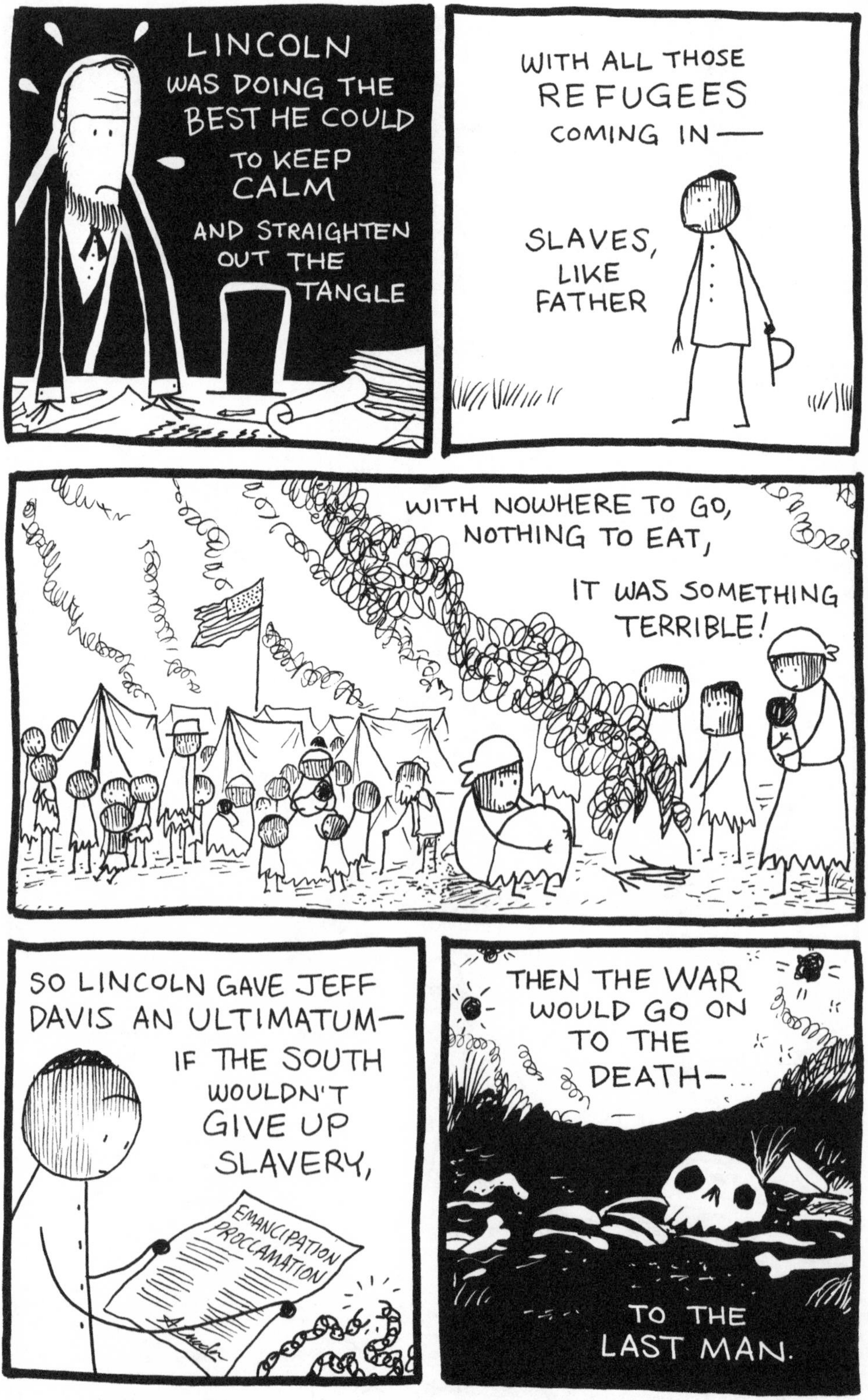
LINCOLN WAS DOING THE BEST HE COULD
TO KEEP CALM
AND STRAIGHTEN OUT THE TANGLE
WITH ALL THOSE REFUGEES COMING IN—
SLAVES, LIKE FATHER
WITH NOWHERE TO GO, NOTHING TO EAT,
IT WAS SOMETHING TERRIBLE!
SO LINCOLN GAVE JEFF DAVIS AN ULTIMATUM—
IF THE SOUTH WOULDN'T GIVE UP SLAVERY,
EMANCIPATION PROCCAMATION
THEN THE WAR WOULD GO ON TO THE DEATH—...
TO THE LAST MAN.

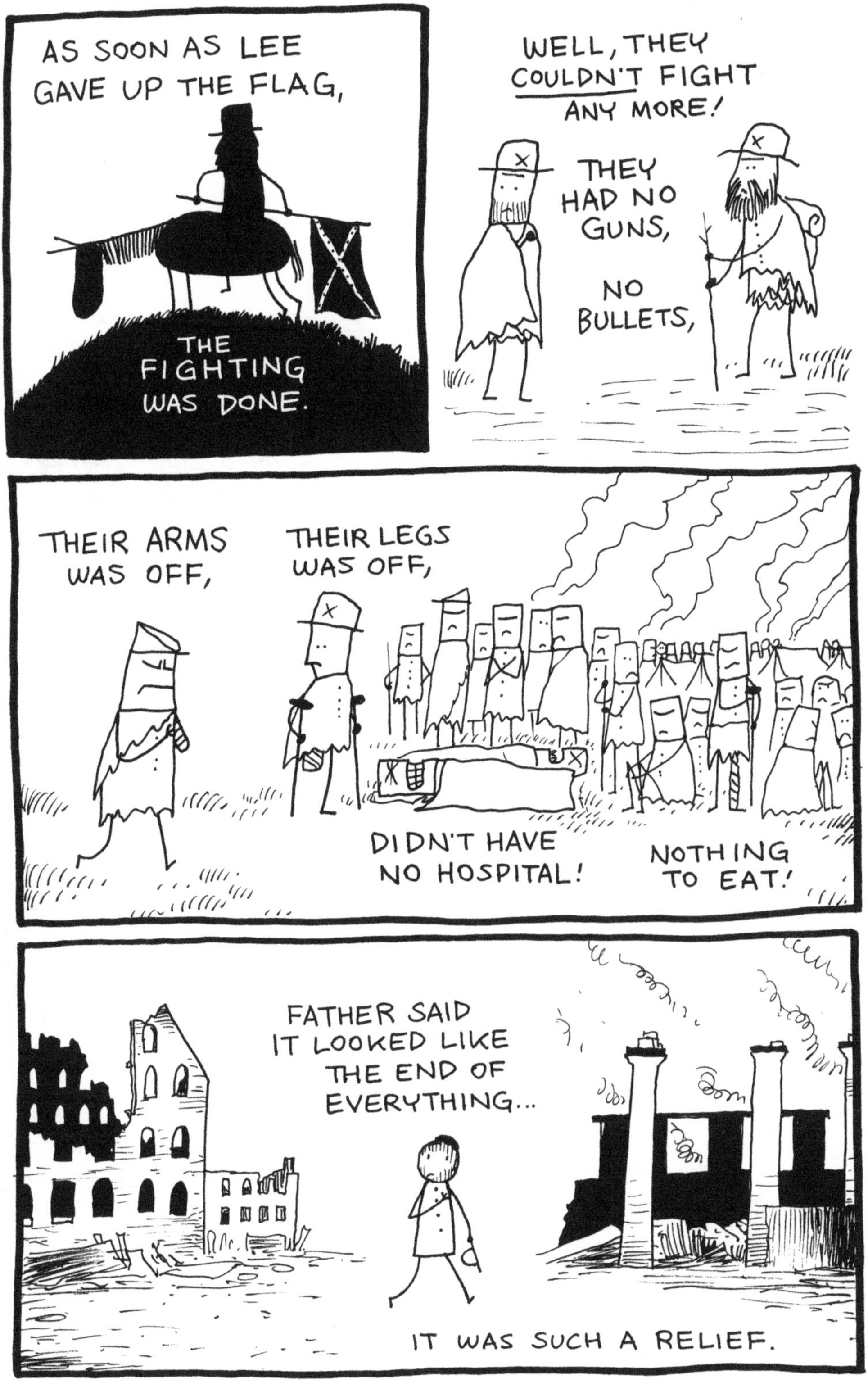
AS SOON AS LEE GAVE UP THE FLAG,
THE FIGHTING WAS DONE.
WELL, THEY COULDN'T FIGHT ANY MORE!
THEY HAD NO GUNS,
NO BULLETS,
THEIR ARMS WAS OFF,
THEIR LEGS WAS OFF,
DIDN'T HAVE NO HOSPITAL!
NOTHING TO EAT!
FATHER SAID IT LOOKED LIKE THE END OF EVERYTHING...
IT WAS SUCH A RELIEF.

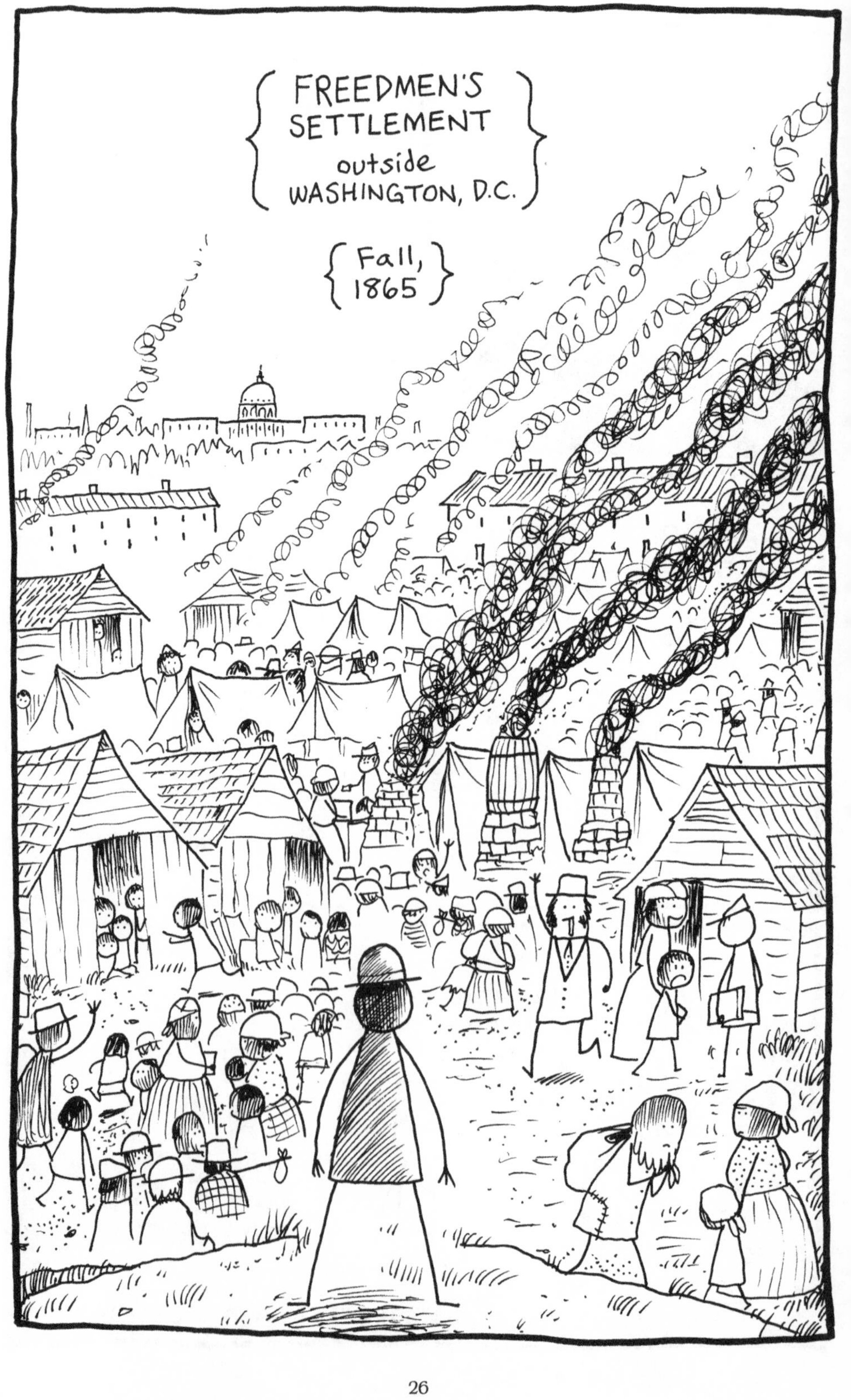
FREEDMEN'S SETTLEMENT outside WASHINGTON, D.C.
Fall, 1865

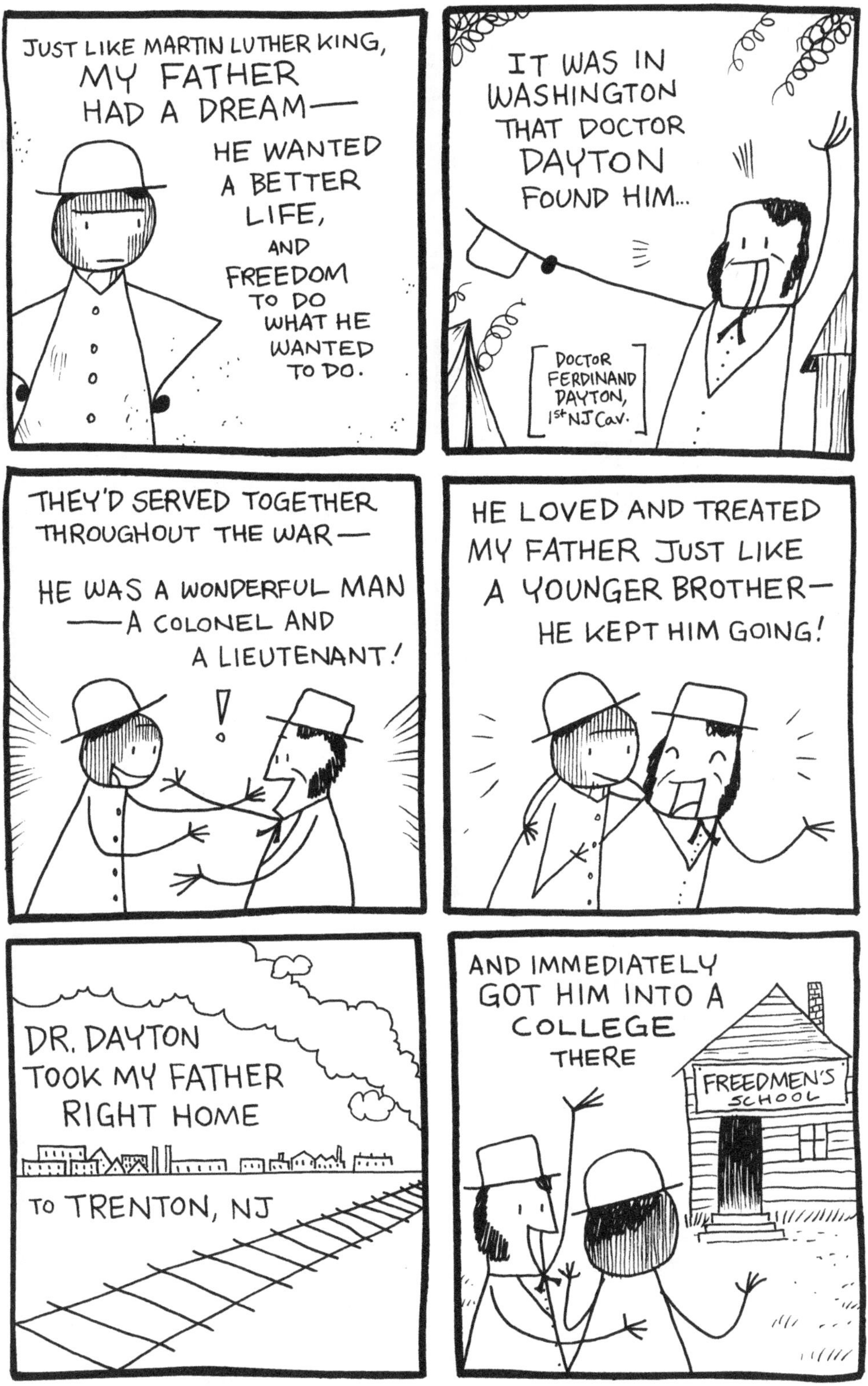
JUST LIKE MARTIN LUTHER KING, MY FATHER HAD A DREAM—
HE WANTED A BETTER LIFE, AND FREEDOM TO DO WHAT HE WANTED TO DO.
IT WAS IN WASHINGTON THAT DOCTOR DAYTON FOUND HIM...
DOCTOR FERDINAND DAYTON, 1st NJ Cav.
THEY'D SERVED TOGETHER THROUGHOUT THE WAR—
HE WAS A WONDERFUL MAN —A COLONEL AND A LIEUTENANT!
!
HE LOVED AND TREATED MY FATHER JUST LIKE A YOUNGER BROTHER—
HE KEPT HIM GOING!
DR. DAYTON TOOK MY FATHER RIGHT HOME
TO TRENTON, NJ
AND IMMEDIATELY GOT HIM INTO A COLLEGE THERE
FREEDMEN'S SCHOOL

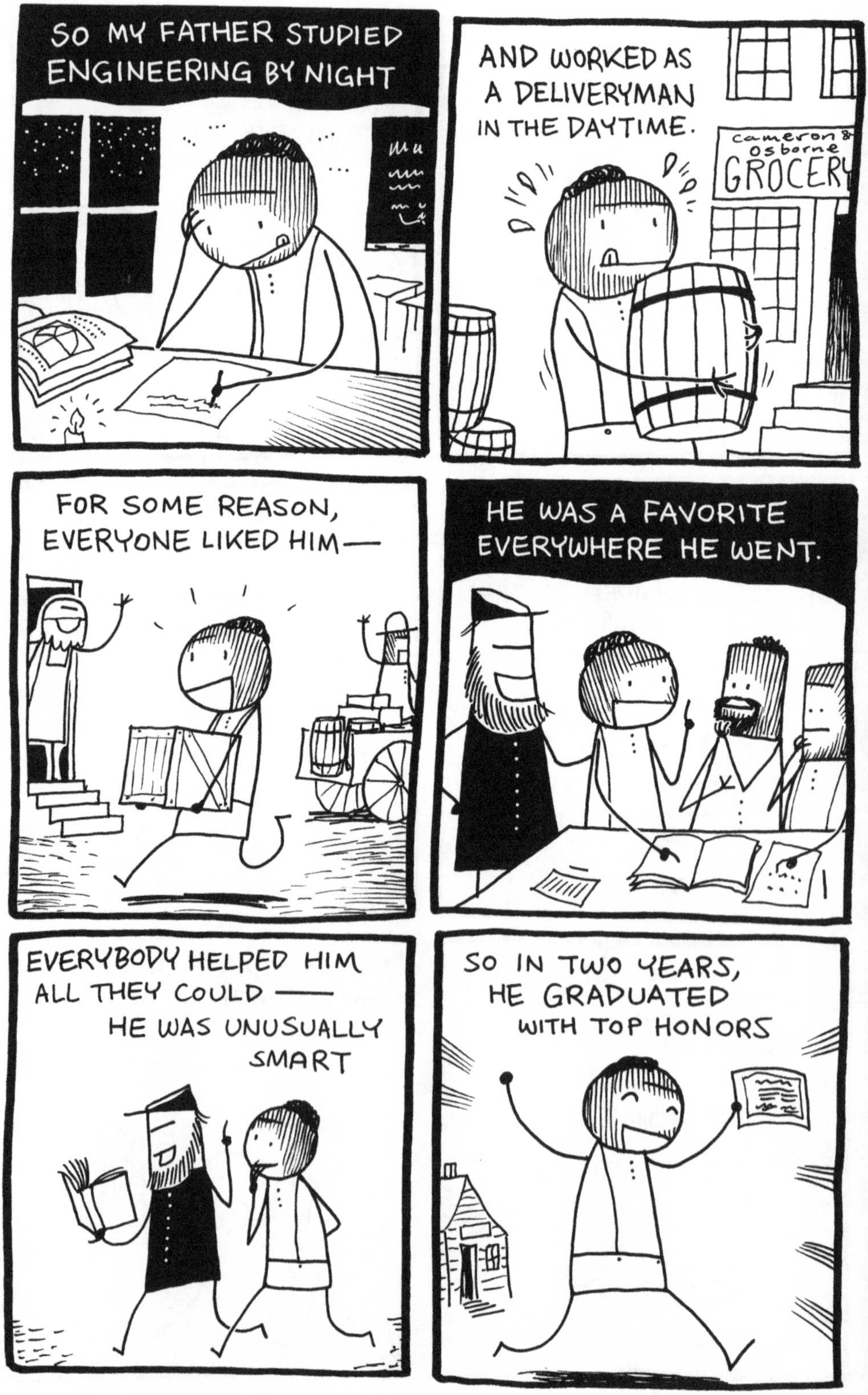
SO MY FATHER STUDIED ENGINEERING BY NIGHT
AND WORKED AS A DELIVERYMAN IN THE DAYTIME.
cameron & osborne GROCERY
FOR SOME REASON, EVERYONE LIKED HIM—
HE WAS A FAVORITE EVERYWHERE HE WENT.
EVERYBODY HELPED HIM ALL THEY COULD —
HE WAS UNUSUALLY SMART
SO IN TWO YEARS, HE GRADUATED WITH TOP HONORS

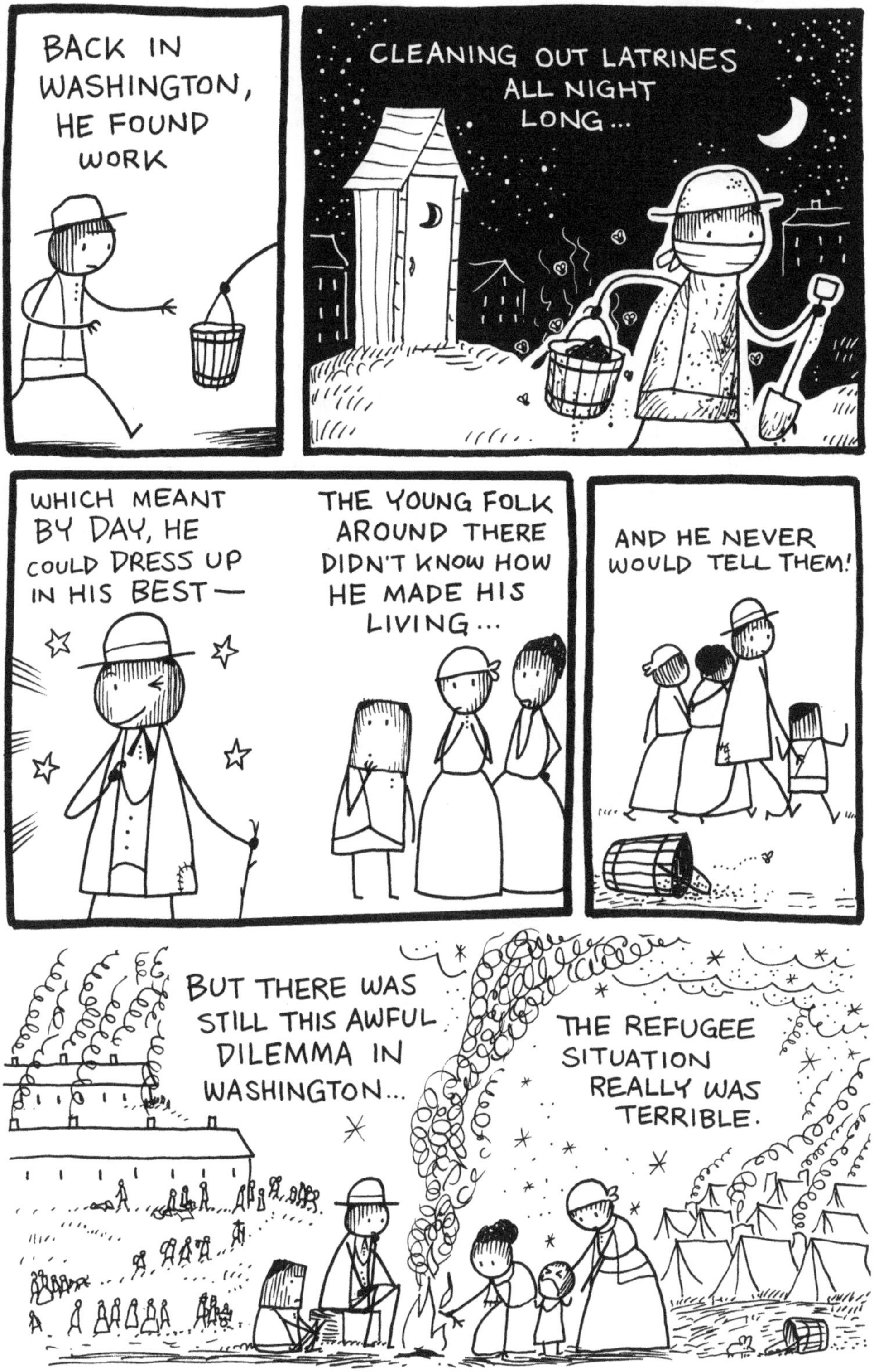
BACK IN WASHINGTON, HE FOUND WORK
CLEANING OUT LATRINES ALL NIGHT LONG...
WHICH MEANT BY DAY, HE COULD DRESS UP IN HIS BEST—
THE YOUNG FOLK AROUND THERE DIDN'T KNOW HOW HE MADE HIS LIVING...
AND HE NEVER WOULD TELL THEM!
BUT THERE WAS STILL THIS AWFUL DILEMMA IN WASHINGTON...
THE REFUGEE SITUATION REALLY WAS TERRIBLE.

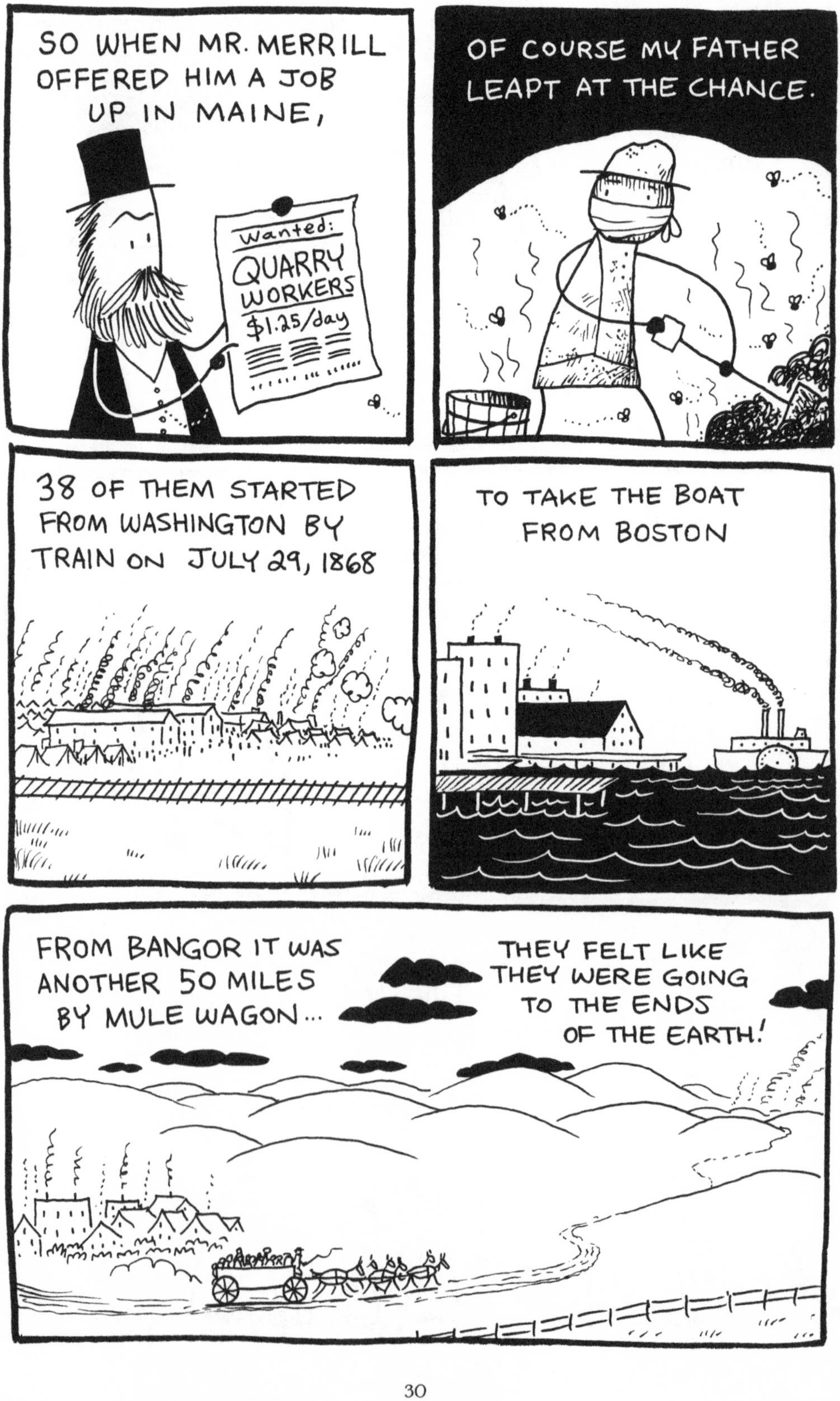
SO WHEN MR. MERRILL OFFERED HIM A JOB UP IN MAINE,
Wanted: QUARRY WORKERS $1.25/day
OF COURSE MY FATHER LEAPT AT THE CHANCE.
38 OF THEM STARTED FROM WASHINGTON BY TRAIN ON JULY 29, 1868
TO TAKE THE BOAT FROM BOSTON
FROM BANGOR IT WAS ANOTHER 50 MILES BY MULE WAGON...
THEY FELT LIKE THEY WERE GOING TO THE ENDS OF THE EARTH!

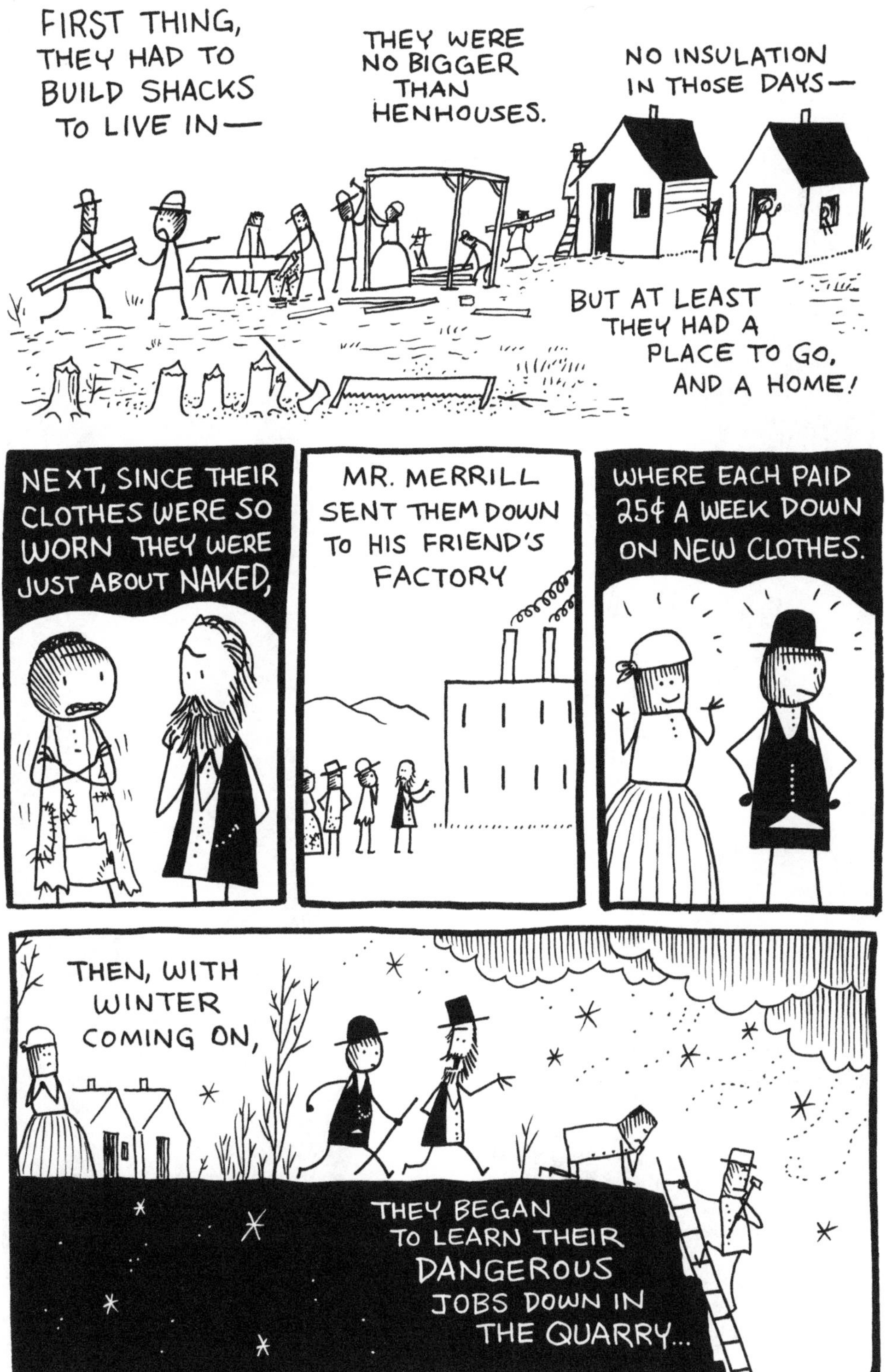
FIRST THING, THEY HAD TO BUILD SHACKS TO LIVE IN—
THEY WERE NO BIGGER THAN HENHOUSES.
NO INSULATION IN THOSE DAYS—
BUT AT LEAST THEY HAD A PLACE TO GO, AND A HOME!
NEXT, SINCE THEIR CLOTHES WERE SO WORN THEY WERE JUST ABOUT NAKED,
MR. MERRILL SENT THEM DOWN TO HIS FRIEND'S FACTORY
WHERE EACH PAID 25¢ A WEEK DOWN ON NEW CLOTHES.
THEN, WITH WINTER COMING ON,
THEY BEGAN TO LEARN THEIR DANGEROUS JOBS DOWN IN THE QUARRY...

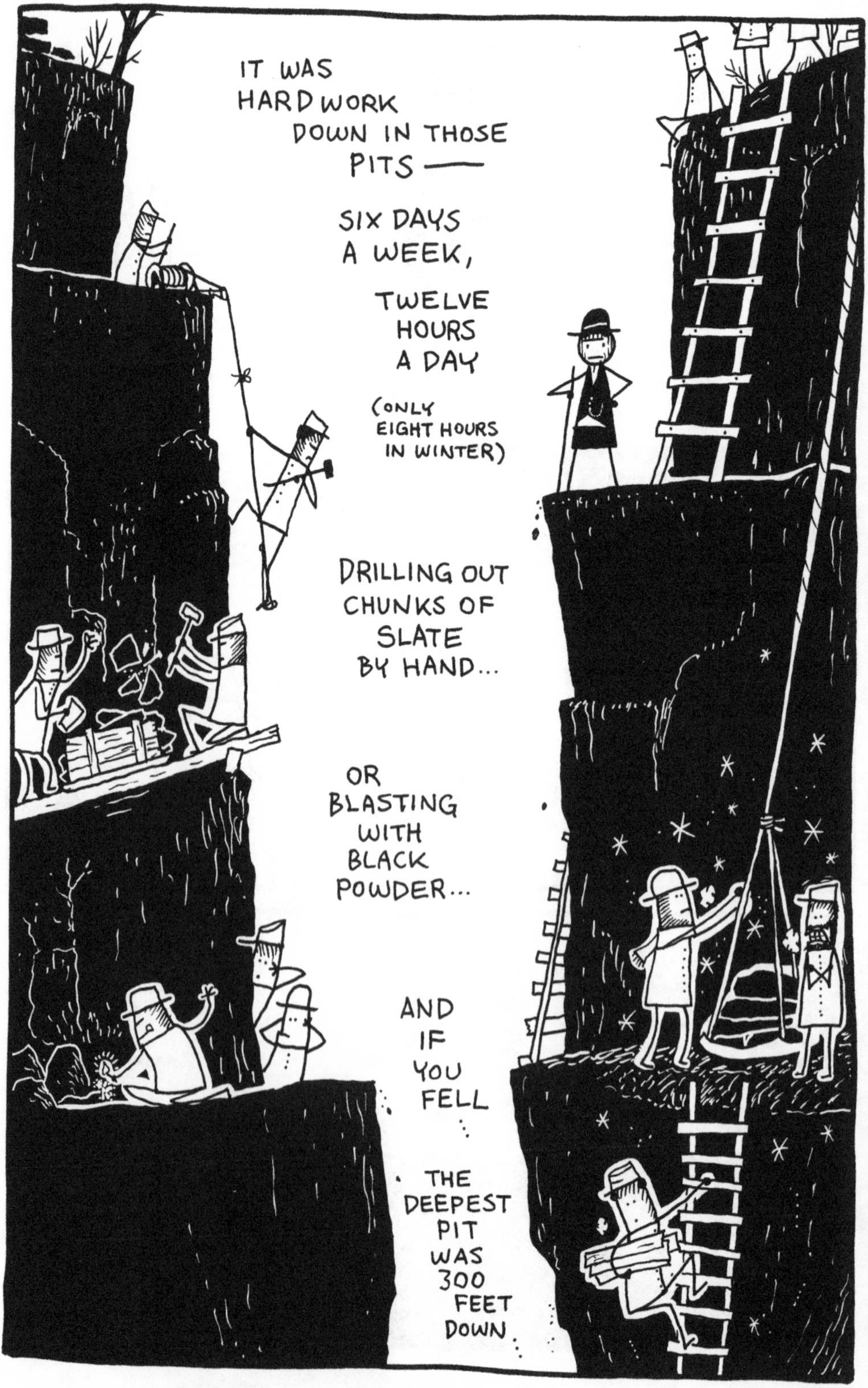
IT WAS HARD WORK DOWN IN THOSE PITS —
SIX DAYS A WEEK,
TWELVE HOURS A DAY
(ONLY EIGHT HOURS IN WINTER)
DRILLING OUT CHUNKS OF SLATE BY HAND...
OR BLASTING WITH BLACK POWDER...
AND IF YOU FELL
THE DEEPEST PIT WAS 300 FEET DOWN.

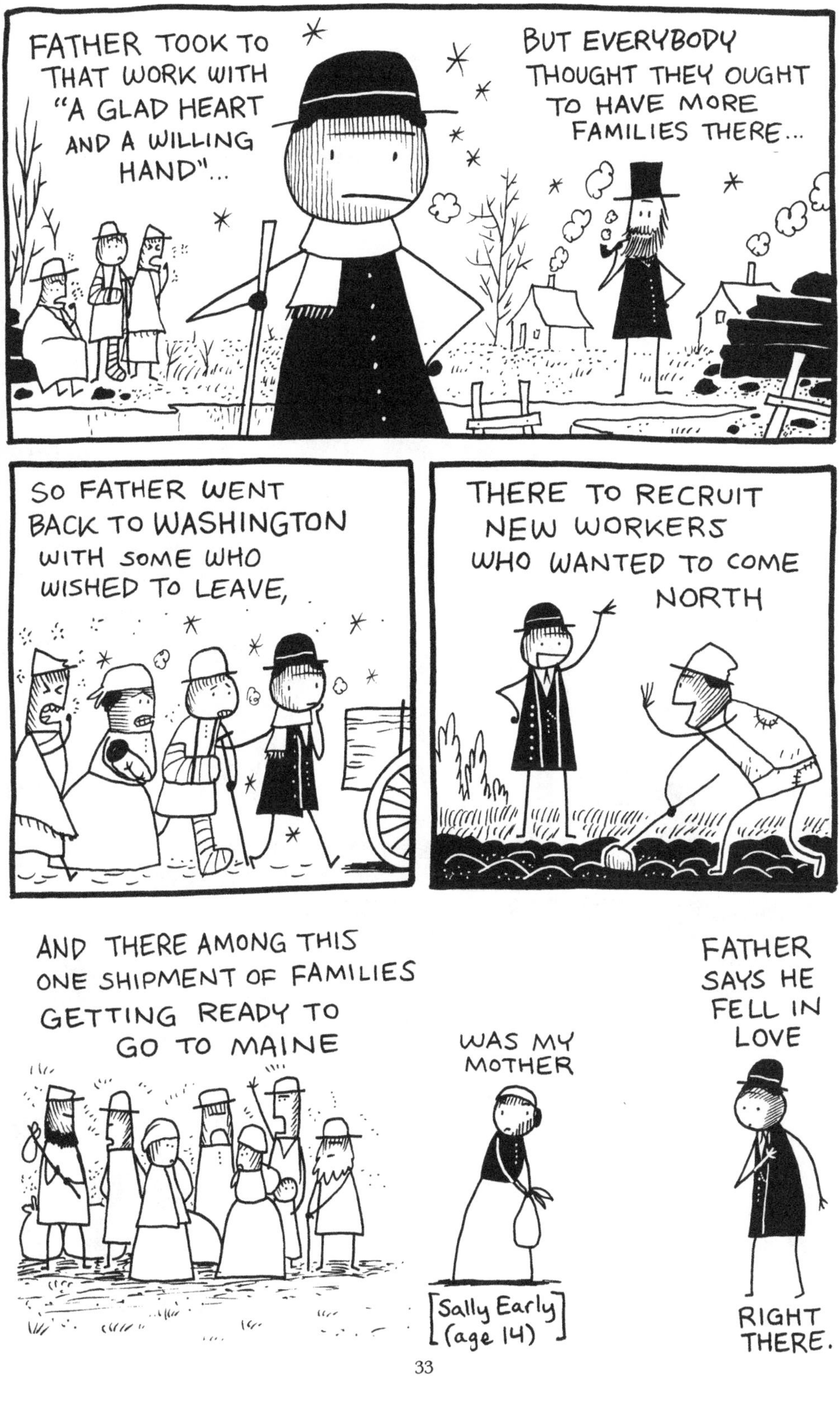
FATHER TOOK TO THAT WORK WITH "A GLAD HEART AND A WILLING HAND"...
BUT EVERYBODY THOUGHT THEY OUGHT TO HAVE MORE FAMILIES THERE...
SO FATHER WENT BACK TO WASHINGTON WITH SOME WHO WISHED TO LEAVE,
THERE TO RECRUIT NEW WORKERS WHO WANTED TO COME NORTH
AND THERE AMONG THIS ONE SHIPMENT OF FAMILIES GETTING READY TO GO TO MAINE
WAS MY MOTHER
[Sally Early (age 14)]
FATHER SAYS HE FELL IN LOVE
RIGHT THERE.

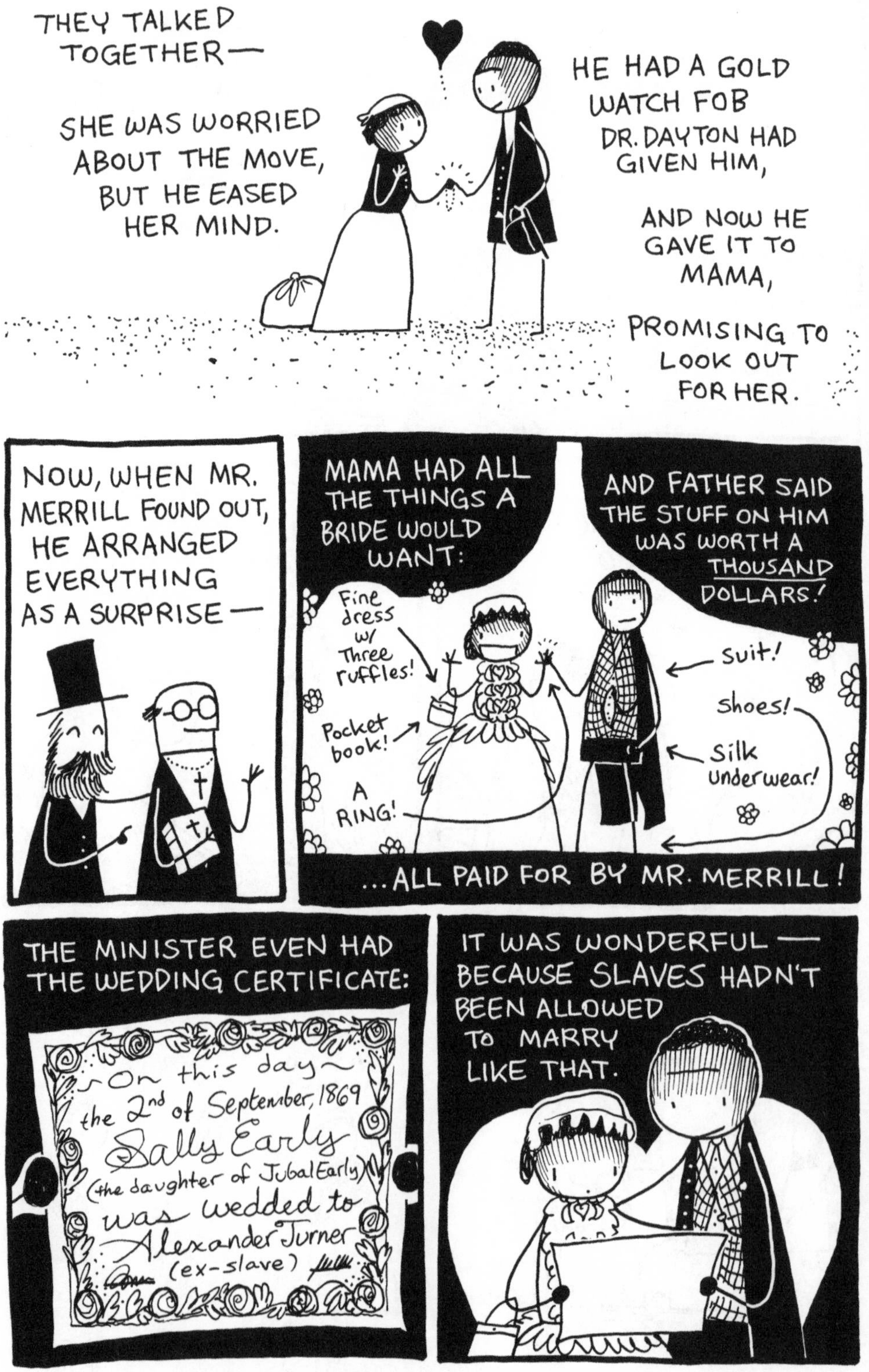
THEY TALKED TOGETHER—
SHE WAS WORRIED ABOUT THE MOVE, BUT HE EASED HER MIND.
HE HAD A GOLD WATCH FOB DR. DAYTON HAD GIVEN HIM,
AND NOW HE GAVE IT TO MAMA,
PROMISING TO LOOK OUT FOR HER.
NOW, WHEN MR. MERRILL FOUND OUT, HE ARRANGED EVERYTHING AS A SURPRISE—
MAMA HAD ALL THE THINGS A BRIDE WOULD WANT:
AND FATHER SAID THE STUFF ON HIM WAS WORTH A THOUSAND DOLLARS!
Fine dress w/ Three ruffles!
Pocket book!
A RING!
Suit!
Shoes!
Silk underwear!
...ALL PAID FOR BY MR. MERRILL!
THE MINISTER EVEN HAD THE WEDDING CERTIFICATE:
~On this day~
the 2nd of September, 1869
Sally Early
(the daughter of Jubal Early)
was wedded to
Alexander Turner
(ex-slave)
IT WAS WONDERFUL— BECAUSE SLAVES HADN'T BEEN ALLOWED TO MARRY LIKE THAT.

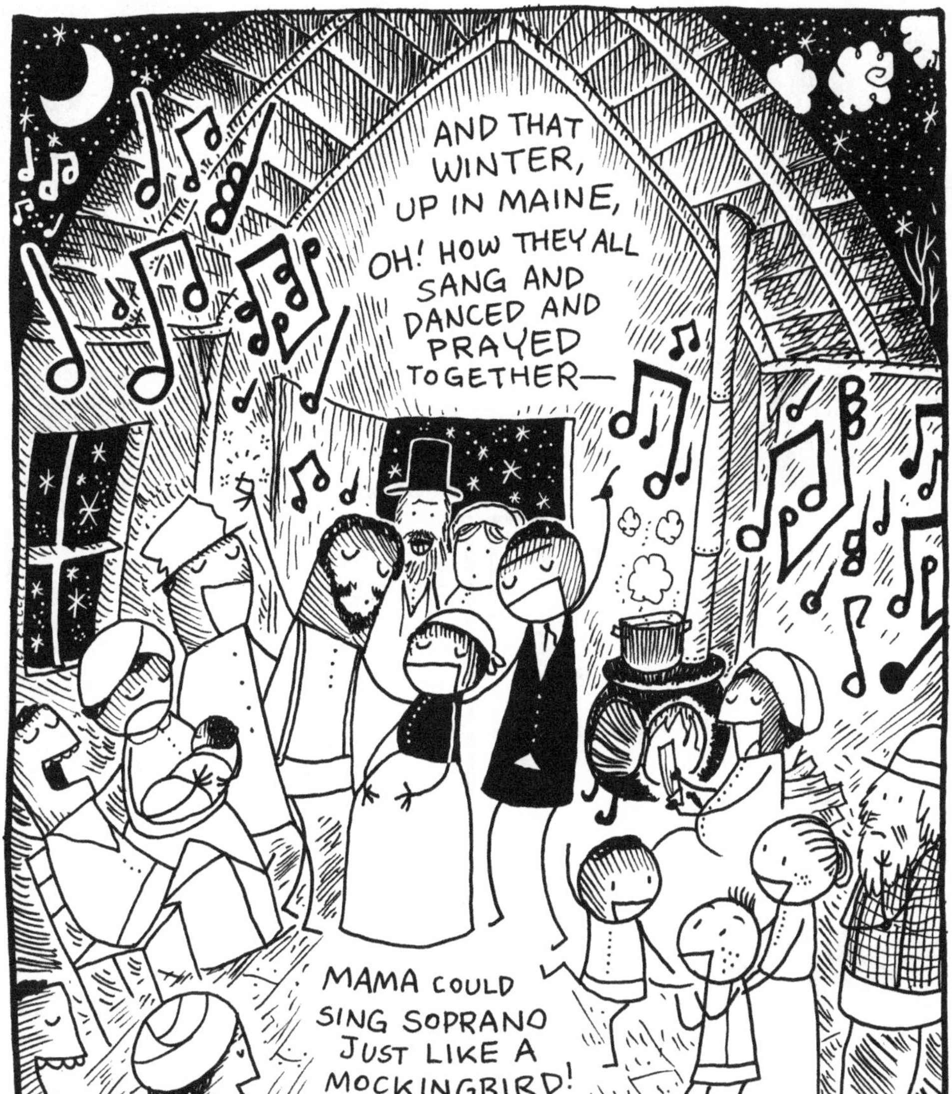
AND THAT WINTER, UP IN MAINE,
OH! HOW THEY ALL SANG AND DANCED AND PRAYED TOGETHER—
MAMA COULD SING SOPRANO JUST LIKE A MOCKINGBIRD!

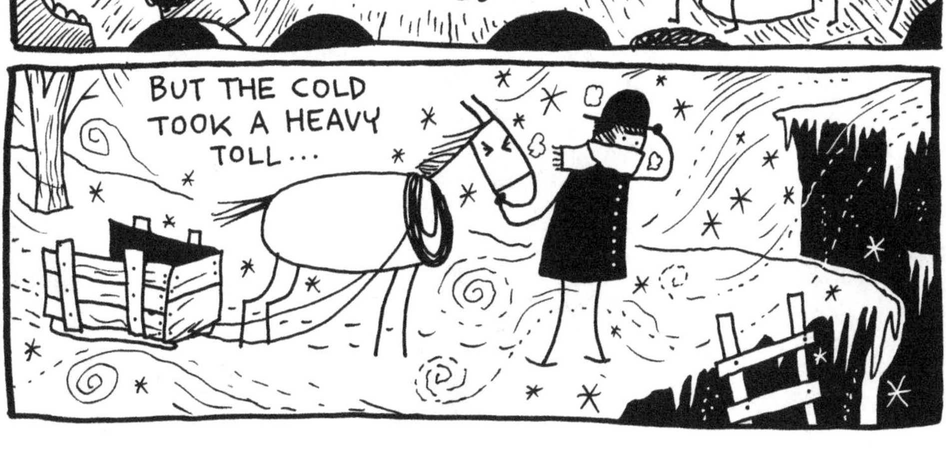
BUT THE COLD TOOK A HEAVY TOLL...

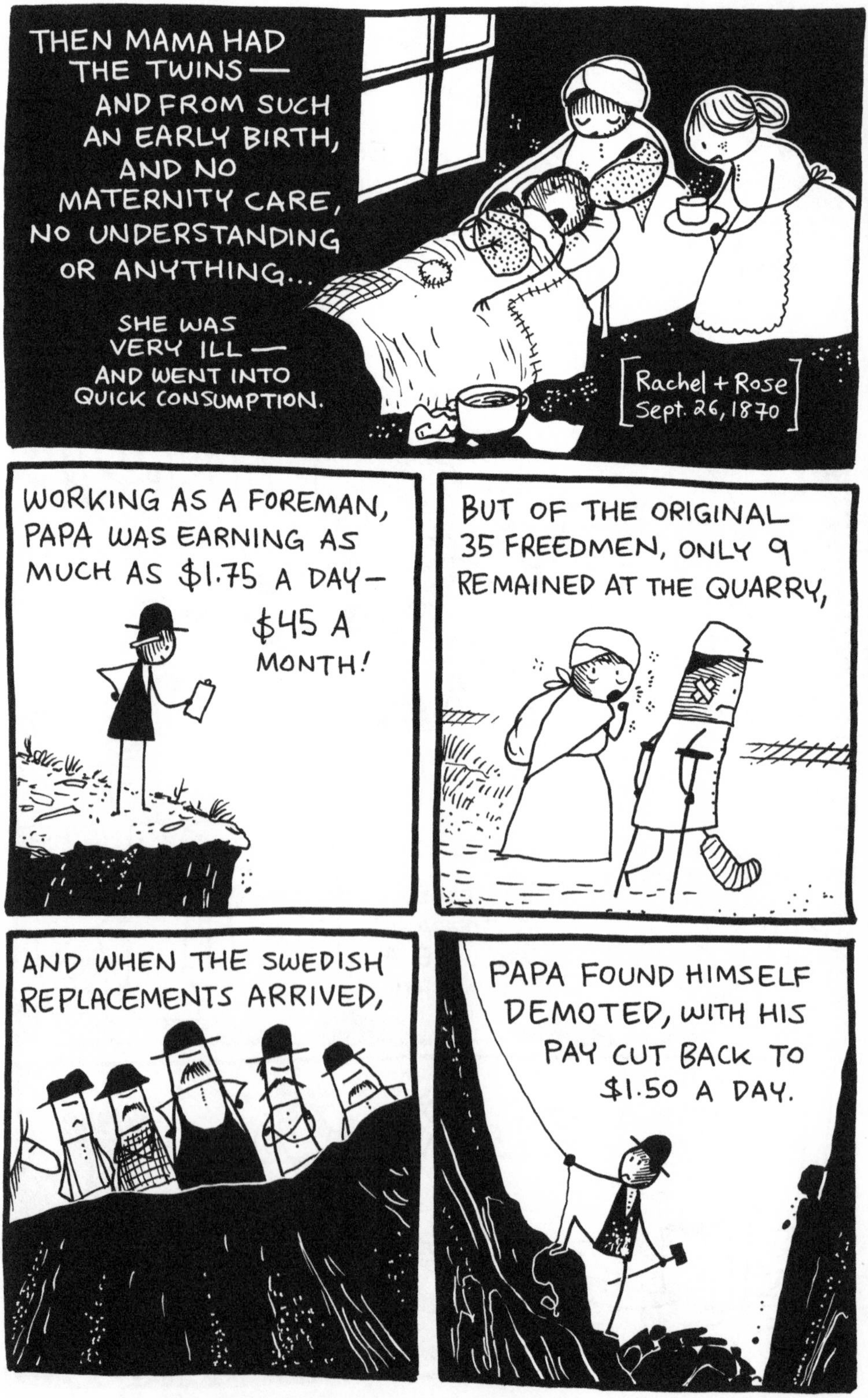
THEN MAMA HAD THE TWINS— AND FROM SUCH AN EARLY BIRTH, AND NO MATERNITY CARE, NO UNDERSTANDING OR ANYTHING...
SHE WAS VERY ILL— AND WENT INTO QUICK CONSUMPTION.
[Rachel + Rose Sept. 26, 1870]
WORKING AS A FOREMAN, PAPA WAS EARNING AS MUCH AS $1.75 A DAY—
$45 A MONTH!
BUT OF THE ORIGINAL 35 FREEDMEN, ONLY 9 REMAINED AT THE QUARRY,
AND WHEN THE SWEDISH REPLACEMENTS ARRIVED,
PAPA FOUND HIMSELF DEMOTED, WITH HIS PAY CUT BACK TO $1.50 A DAY.

MAMA WAS ONLY GETTING WORSE, ON ACCOUNT OF THE HEMORRHAGES SETTING IN —

NELLIE
May 24,
1873

SO QUICK AS HE COULD, MR. MERRILL CONTACTED A DOCTOR

WHO TOLD THEM TO GET MAMA DOWN TO BOSTON TO SEE WHAT COULD BE DONE...

HE FOUND A PLACE FOR THEM NEAR THE HOSPITAL —

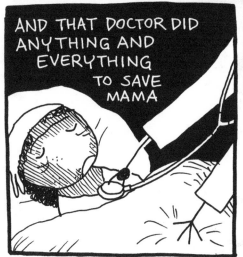

AND THAT DOCTOR DID ANYTHING AND EVERYTHING TO SAVE MAMA

BUT SHE KEPT A'FAILING...

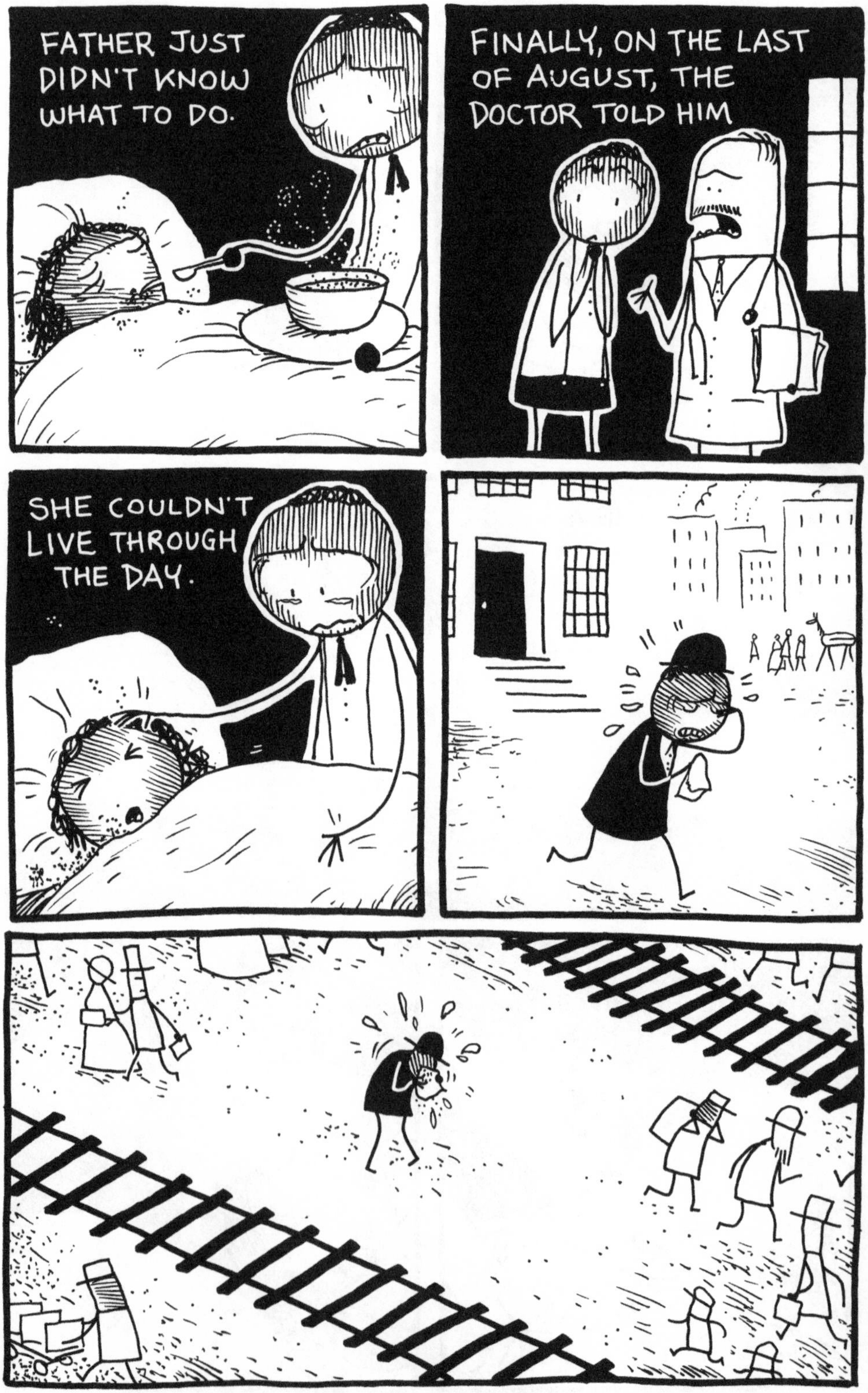
FATHER JUST DIDN'T KNOW WHAT TO DO.
FINALLY, ON THE LAST OF AUGUST, THE DOCTOR TOLD HIM
SHE COULDN'T LIVE THROUGH THE DAY.

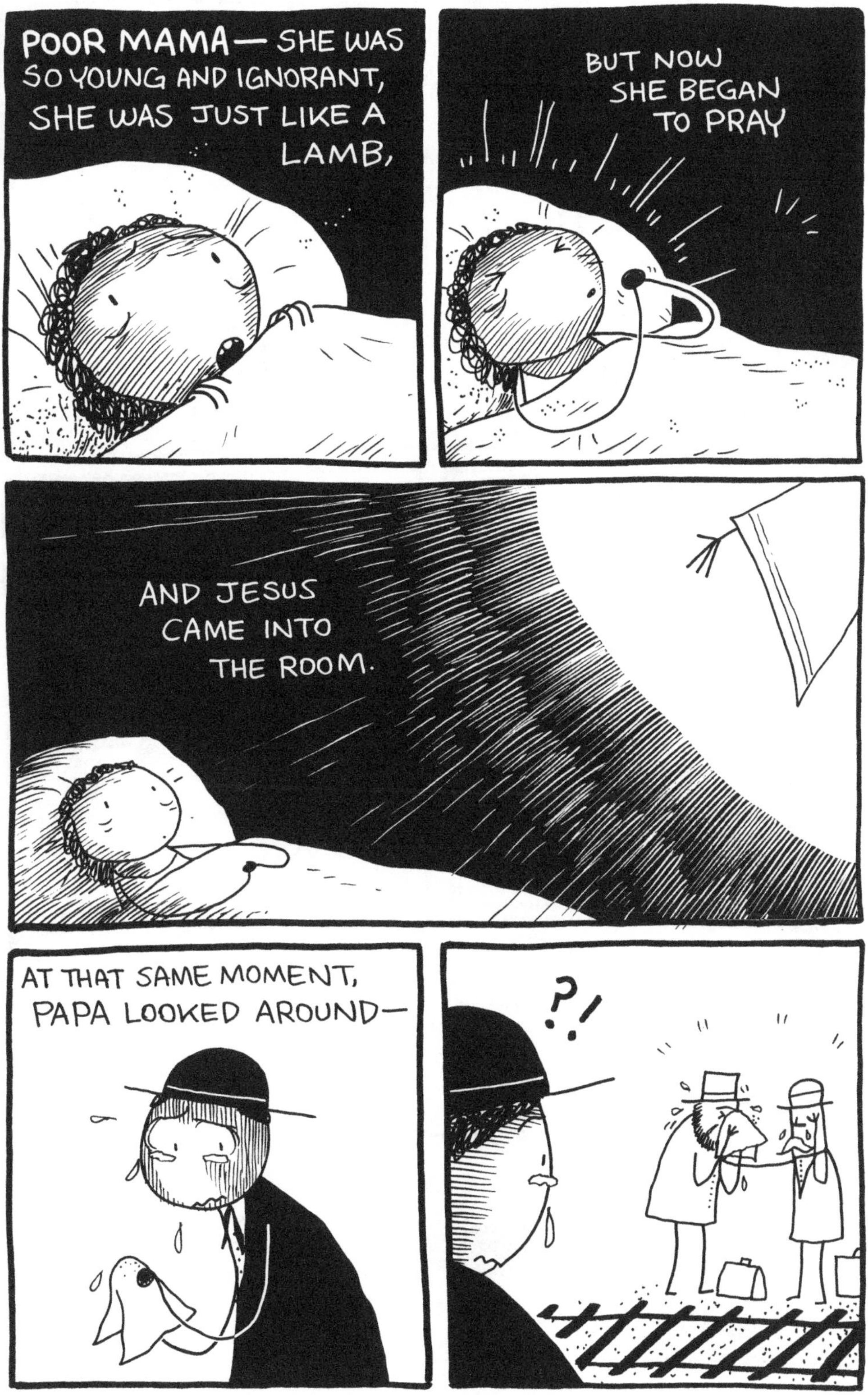
POOR MAMA— SHE WAS SO YOUNG AND IGNORANT, SHE WAS JUST LIKE A LAMB,
BUT NOW SHE BEGAN TO PRAY
AND JESUS CAME INTO THE ROOM.
AT THAT SAME MOMENT, PAPA LOOKED AROUND—
?!

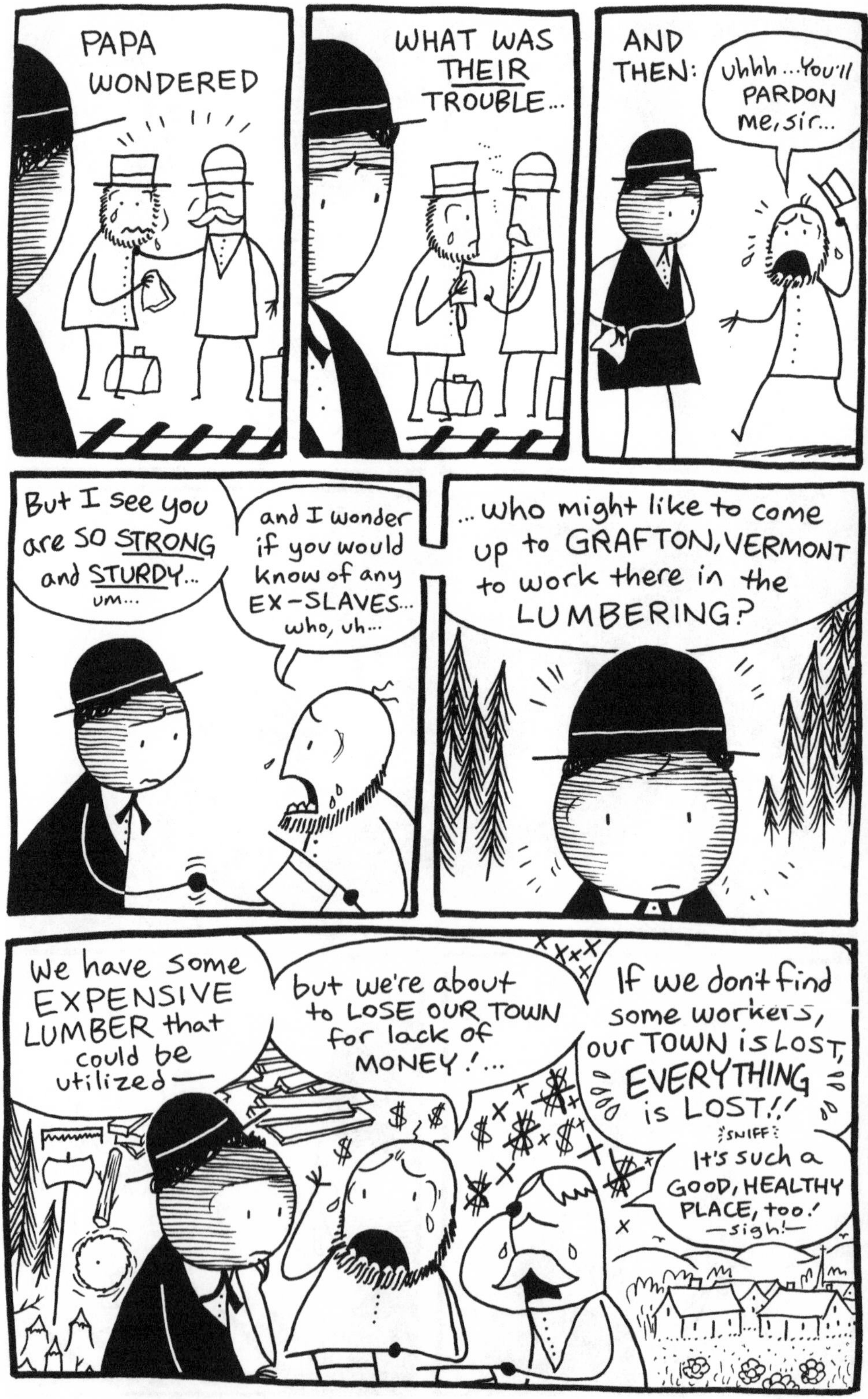
PAPA WONDERED
WHAT WAS THEIR TROUBLE...
AND THEN:
uhhh... You'll PARDON me, sir...
But I see you are SO STRONG and STURDY... um...
and I wonder if you would know of any EX-SLAVES... who, uh...
...who might like to come up to GRAFTON, VERMONT to work there in the LUMBERING?
We have some EXPENSIVE LUMBER that could be utilized—
but we're about to LOSE OUR TOWN for lack of MONEY!...
If we don't find some workers, our TOWN is LOST, EVERYTHING is LOST!!
SNIFF
It's such a GOOD, HEALTHY PLACE, too! —sigh!—

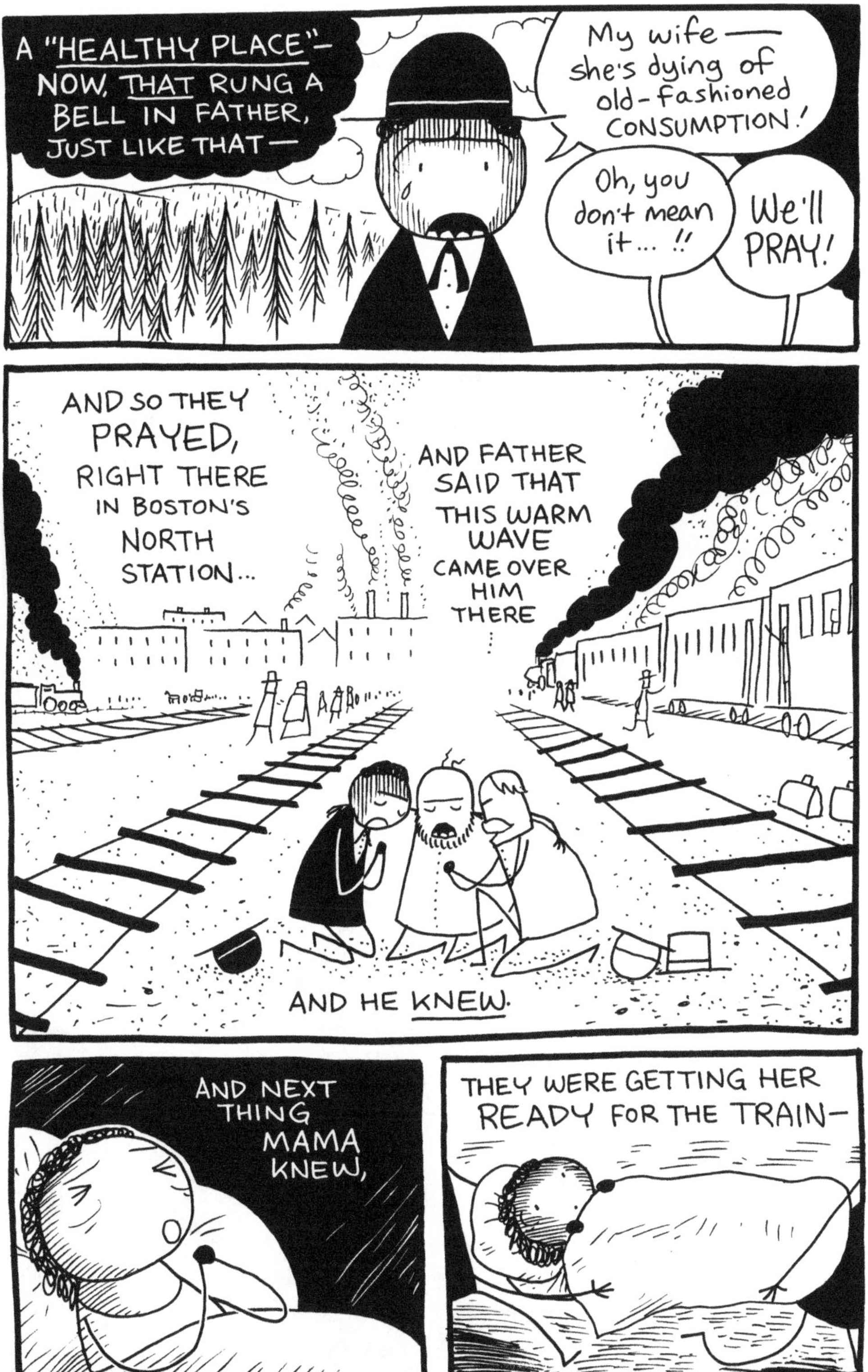
A "HEALTHY PLACE"– NOW, THAT RUNG A BELL IN FATHER, JUST LIKE THAT—
My wife— she's dying of old-fashioned CONSUMPTION!
Oh, you don't mean it... !!
We'll PRAY!
AND SO THEY PRAYED, RIGHT THERE IN BOSTON'S NORTH STATION...
AND FATHER SAID THAT THIS WARM WAVE CAME OVER HIM THERE
AND HE KNEW.
AND NEXT THING MAMA KNEW,
THEY WERE GETTING HER READY FOR THE TRAIN–

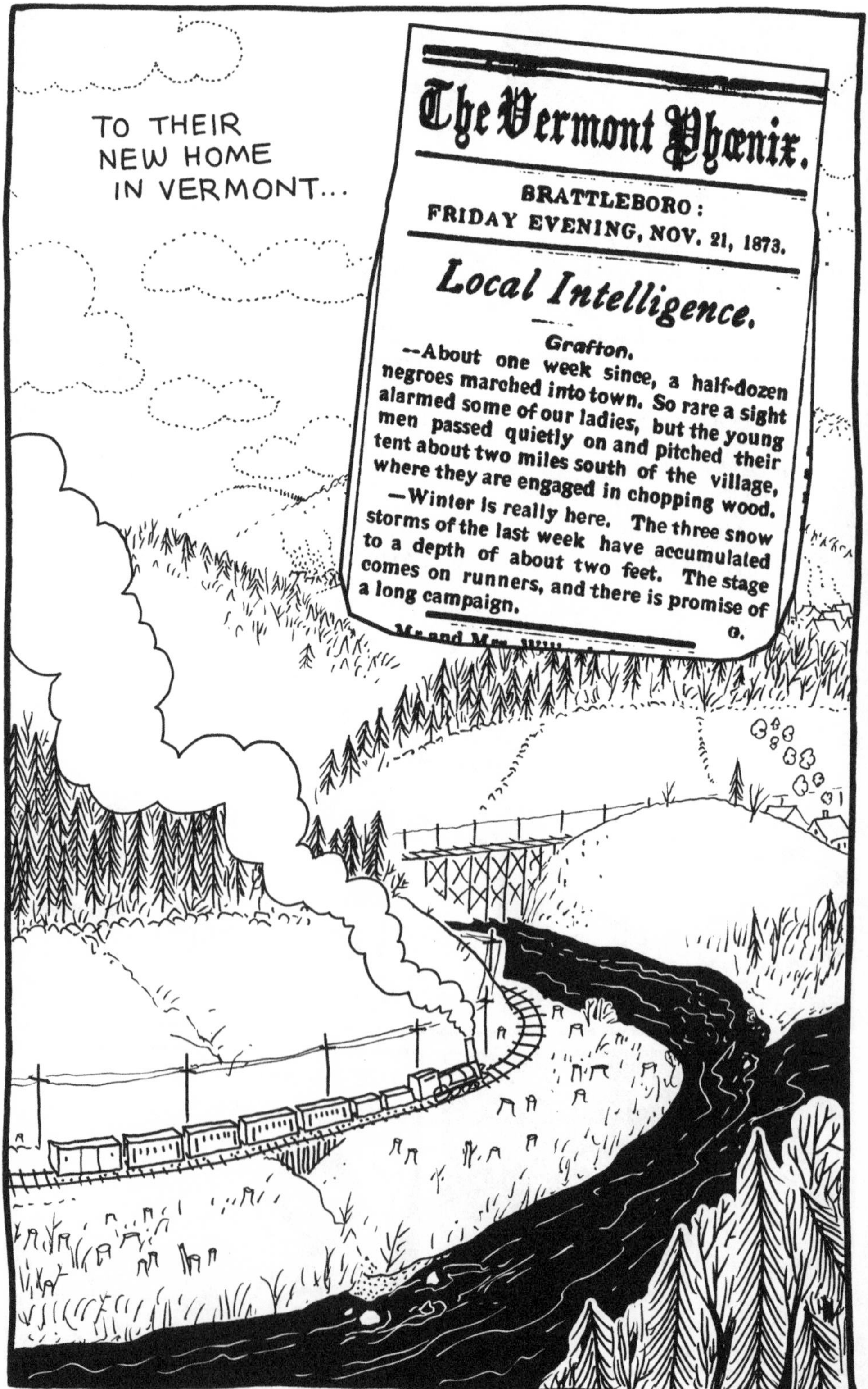
TO THEIR NEW HOME IN VERMONT...
The Vermont Phœnix.
BRATTLEBORO:
FRIDAY EVENING, NOV. 21, 1873.
Local Intelligence.
Grafton.
--About one week since, a half-dozen negroes marched into town. So rare a sight alarmed some of our ladies, but the young men passed quietly on and pitched their tent about two miles south of the village, where they are engaged in chopping wood.
—Winter is really here. The three snow storms of the last week have accumulaled to a depth of about two feet. The stage comes on runners, and there is promise of a long campaign.
G.

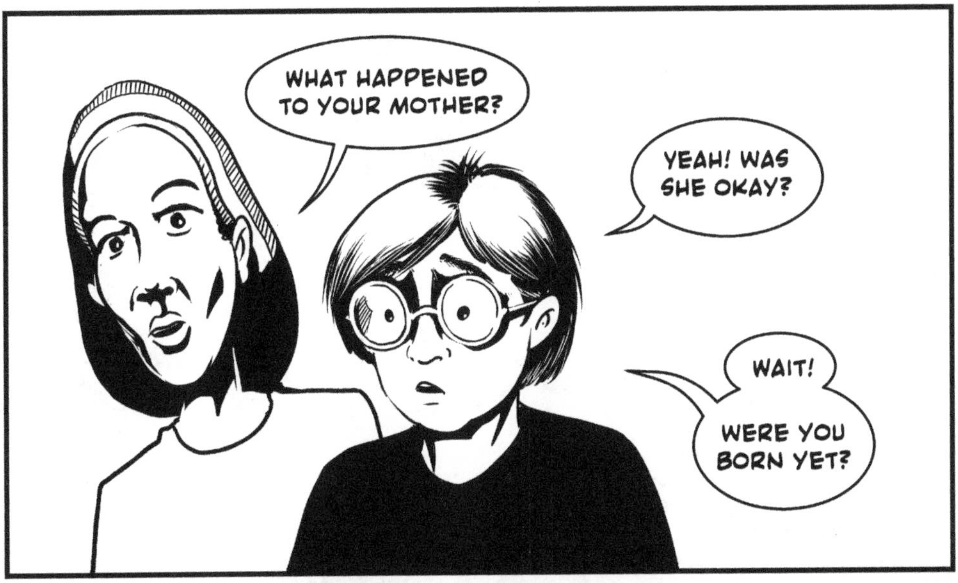
WHAT HAPPENED TO YOUR MOTHER?
YEAH! WAS SHE OKAY?
WAIT!
WERE YOU BORN YET?

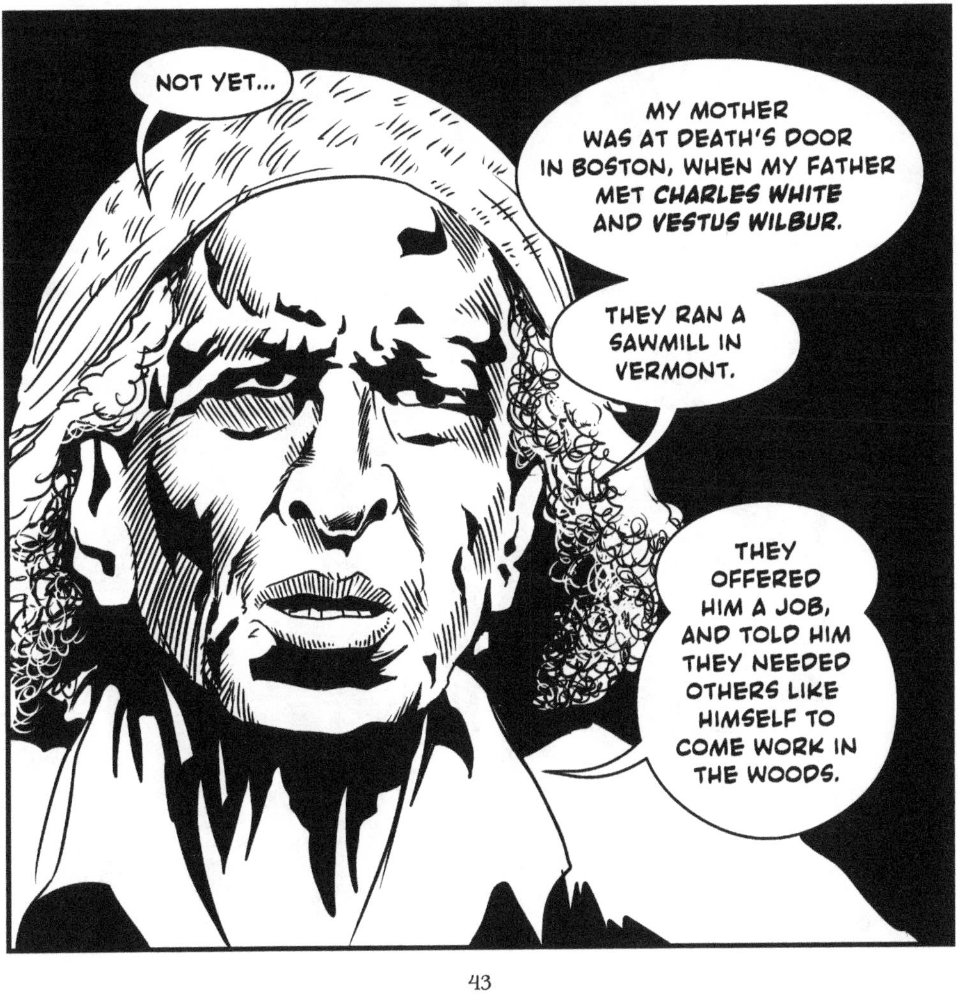
NOT YET...
MY MOTHER WAS AT DEATH'S DOOR IN BOSTON, WHEN MY FATHER MET CHARLES WHITE AND VESTUS WILBUR.
THEY RAN A SAWMILL IN VERMONT.
THEY OFFERED HIM A JOB, AND TOLD HIM THEY NEEDED OTHERS LIKE HIMSELF TO COME WORK IN THE WOODS.

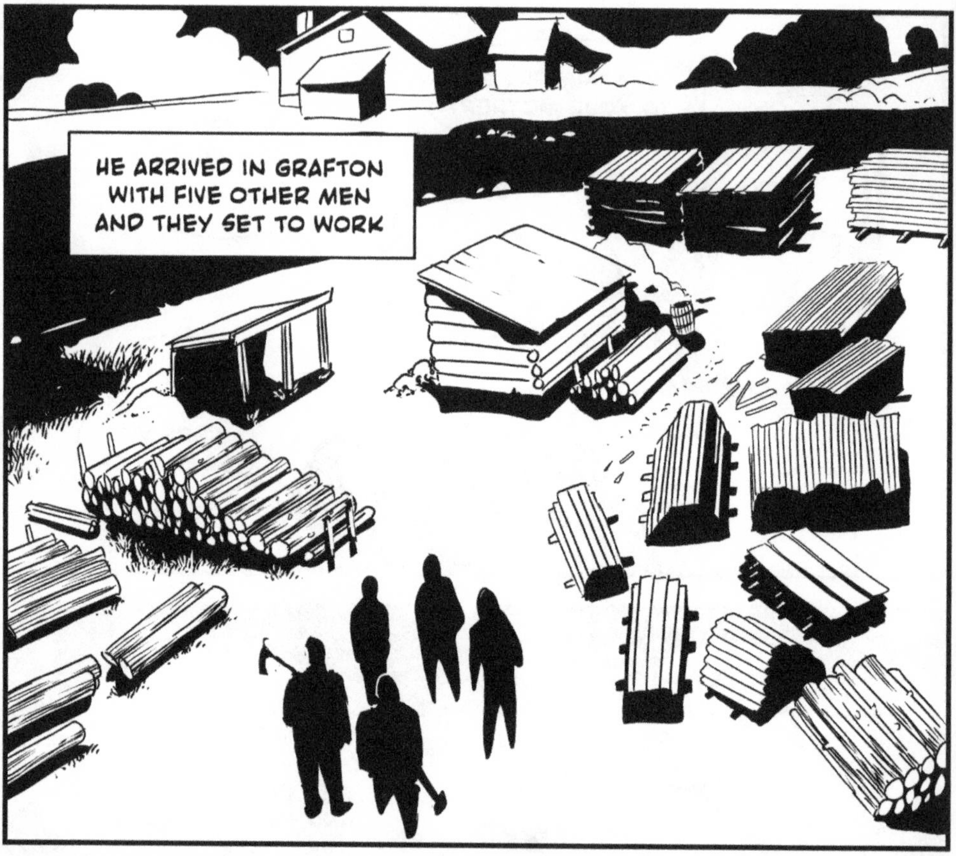
HE ARRIVED IN GRAFTON WITH FIVE OTHER MEN AND THEY SET TO WORK

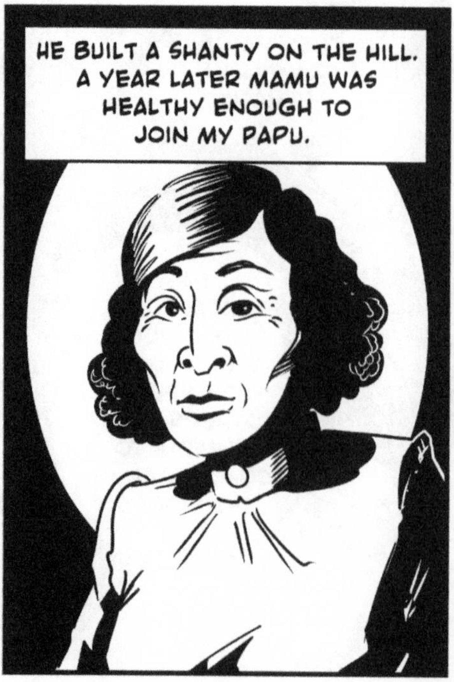
HE BUILT A SHANTY ON THE HILL. A YEAR LATER MAMU WAS HEALTHY ENOUGH TO JOIN MY PAPU.

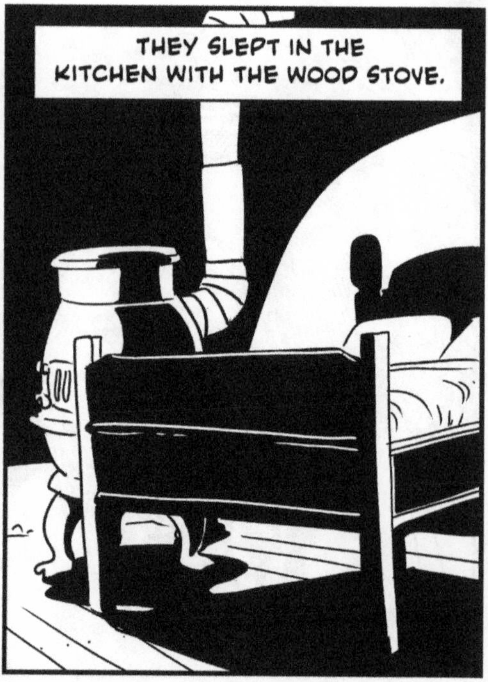
THEY SLEPT IN THE KITCHEN WITH THE WOOD STOVE.

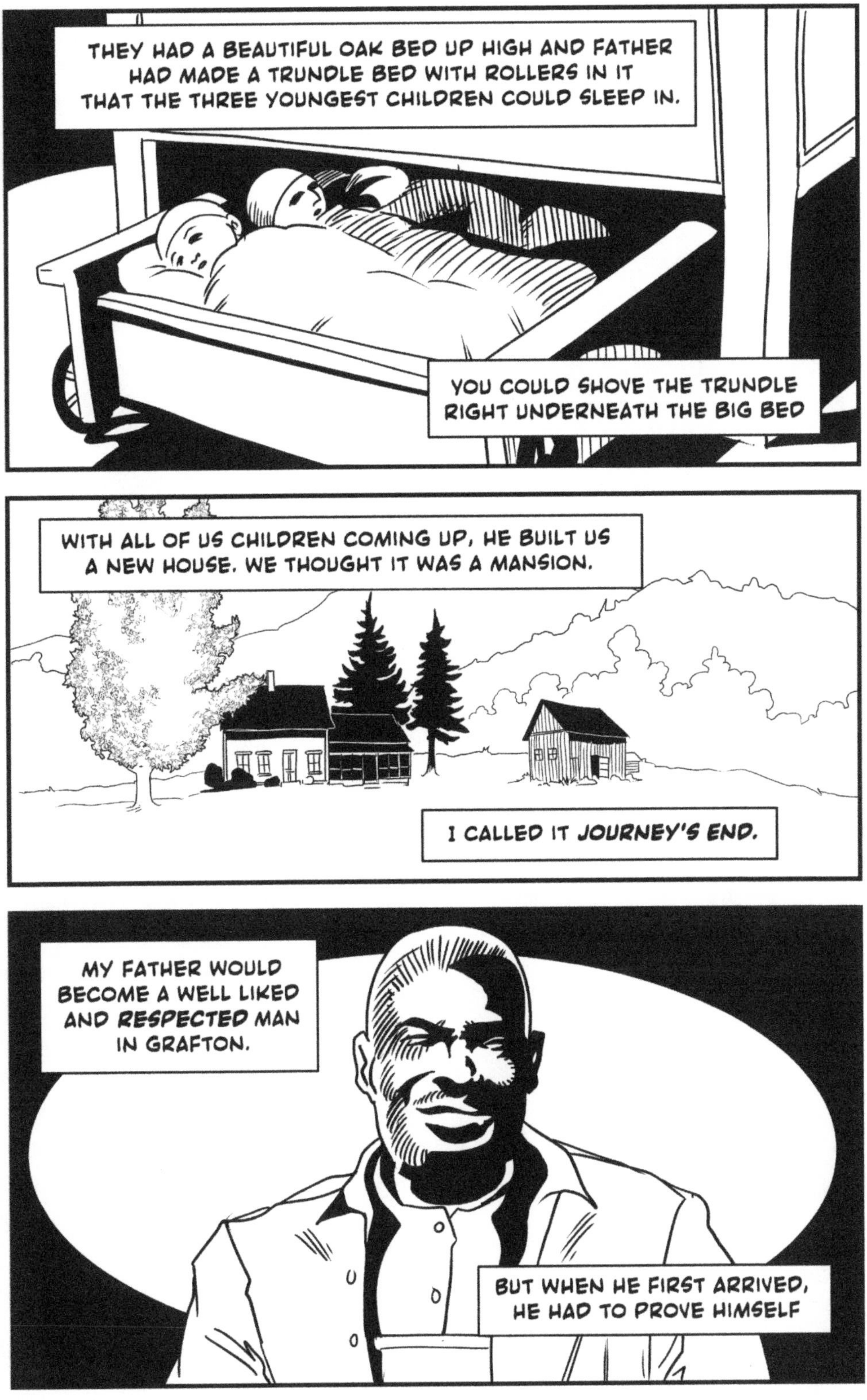
THEY HAD A BEAUTIFUL OAK BED UP HIGH AND FATHER HAD MADE A TRUNDLE BED WITH ROLLERS IN IT THAT THE THREE YOUNGEST CHILDREN COULD SLEEP IN.
YOU COULD SHOVE THE TRUNDLE RIGHT UNDERNEATH THE BIG BED
WITH ALL OF US CHILDREN COMING UP, HE BUILT US A NEW HOUSE. WE THOUGHT IT WAS A MANSION.
I CALLED IT *JOURNEY'S END.*
MY FATHER WOULD BECOME A WELL LIKED AND *RESPECTED* MAN IN GRAFTON.
BUT WHEN HE FIRST ARRIVED, HE HAD TO PROVE HIMSELF

STRONGEST MAN IN TOWN

By Joel Christian Gill

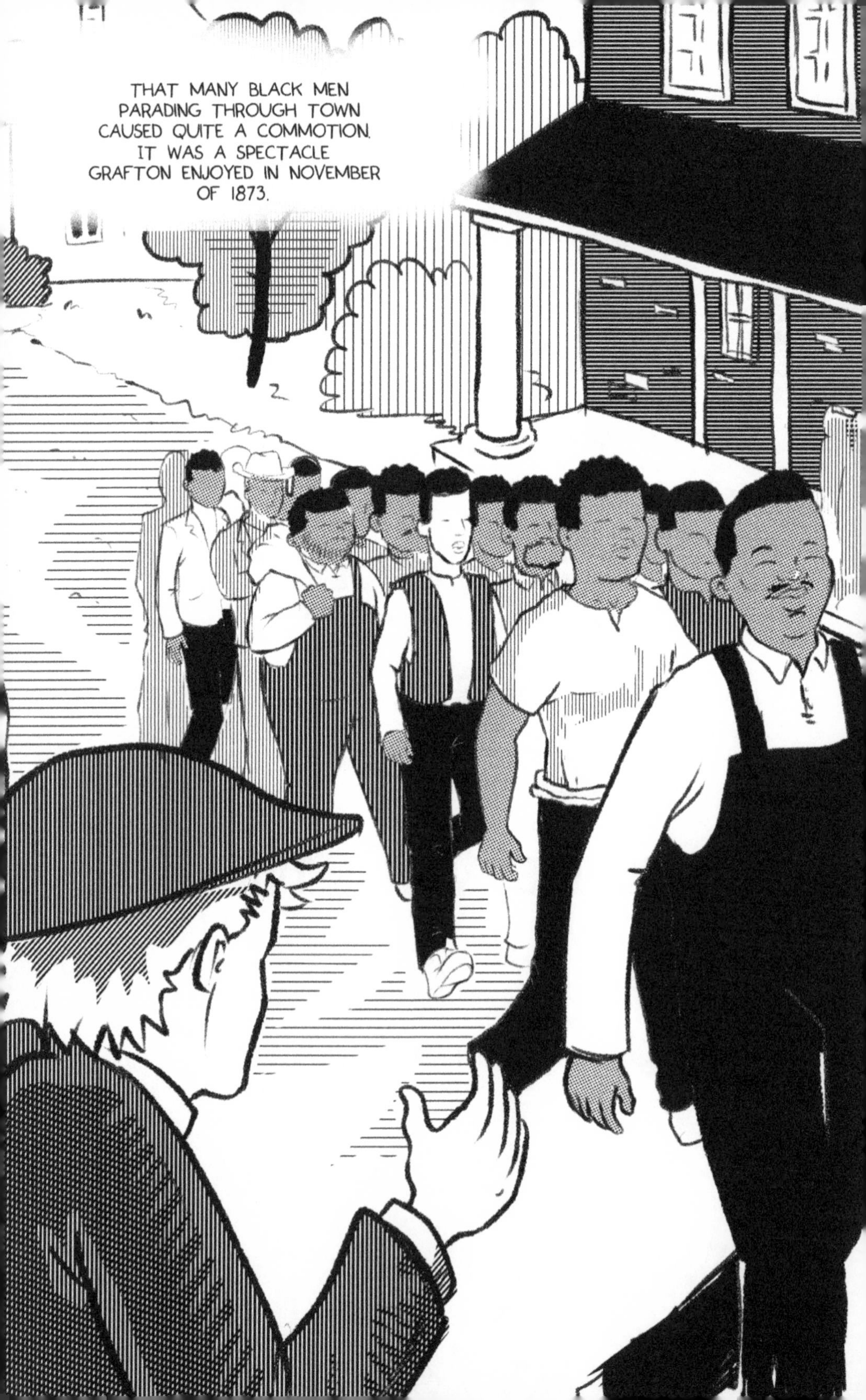
THAT MANY BLACK MEN PARADING THROUGH TOWN CAUSED QUITE A COMMOTION. IT WAS A SPECTACLE GRAFTON ENJOYED IN NOVEMBER OF 1873.

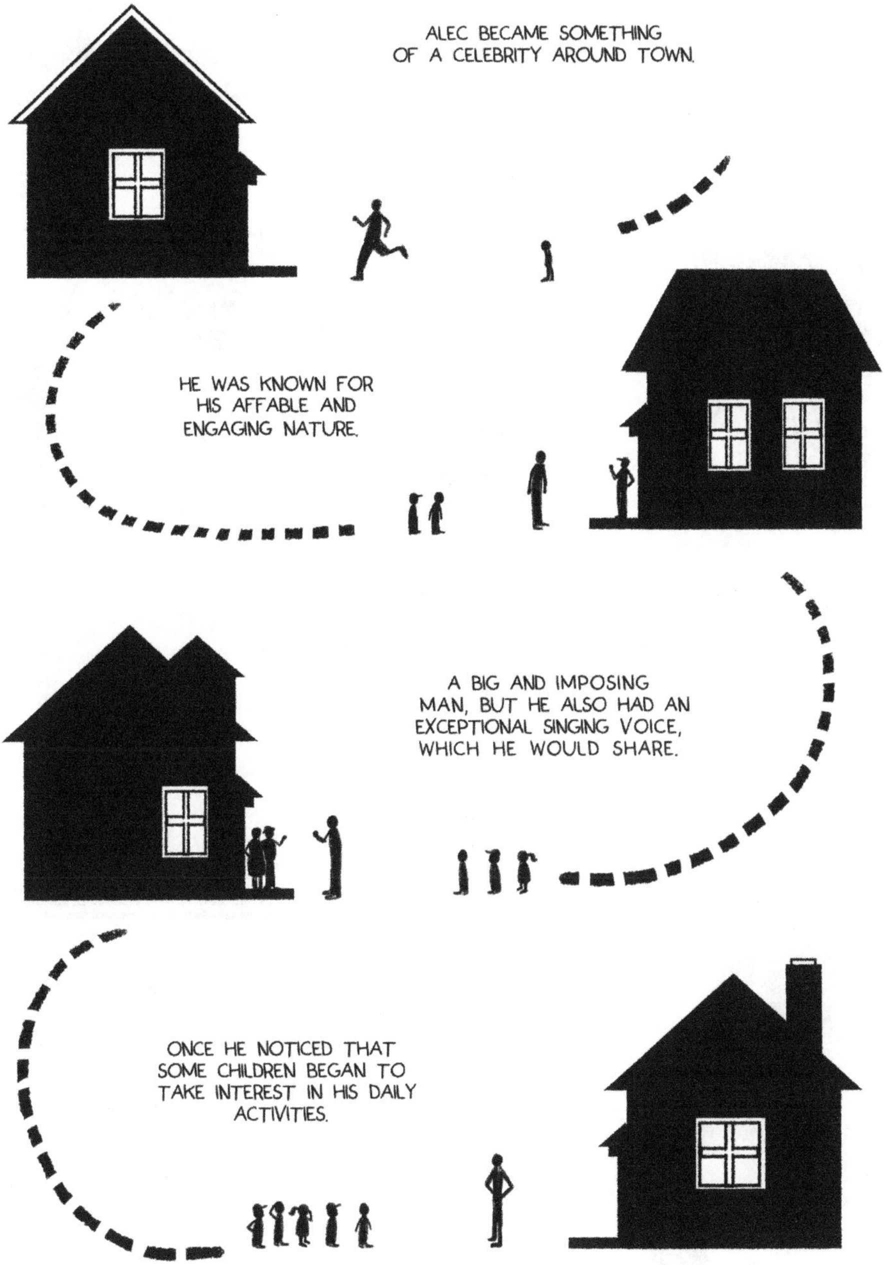
ALEC BECAME SOMETHING OF A CELEBRITY AROUND TOWN.
HE WAS KNOWN FOR HIS AFFABLE AND ENGAGING NATURE.
A BIG AND IMPOSING MAN, BUT HE ALSO HAD AN EXCEPTIONAL SINGING VOICE, WHICH HE WOULD SHARE.
ONCE HE NOTICED THAT SOME CHILDREN BEGAN TO TAKE INTEREST IN HIS DAILY ACTIVITIES.

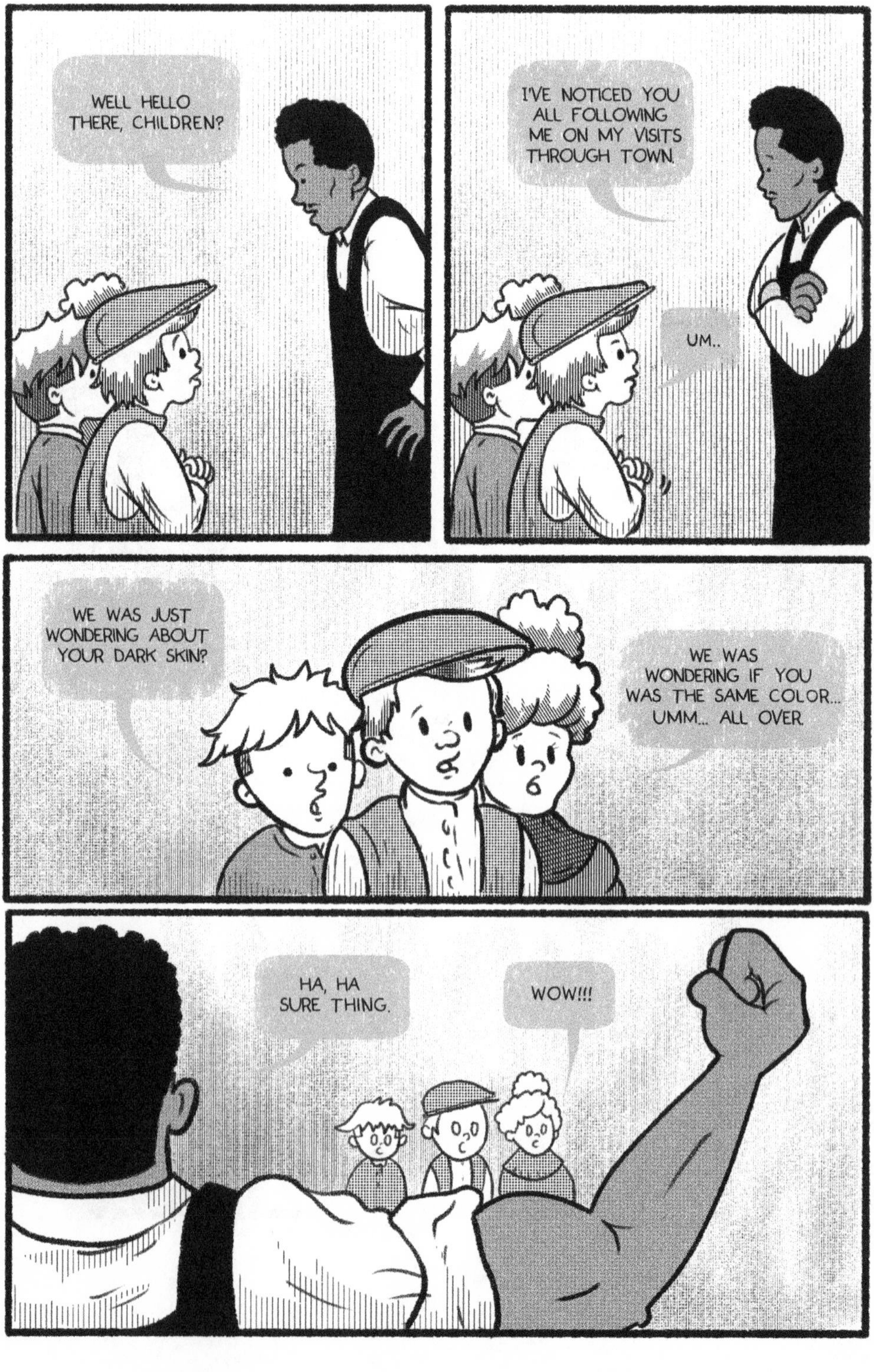
WELL HELLO THERE, CHILDREN?
I'VE NOTICED YOU ALL FOLLOWING ME ON MY VISITS THROUGH TOWN.
UM..
WE WAS JUST WONDERING ABOUT YOUR DARK SKIN?
WE WAS WONDERING IF YOU WAS THE SAME COLOR... UMM... ALL OVER.
HA, HA SURE THING.
WOW!!!

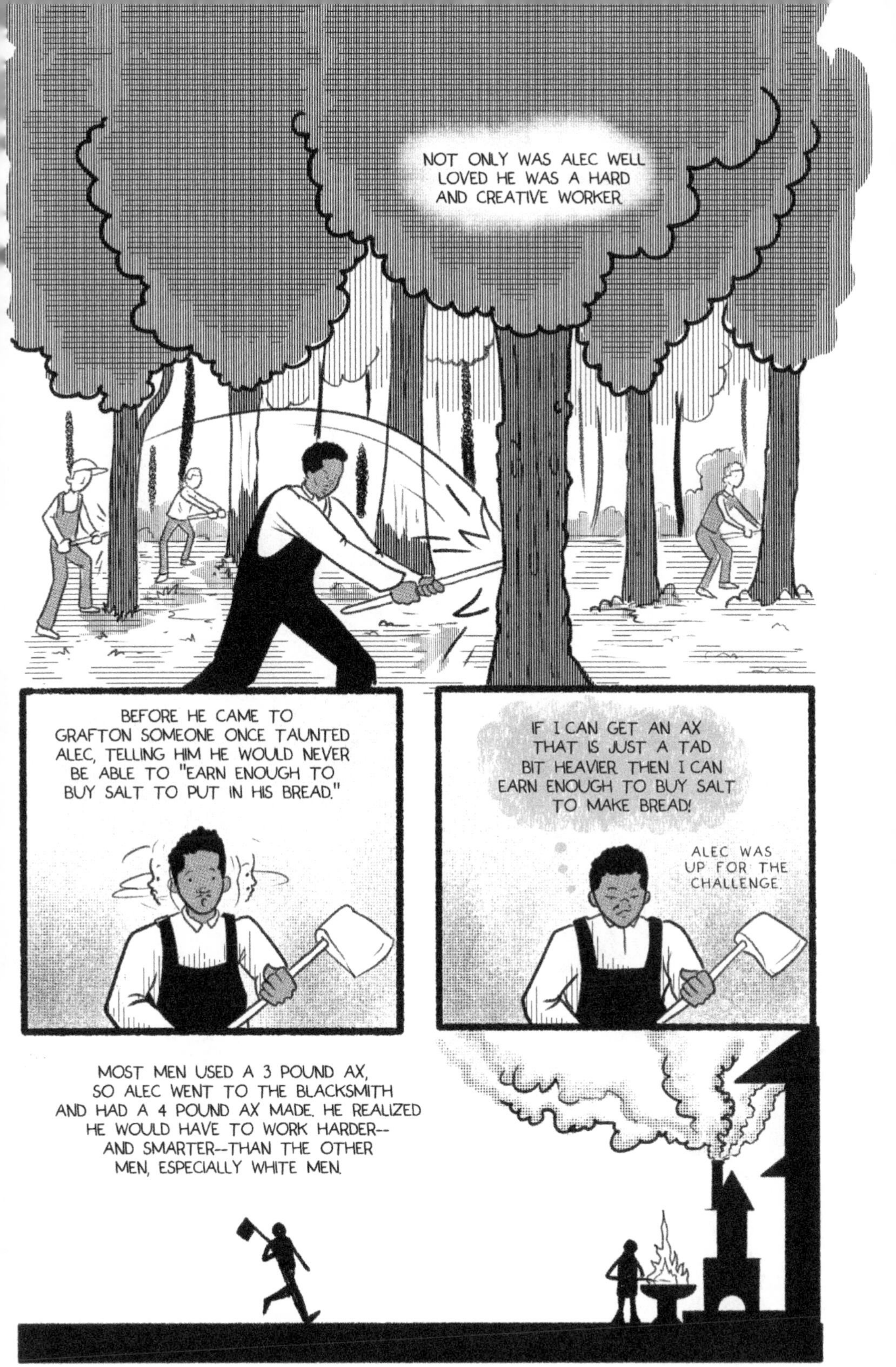
NOT ONLY WAS ALEC WELL LOVED HE WAS A HARD AND CREATIVE WORKER.
BEFORE HE CAME TO GRAFTON SOMEONE ONCE TAUNTED ALEC, TELLING HIM HE WOULD NEVER BE ABLE TO "EARN ENOUGH TO BUY SALT TO PUT IN HIS BREAD."
IF I CAN GET AN AX THAT IS JUST A TAD BIT HEAVIER THEN I CAN EARN ENOUGH TO BUY SALT TO MAKE BREAD!
ALEC WAS UP FOR THE CHALLENGE.
MOST MEN USED A 3 POUND AX, SO ALEC WENT TO THE BLACKSMITH AND HAD A 4 POUND AX MADE. HE REALIZED HE WOULD HAVE TO WORK HARDER-- AND SMARTER--THAN THE OTHER MEN, ESPECIALLY WHITE MEN.

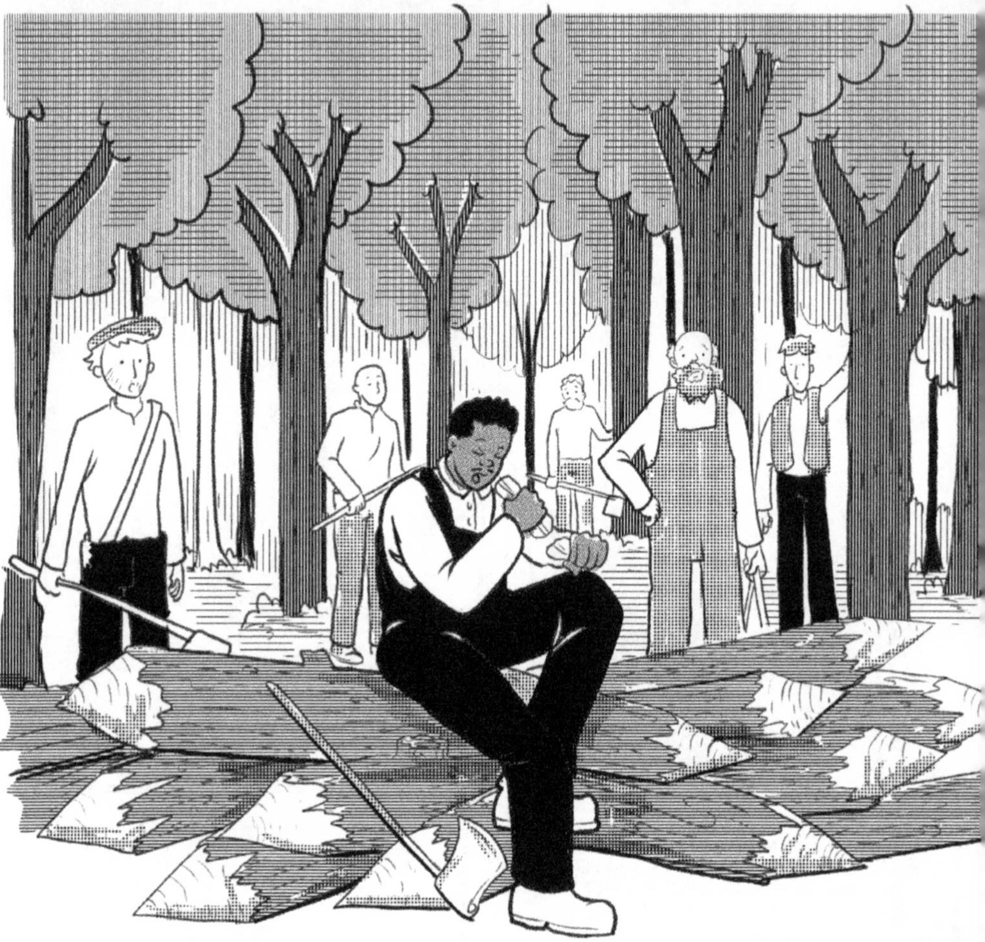

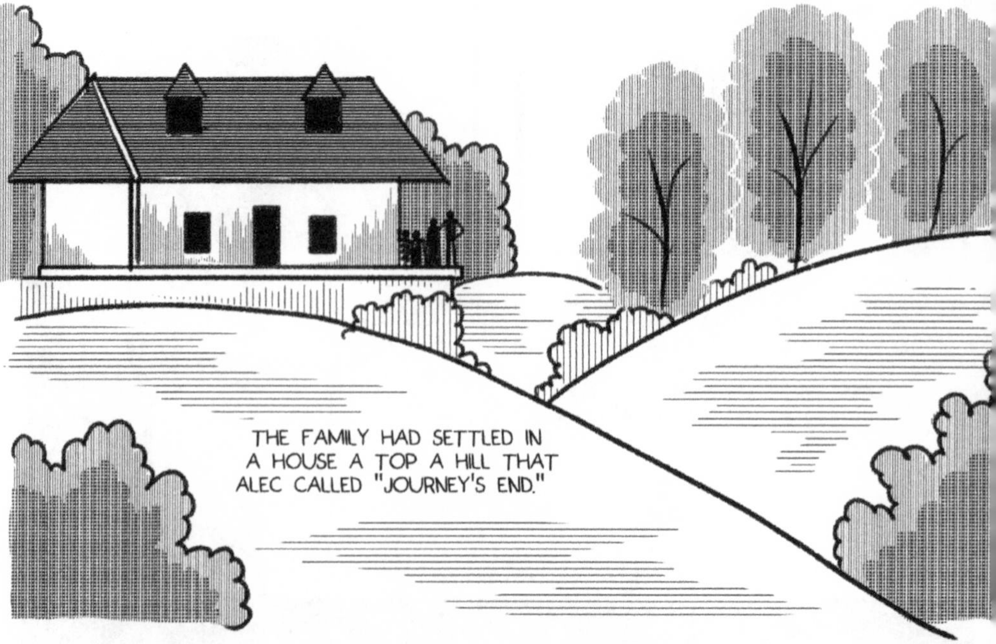
THE FAMILY HAD SETTLED IN A HOUSE A TOP A HILL THAT ALEC CALLED "JOURNEY'S END."

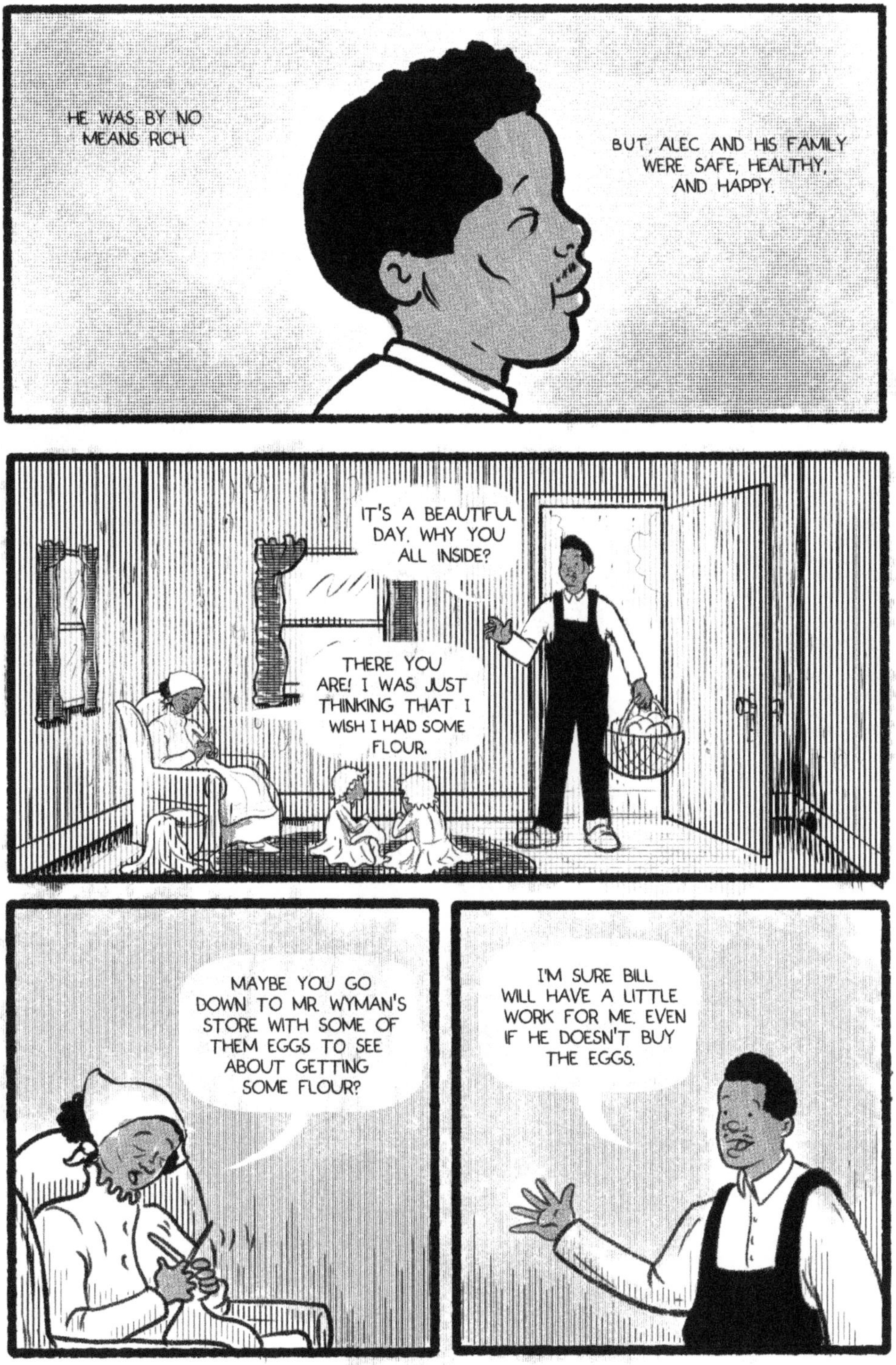
HE WAS BY NO MEANS RICH.
BUT, ALEC AND HIS FAMILY WERE SAFE, HEALTHY, AND HAPPY.
IT'S A BEAUTIFUL DAY. WHY YOU ALL INSIDE?
THERE YOU ARE! I WAS JUST THINKING THAT I WISH I HAD SOME FLOUR.
MAYBE YOU GO DOWN TO MR. WYMAN'S STORE WITH SOME OF THEM EGGS TO SEE ABOUT GETTING SOME FLOUR?
I'M SURE BILL WILL HAVE A LITTLE WORK FOR ME. EVEN IF HE DOESN'T BUY THE EGGS.

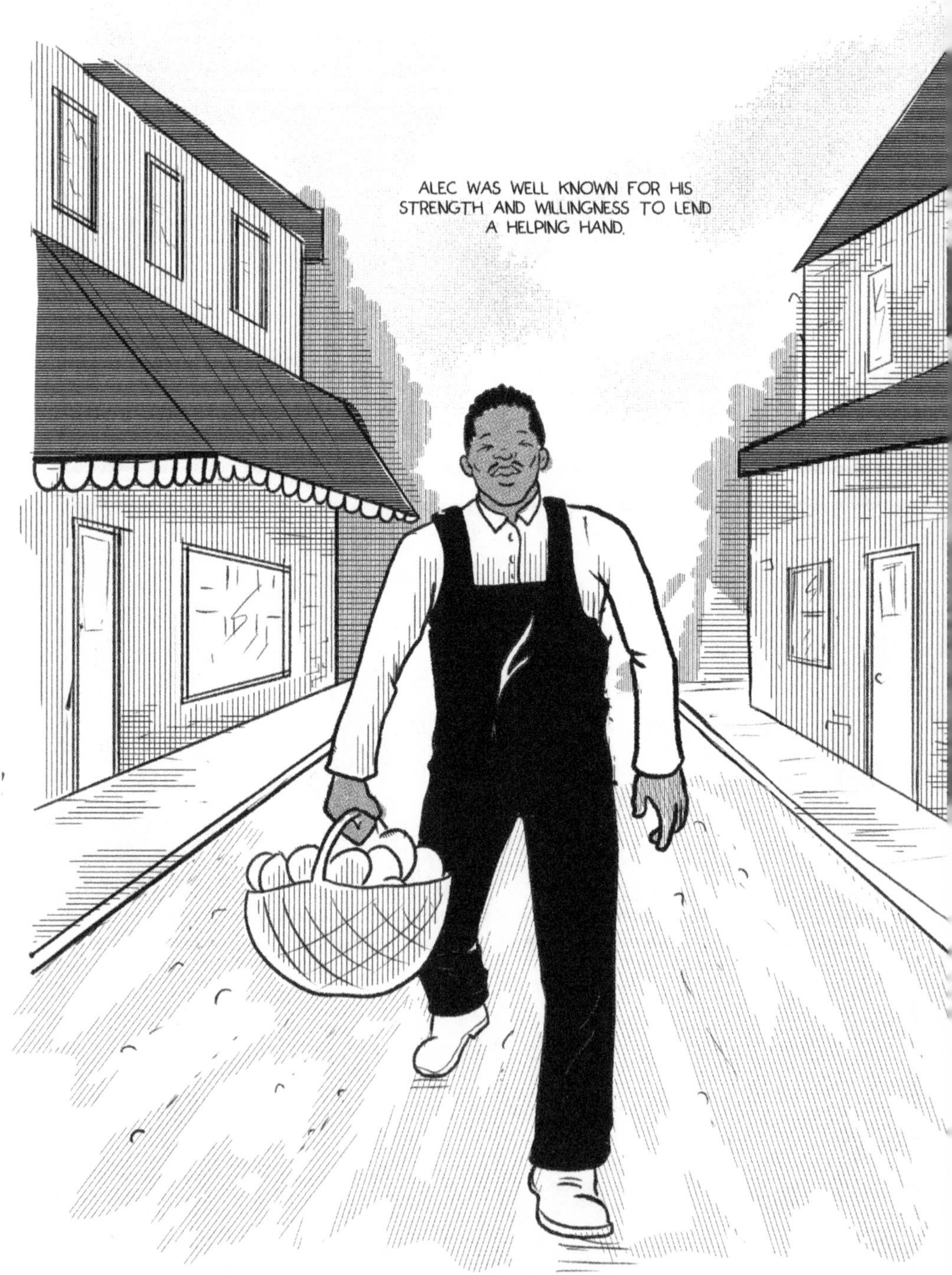
ALEC WAS WELL KNOWN FOR HIS STRENGTH AND WILLINGNESS TO LEND A HELPING HAND.

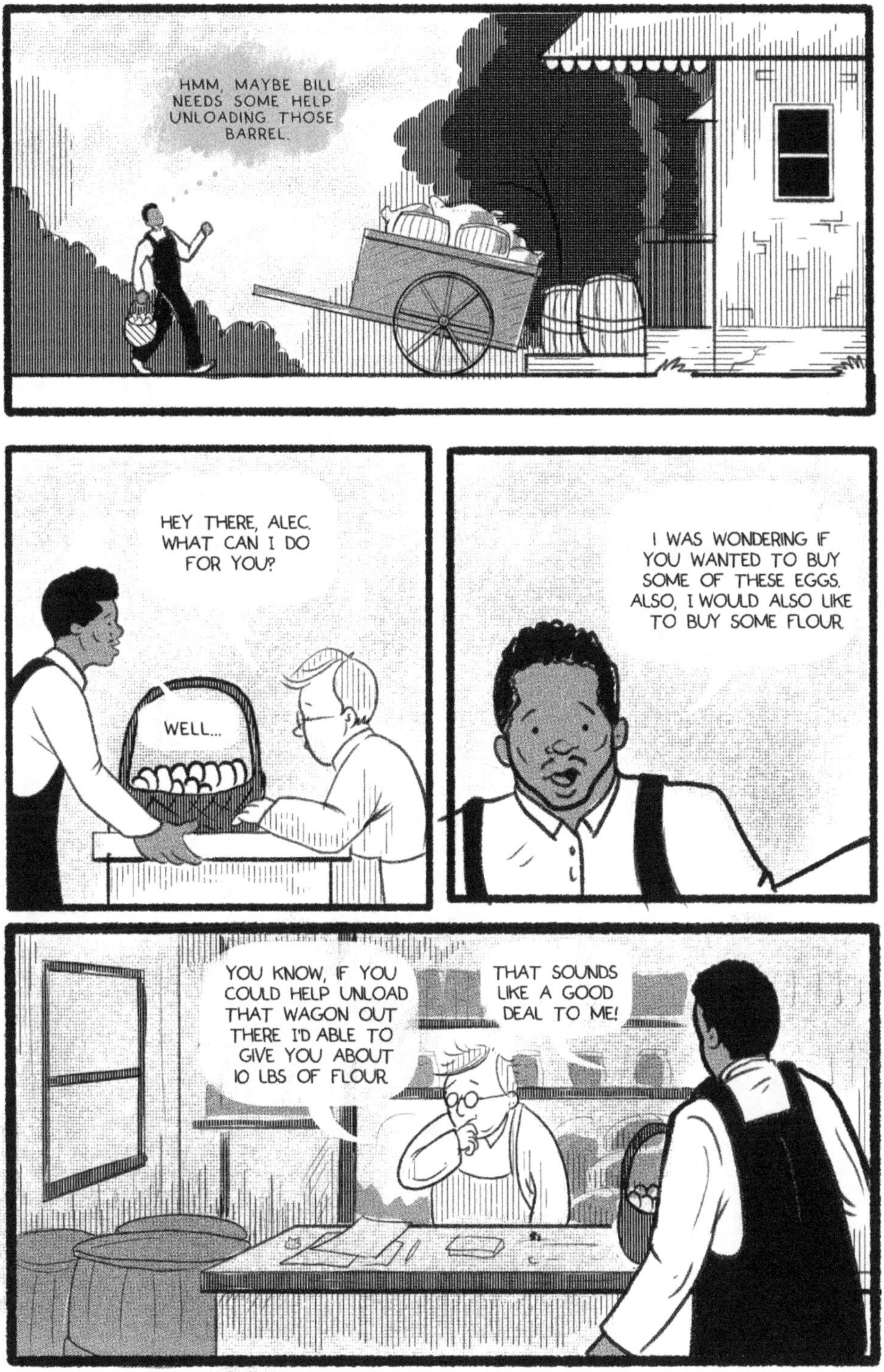
HMM, MAYBE BILL NEEDS SOME HELP UNLOADING THOSE BARREL.
HEY THERE, ALEC. WHAT CAN I DO FOR YOU?
WELL...
I WAS WONDERING IF YOU WANTED TO BUY SOME OF THESE EGGS. ALSO, I WOULD ALSO LIKE TO BUY SOME FLOUR.
YOU KNOW, IF YOU COULD HELP UNLOAD THAT WAGON OUT THERE I'D ABLE TO GIVE YOU ABOUT 10 LBS OF FLOUR.
THAT SOUNDS LIKE A GOOD DEAL TO ME!

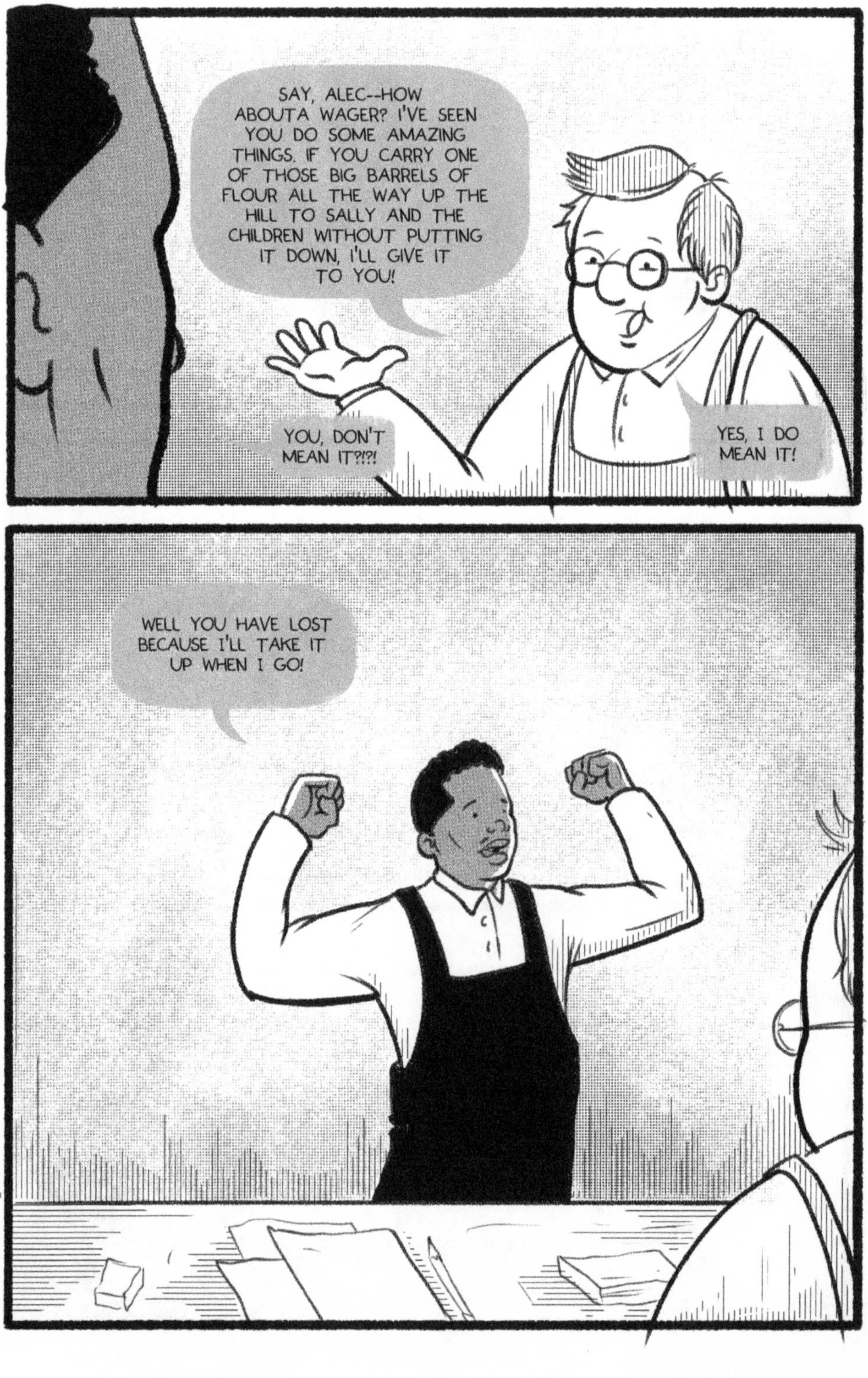
SAY, ALEC--HOW ABOUTA WAGER? I'VE SEEN YOU DO SOME AMAZING THINGS. IF YOU CARRY ONE OF THOSE BIG BARRELS OF FLOUR ALL THE WAY UP THE HILL TO SALLY AND THE CHILDREN WITHOUT PUTTING IT DOWN, I'LL GIVE IT TO YOU!
YOU, DON'T MEAN IT?!?!
YES, I DO MEAN IT!
WELL YOU HAVE LOST BECAUSE I'LL TAKE IT UP WHEN I GO!

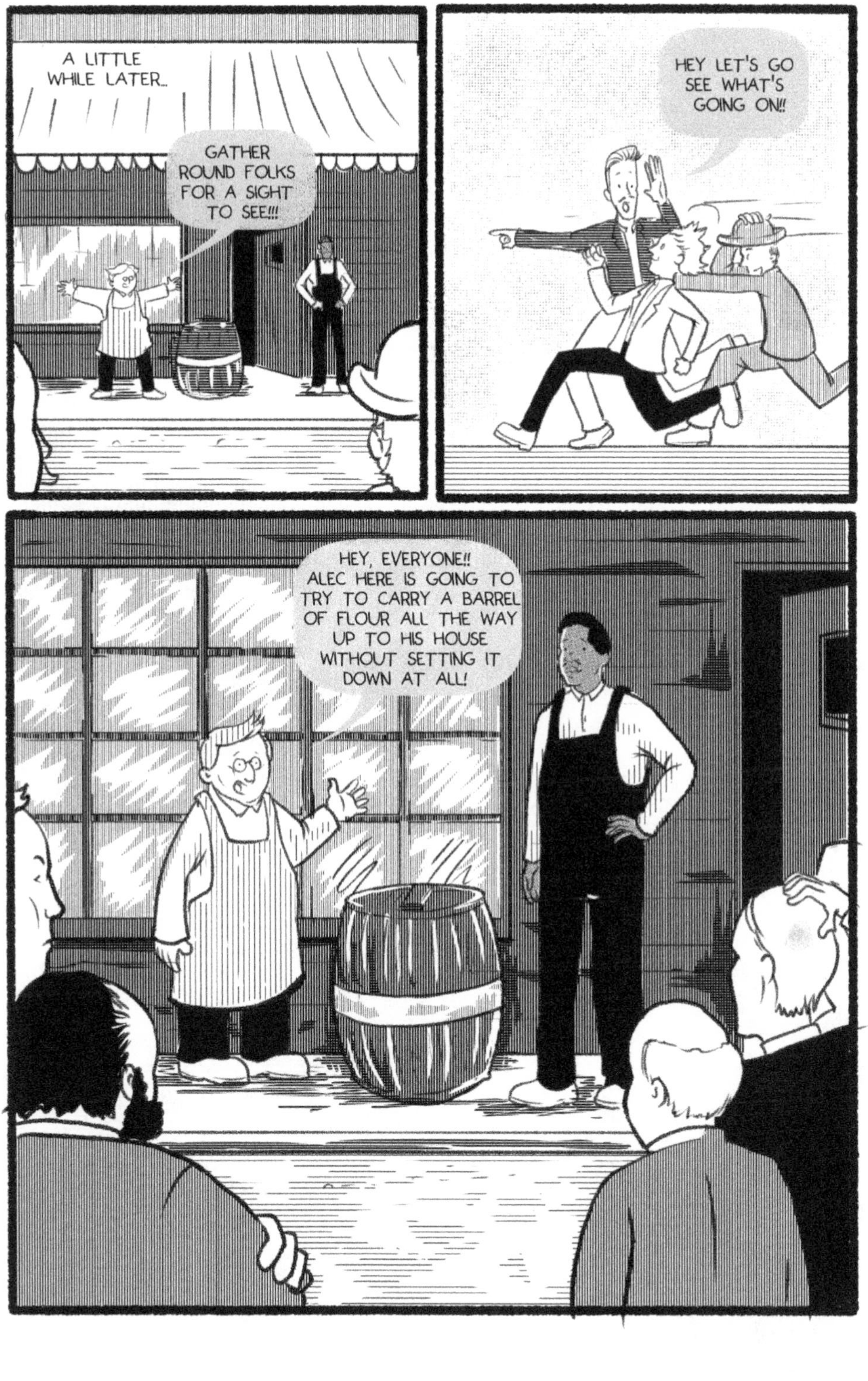
A LITTLE WHILE LATER..
GATHER ROUND FOLKS FOR A SIGHT TO SEE!!!
HEY LET'S GO SEE WHAT'S GOING ON!!
HEY, EVERYONE!! ALEC HERE IS GOING TO TRY TO CARRY A BARREL OF FLOUR ALL THE WAY UP TO HIS HOUSE WITHOUT SETTING IT DOWN AT ALL!

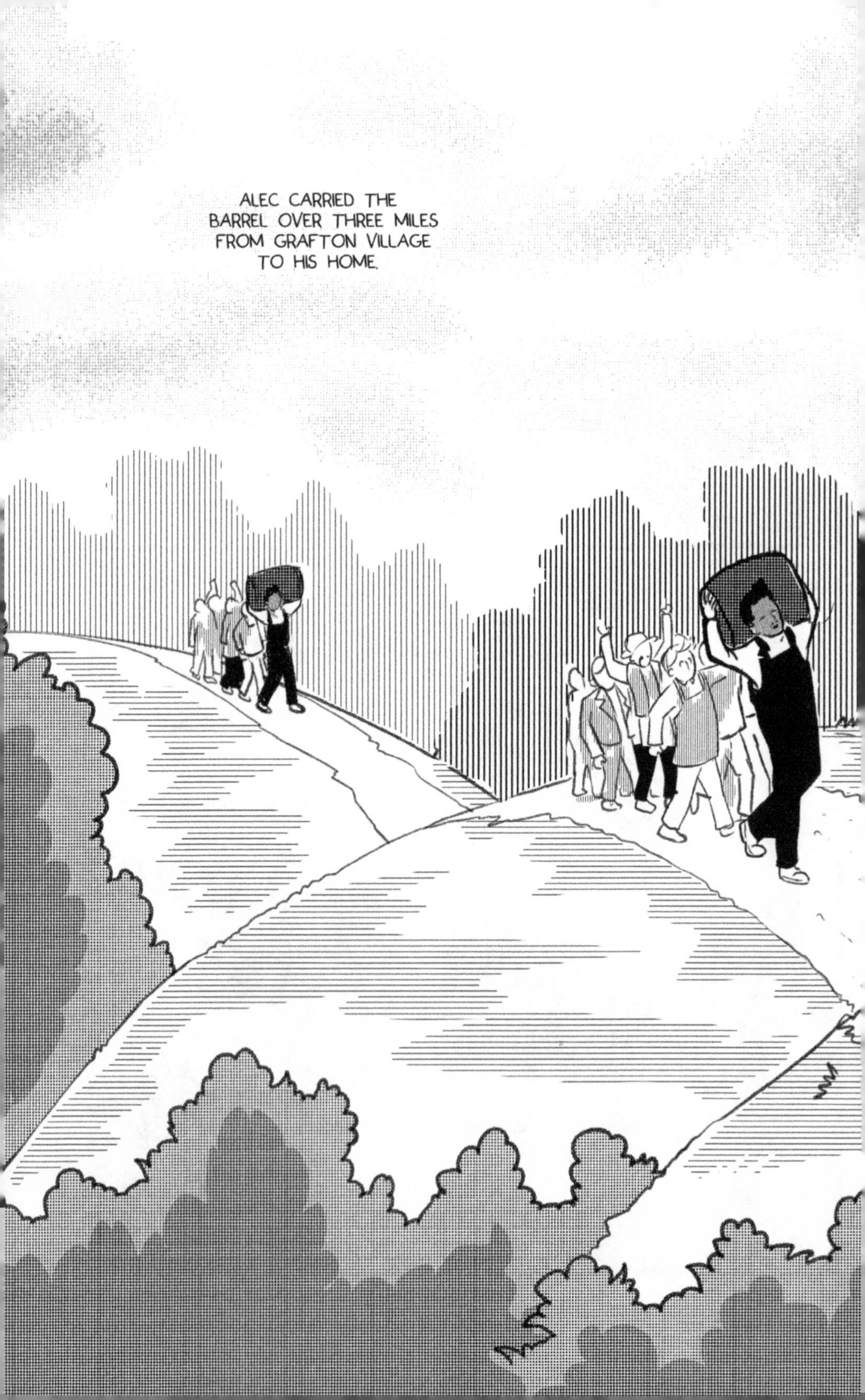
ALEC CARRIED THE BARREL OVER THREE MILES FROM GRAFTON VILLAGE TO HIS HOME.

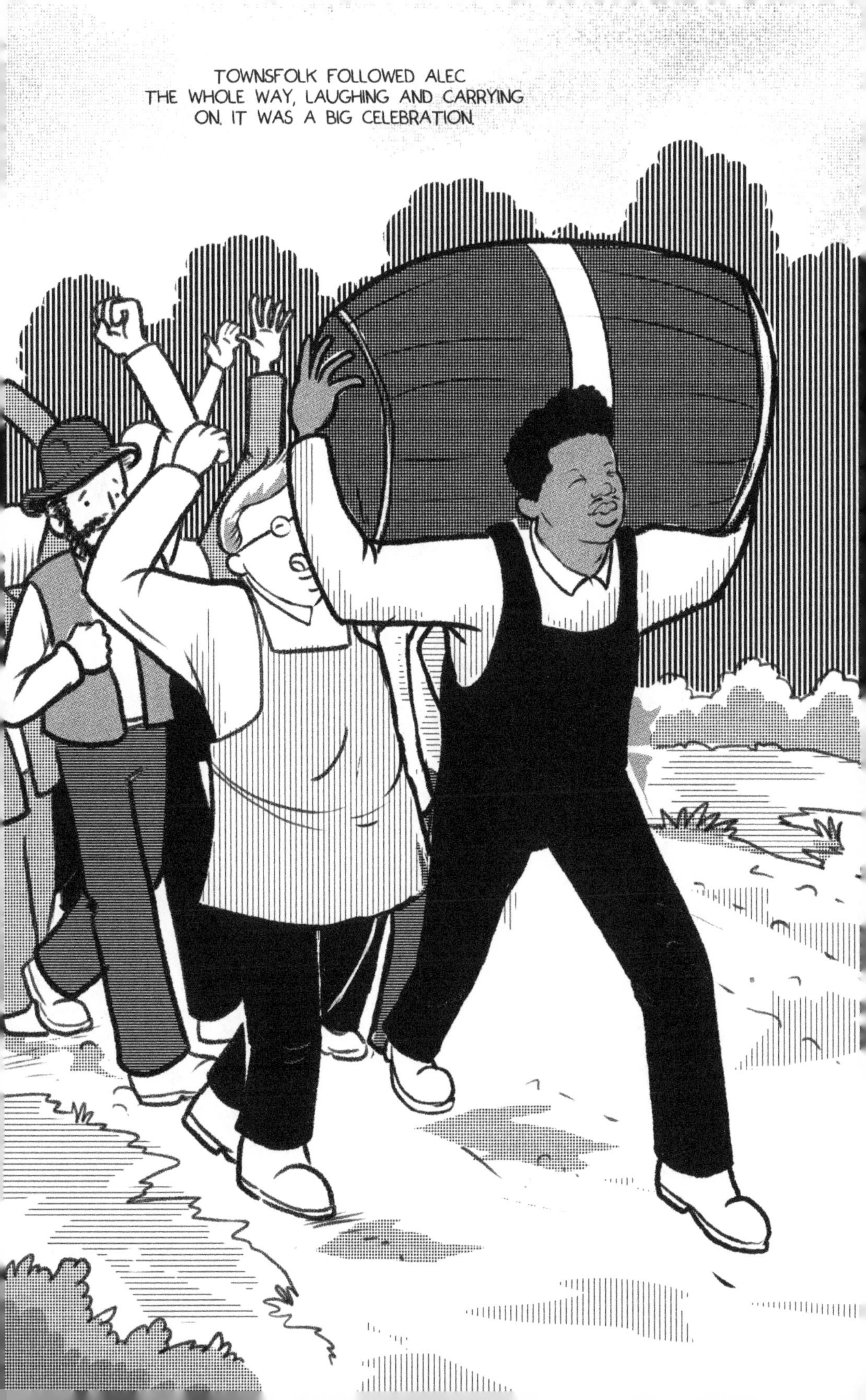
TOWNSFOLK FOLLOWED ALEC THE WHOLE WAY, LAUGHING AND CARRYING ON. IT WAS A BIG CELEBRATION.

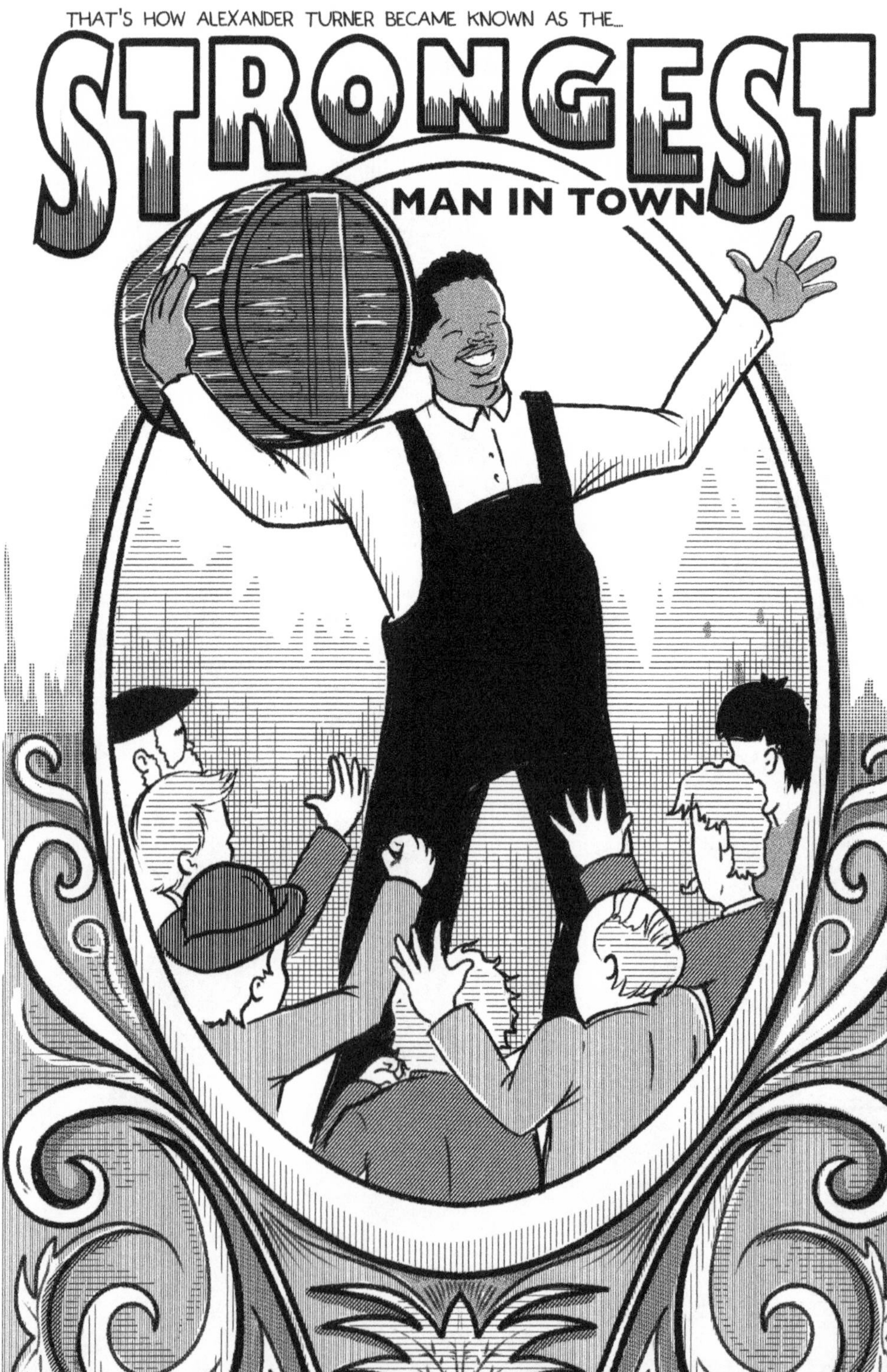
THAT'S HOW ALEXANDER TURNER BECAME KNOWN AS THE....
STRONGEST
MAN IN TOWN

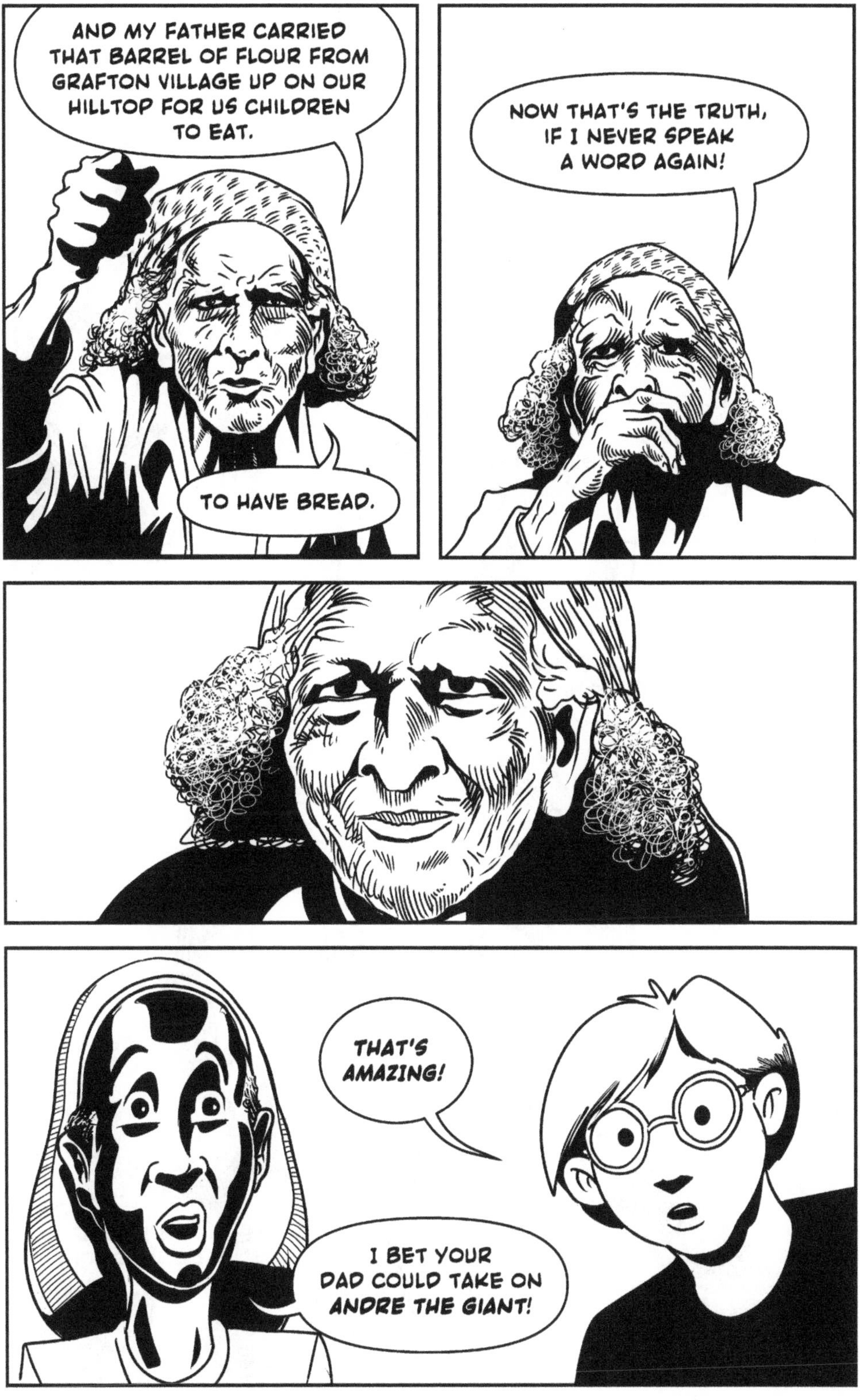
AND MY FATHER CARRIED THAT BARREL OF FLOUR FROM GRAFTON VILLAGE UP ON OUR HILLTOP FOR US CHILDREN TO EAT.
TO HAVE BREAD.
NOW THAT'S THE TRUTH, IF I NEVER SPEAK A WORD AGAIN!
THAT'S AMAZING!
I BET YOUR DAD COULD TAKE ON ANDRE THE GIANT!

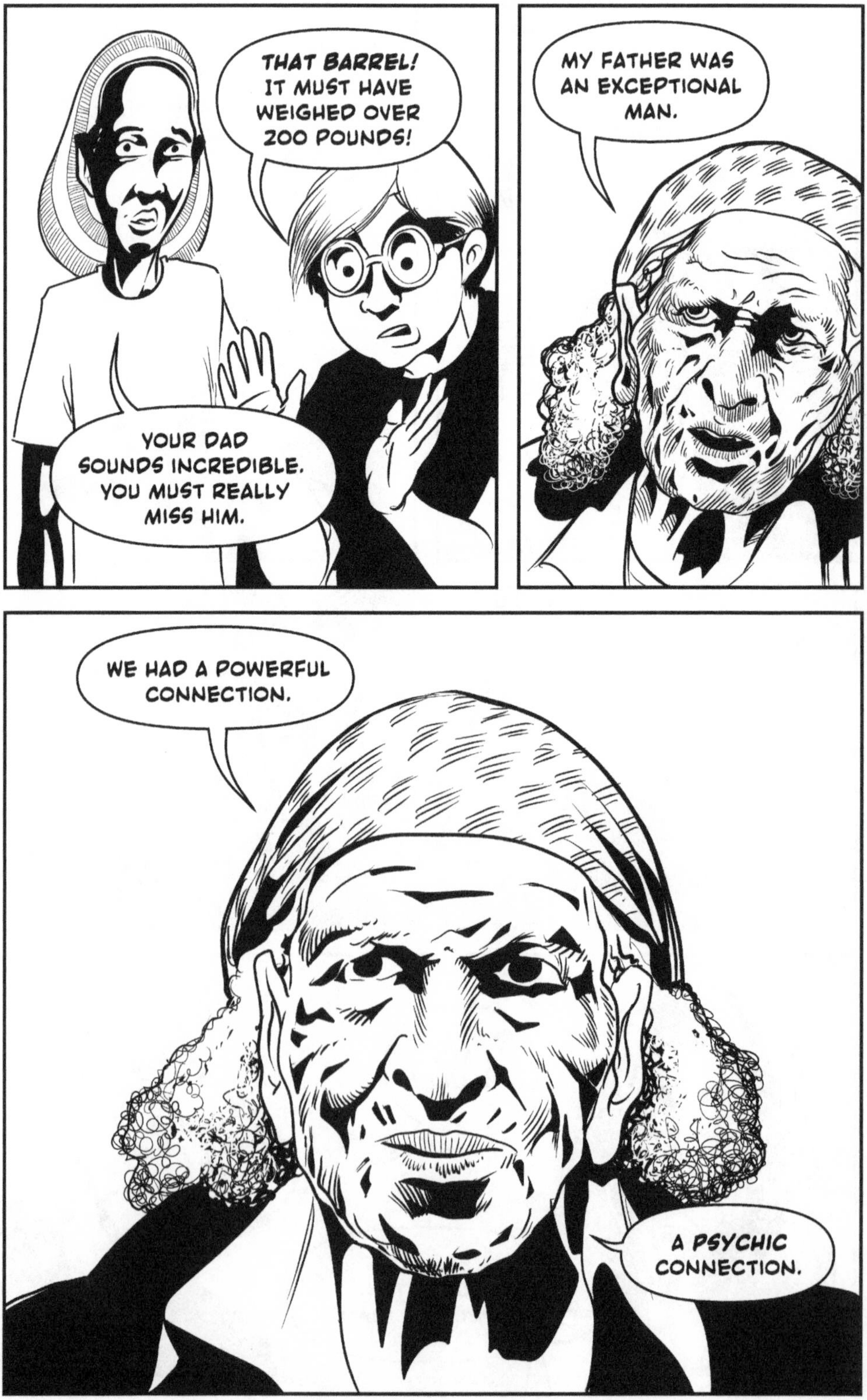
THAT BARREL! IT MUST HAVE WEIGHED OVER 200 POUNDS!
YOUR DAD SOUNDS INCREDIBLE. YOU MUST REALLY MISS HIM.
MY FATHER WAS AN EXCEPTIONAL MAN.
WE HAD A POWERFUL CONNECTION.
A PSYCHIC CONNECTION.

DAISY'S PREMONITION

By Lillie Harris

DAISY'S PREMONITION

DAISY TURNER USED TO SAY
THAT SHE AND HER FATHER WERE SO CLOSE...

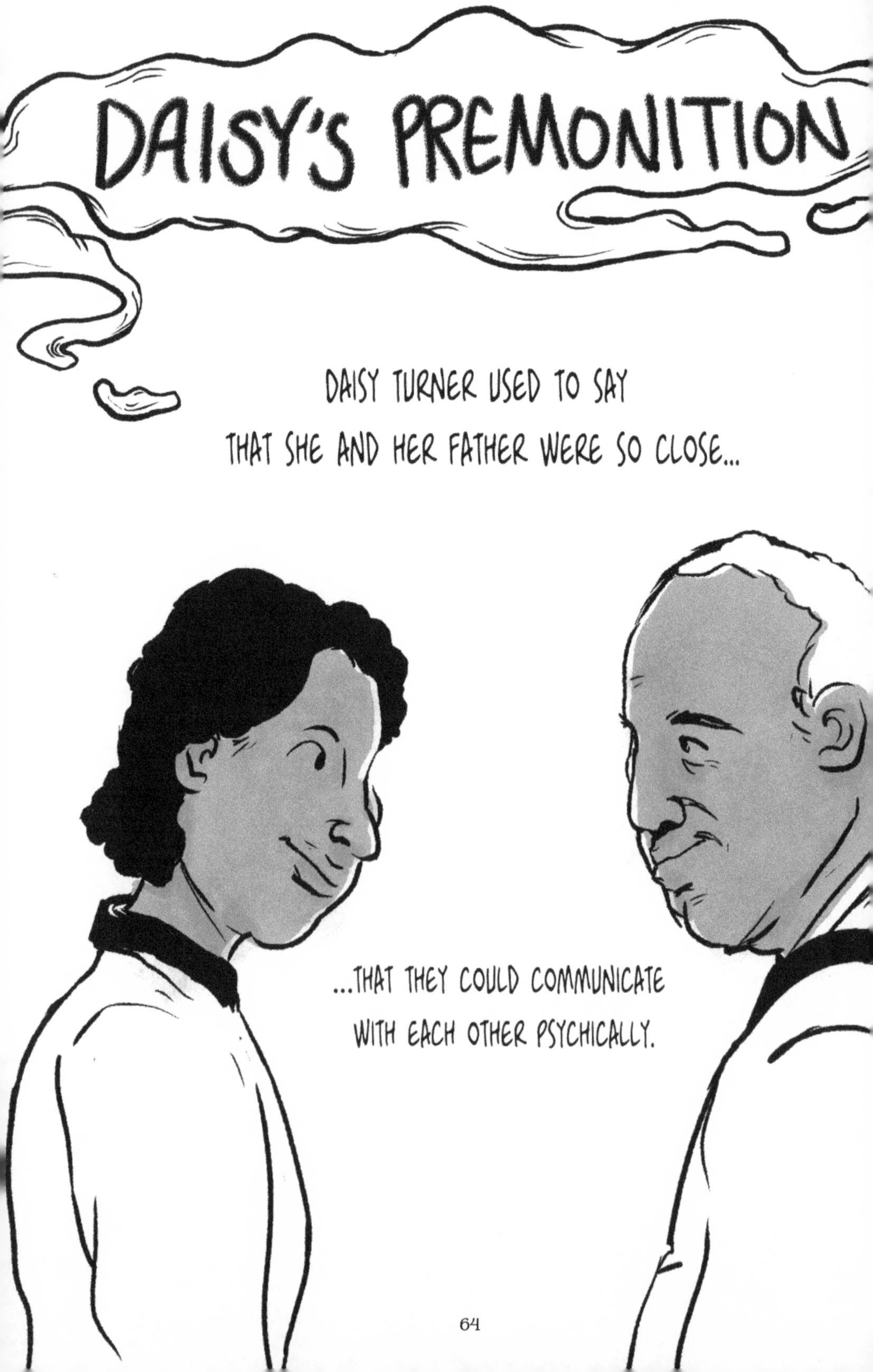
...THAT THEY COULD COMMUNICATE
WITH EACH OTHER PSYCHICALLY.

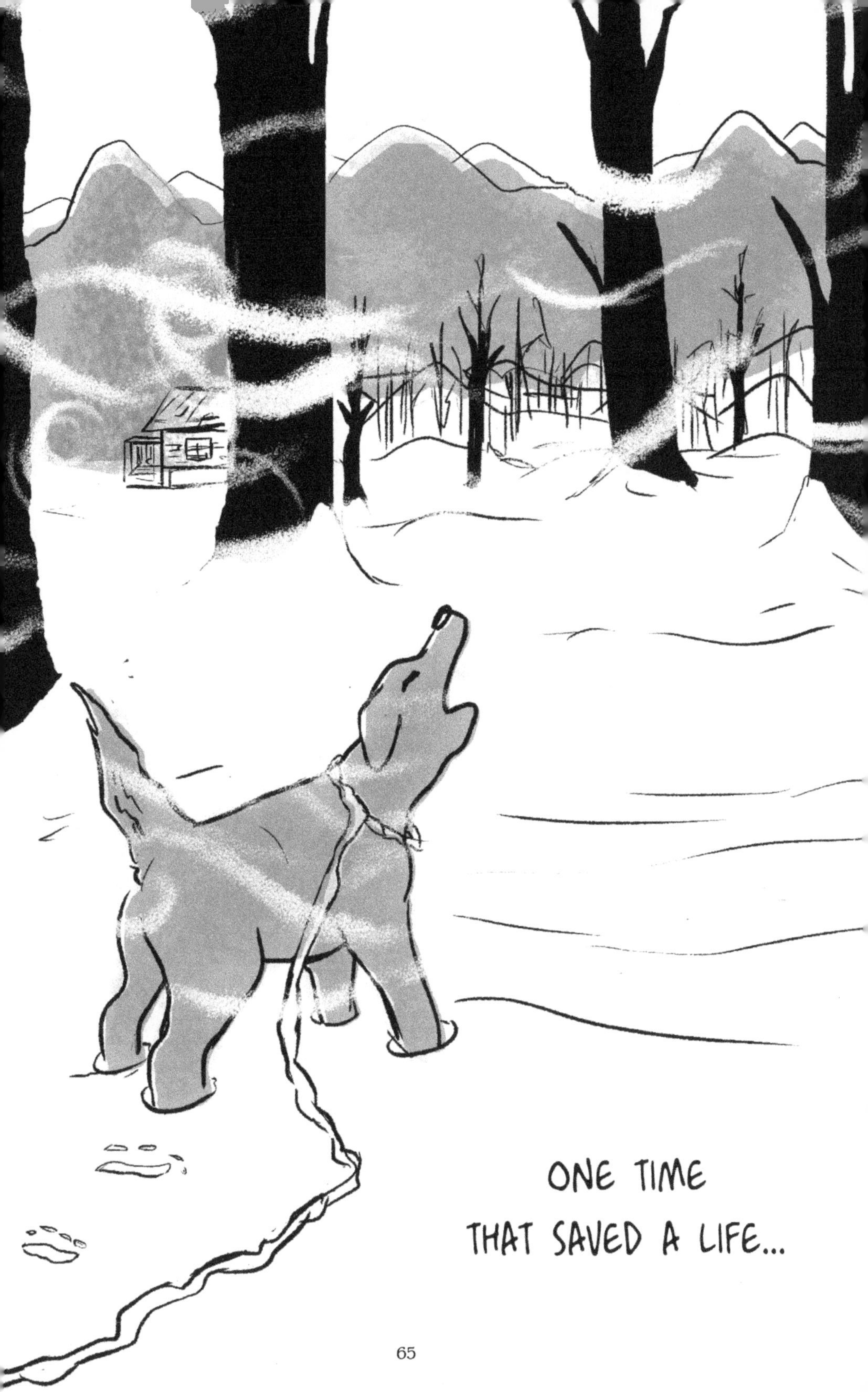
ONE TIME
THAT SAVED A LIFE...

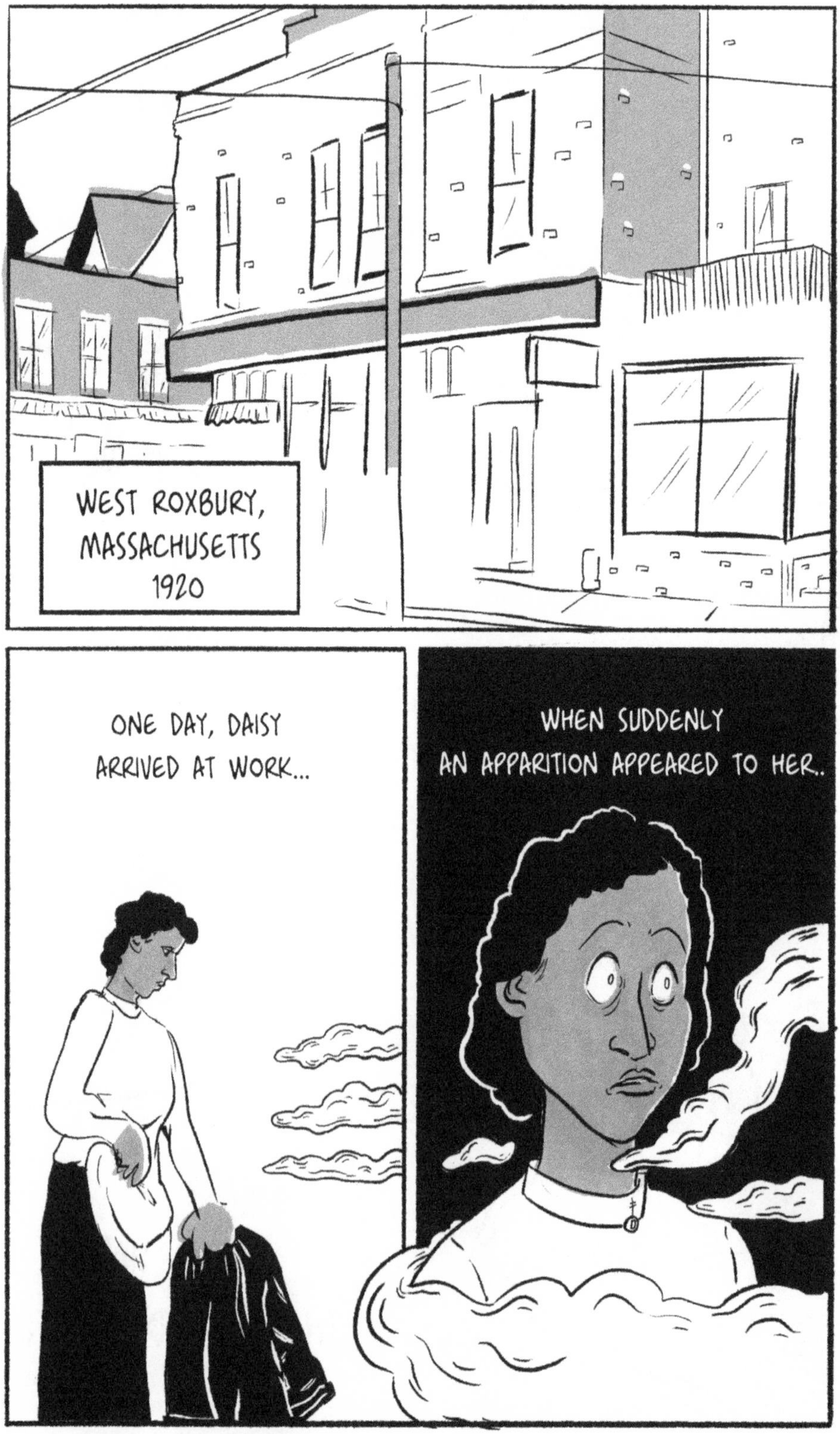
WEST ROXBURY, MASSACHUSETTS 1920
ONE DAY, DAISY ARRIVED AT WORK...
WHEN SUDDENLY AN APPARITION APPEARED TO HER..

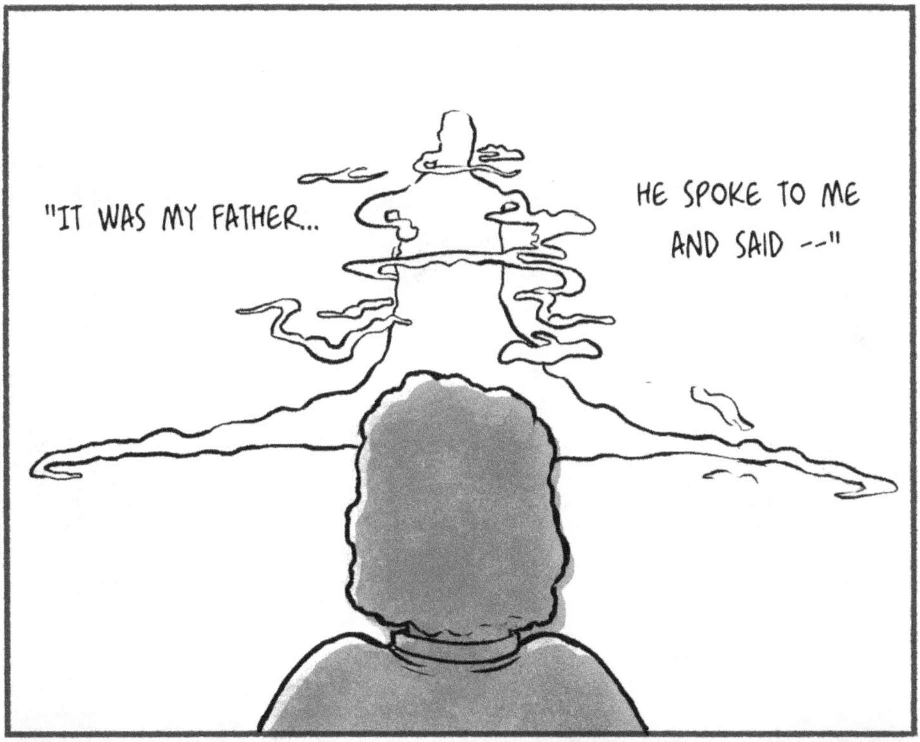
"IT WAS MY FATHER...
HE SPOKE TO ME AND SAID --"

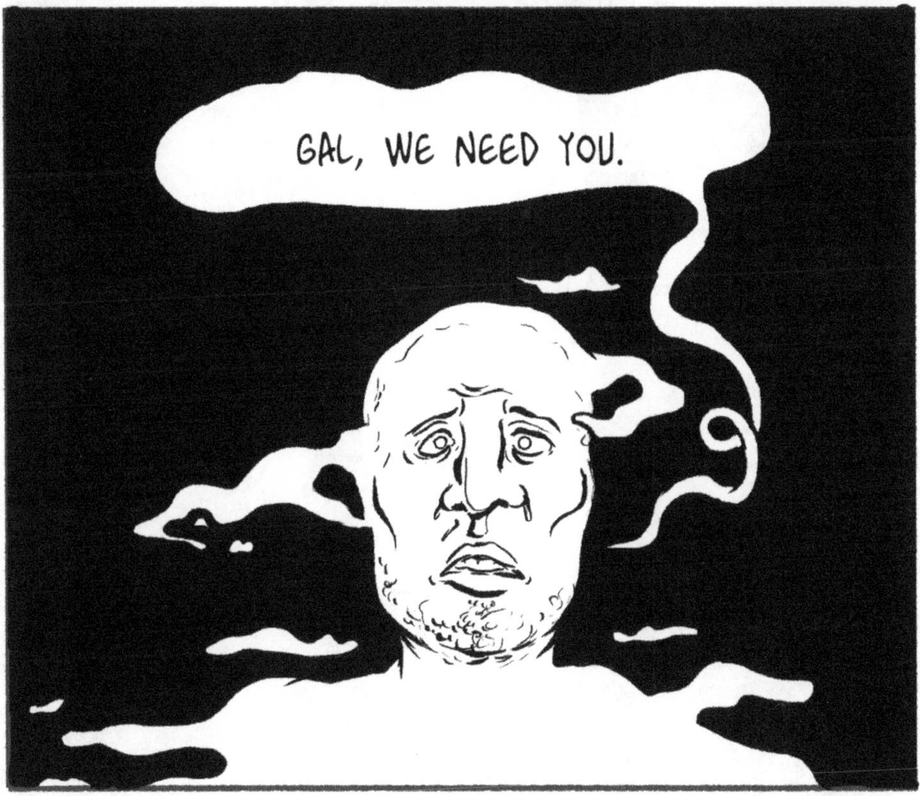
GAL, WE NEED YOU.

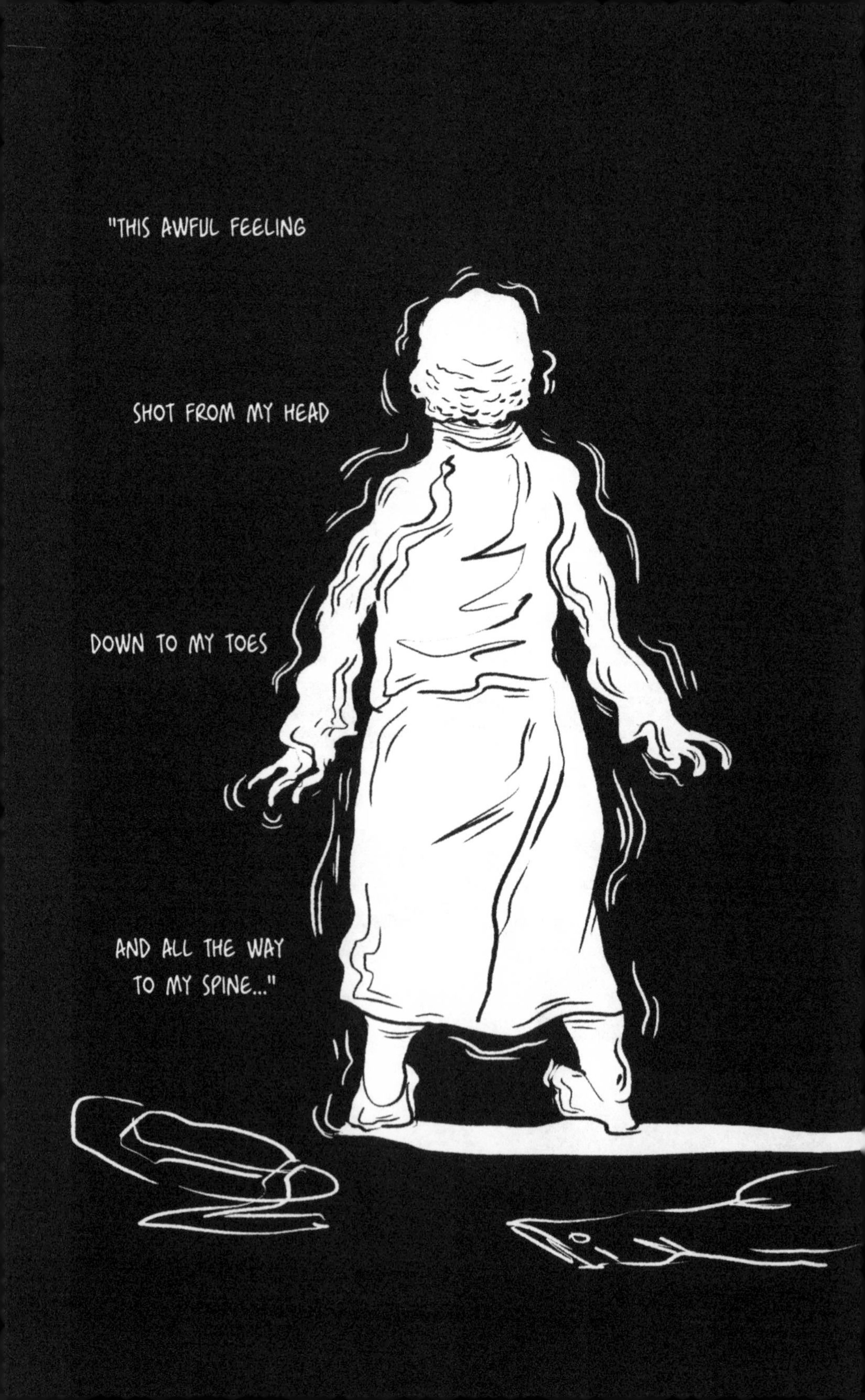
"THIS AWFUL FEELING
SHOT FROM MY HEAD
DOWN TO MY TOES
AND ALL THE WAY TO MY SPINE..."

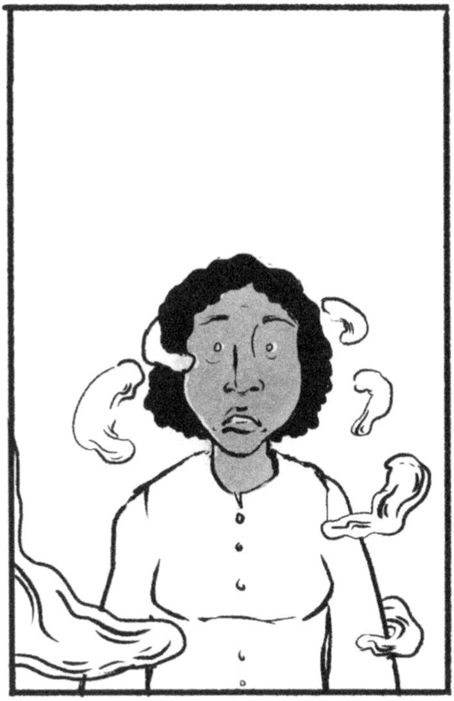

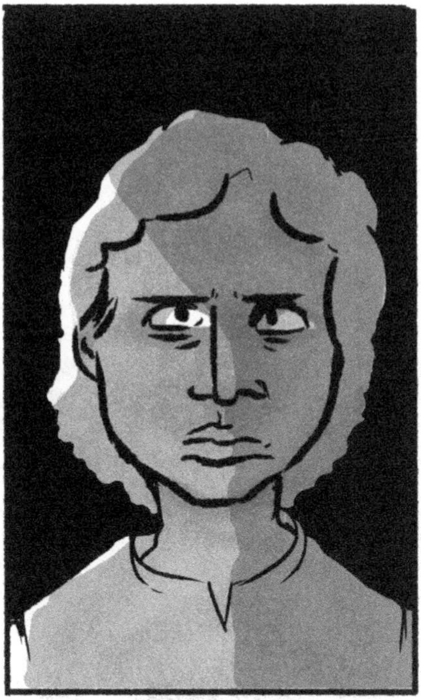

DAISY PUT HER COAT
RIGHT BACK ON

AND TOOK THE NEXT
TRAIN HOME...

...TO VERMONT.

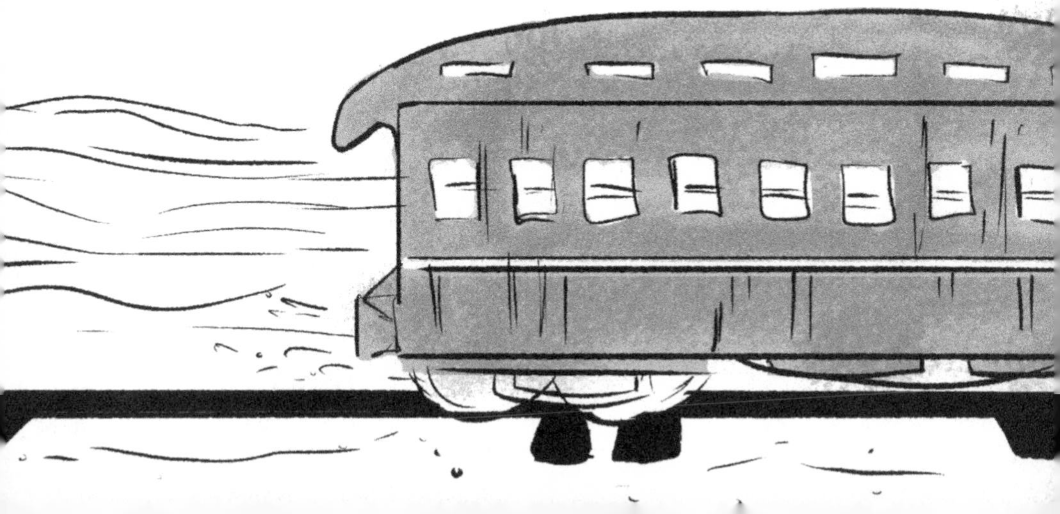

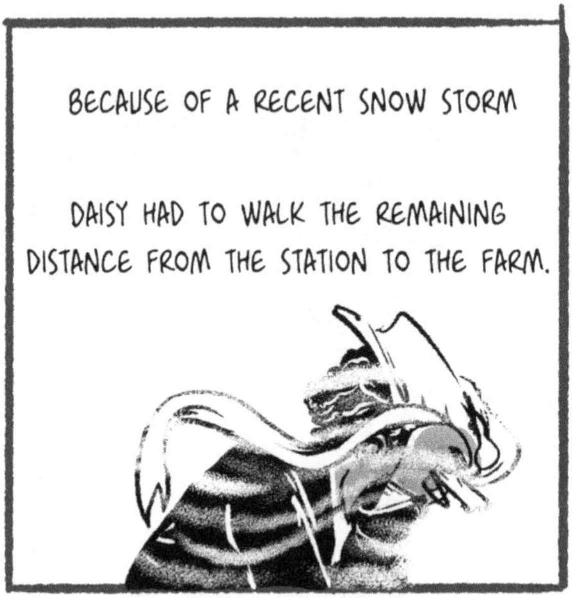
BECAUSE OF A RECENT SNOW STORM
DAISY HAD TO WALK THE REMAINING DISTANCE FROM THE STATION TO THE FARM.

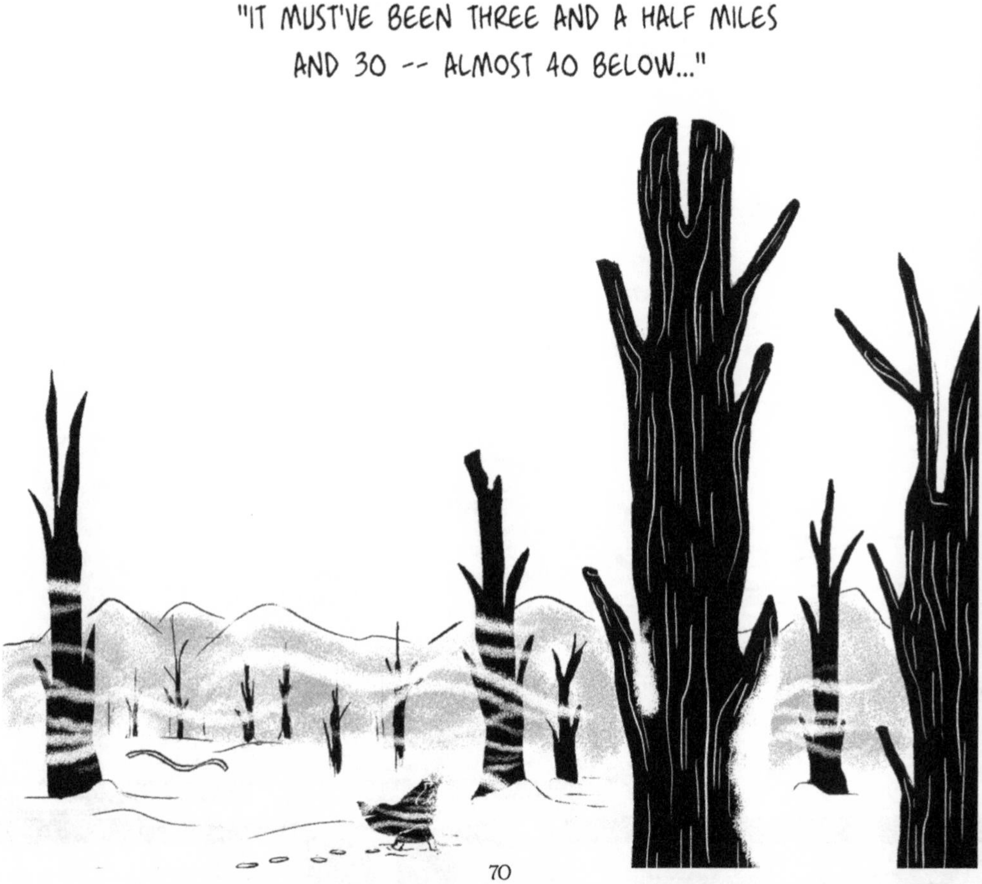
"IT MUST'VE BEEN THREE AND A HALF MILES AND 30 -- ALMOST 40 BELOW..."

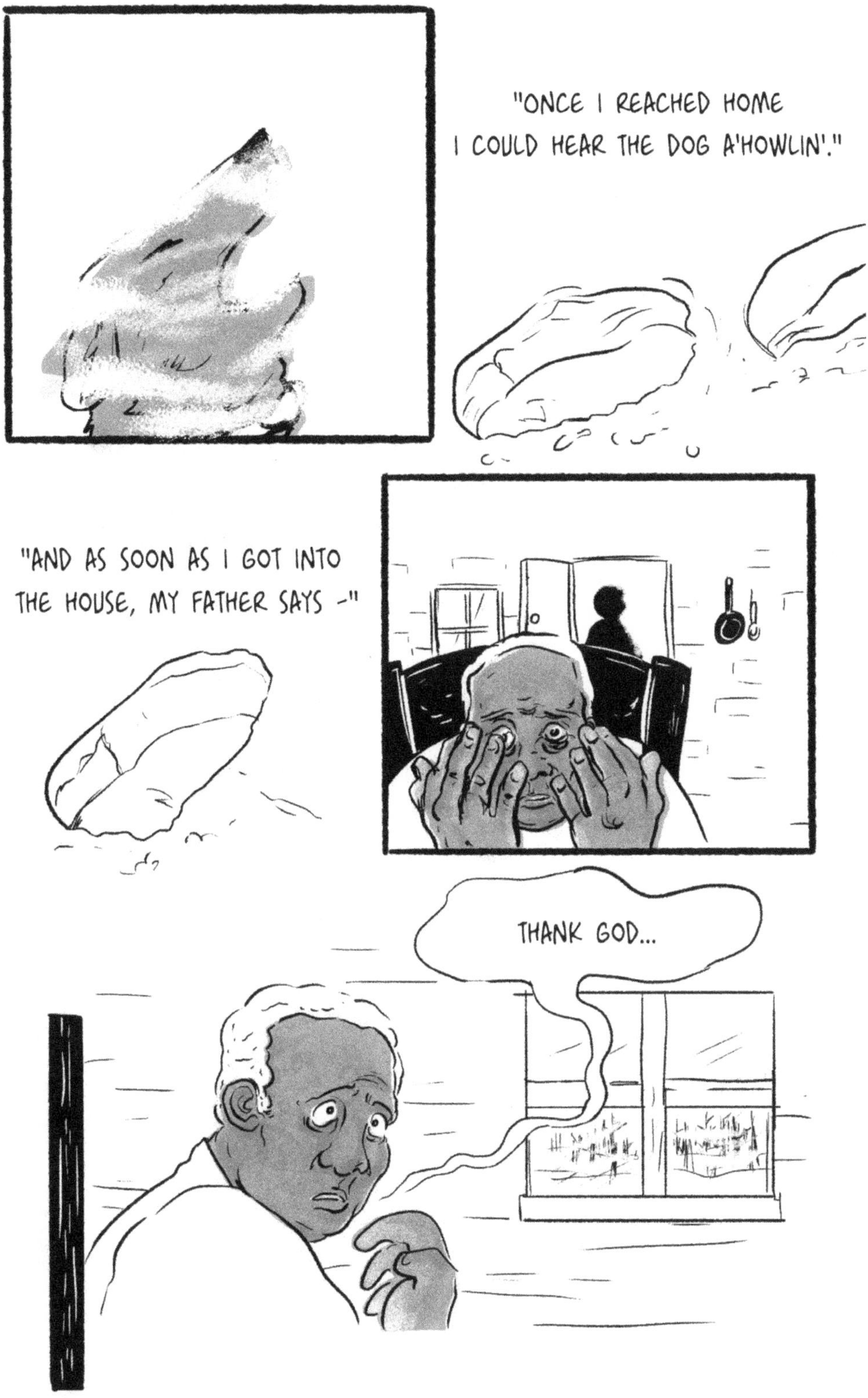
"ONCE I REACHED HOME I COULD HEAR THE DOG A'HOWLIN'."
"AND AS SOON AS I GOT INTO THE HOUSE, MY FATHER SAYS -"
THANK GOD...

"MY MOTHER HAD GONE OUT TO TEND TO THE CHICKENS, BUT HAD LOST HER WAY."

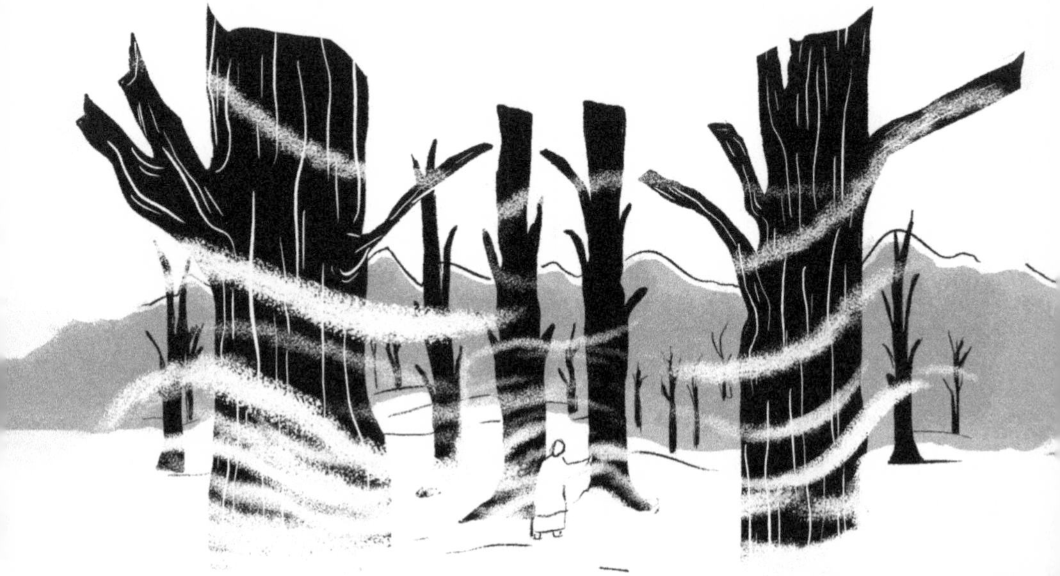

"SHE HAD CALLED AND CALLED FOR HELP, BUT NO ONE COULD HEAR HER."

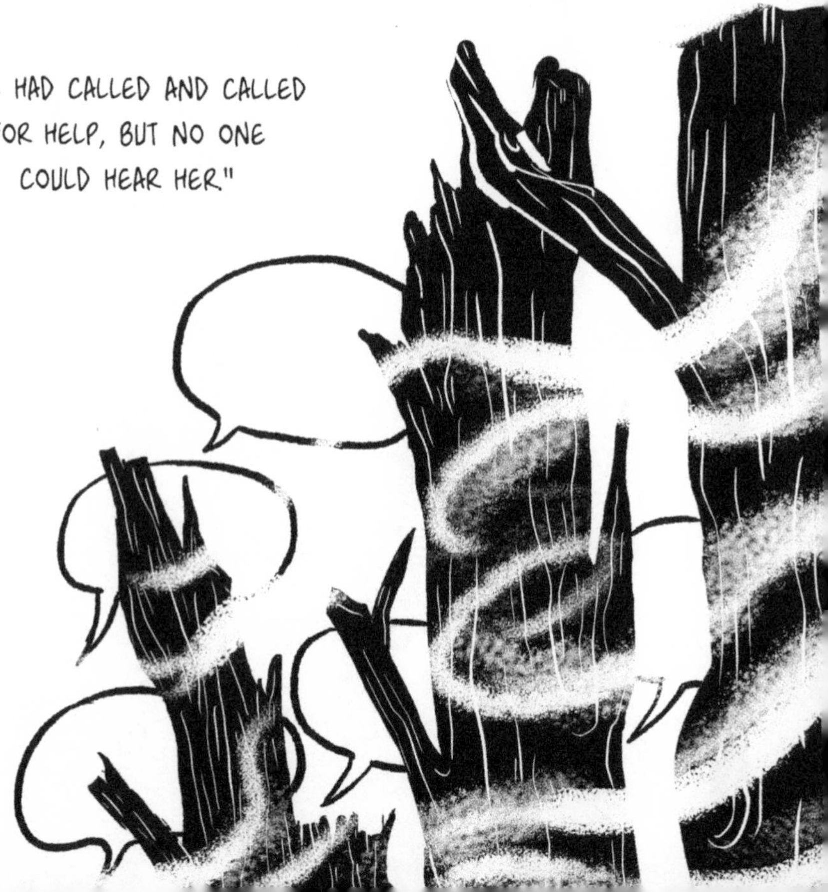

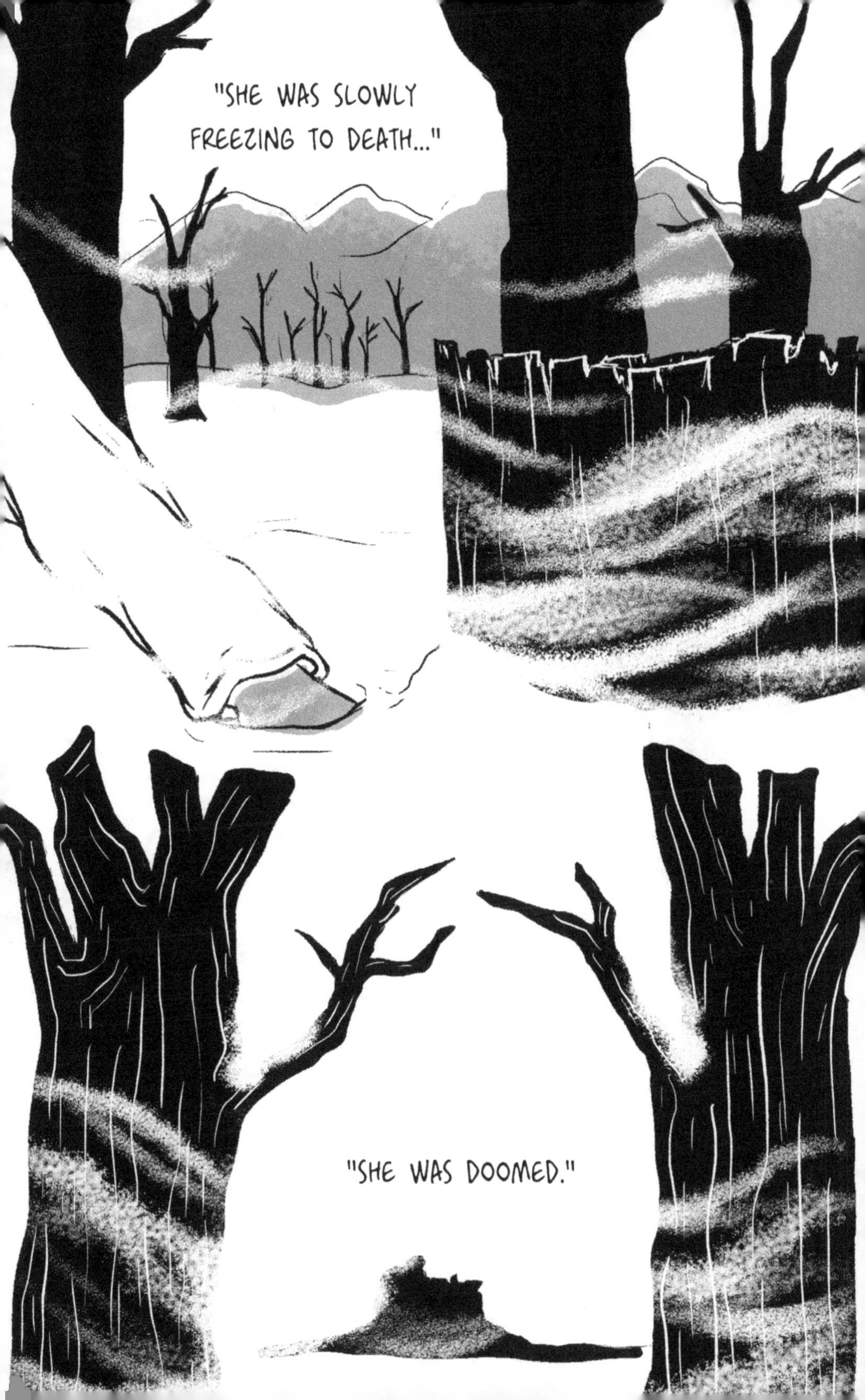
"SHE WAS SLOWLY FREEZING TO DEATH..."
"SHE WAS DOOMED."

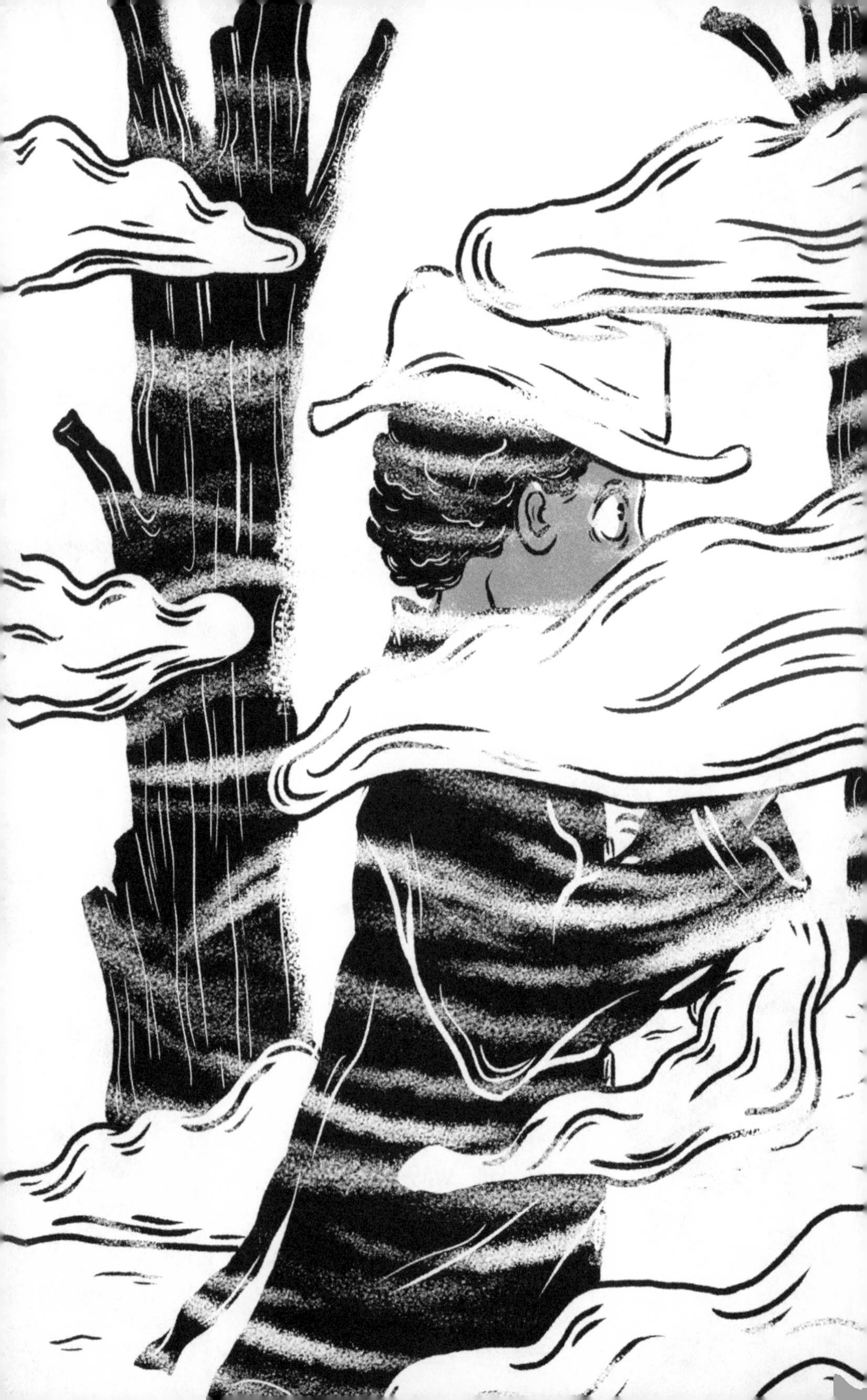

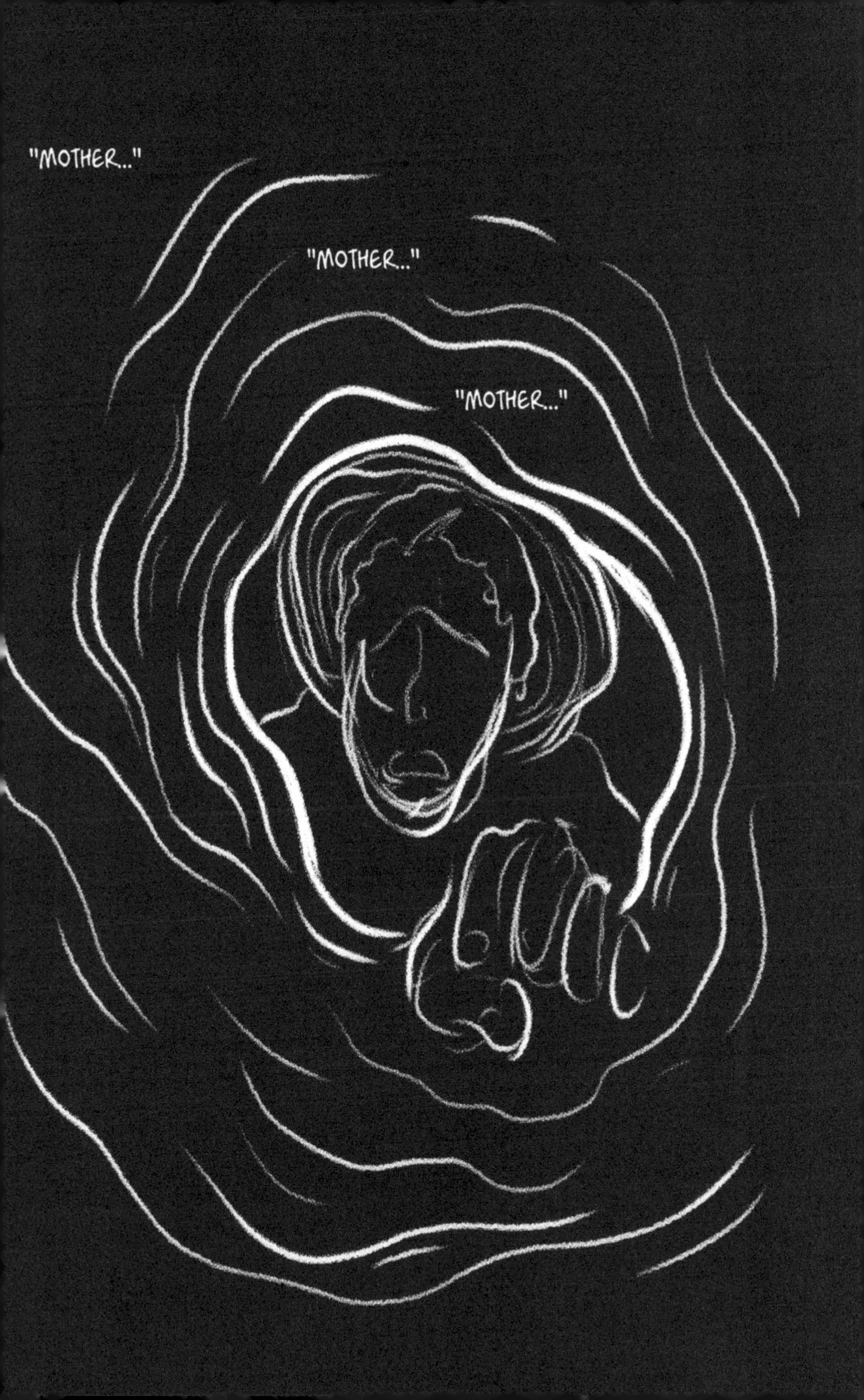
"MOTHER..."
"MOTHER..."
"MOTHER..."

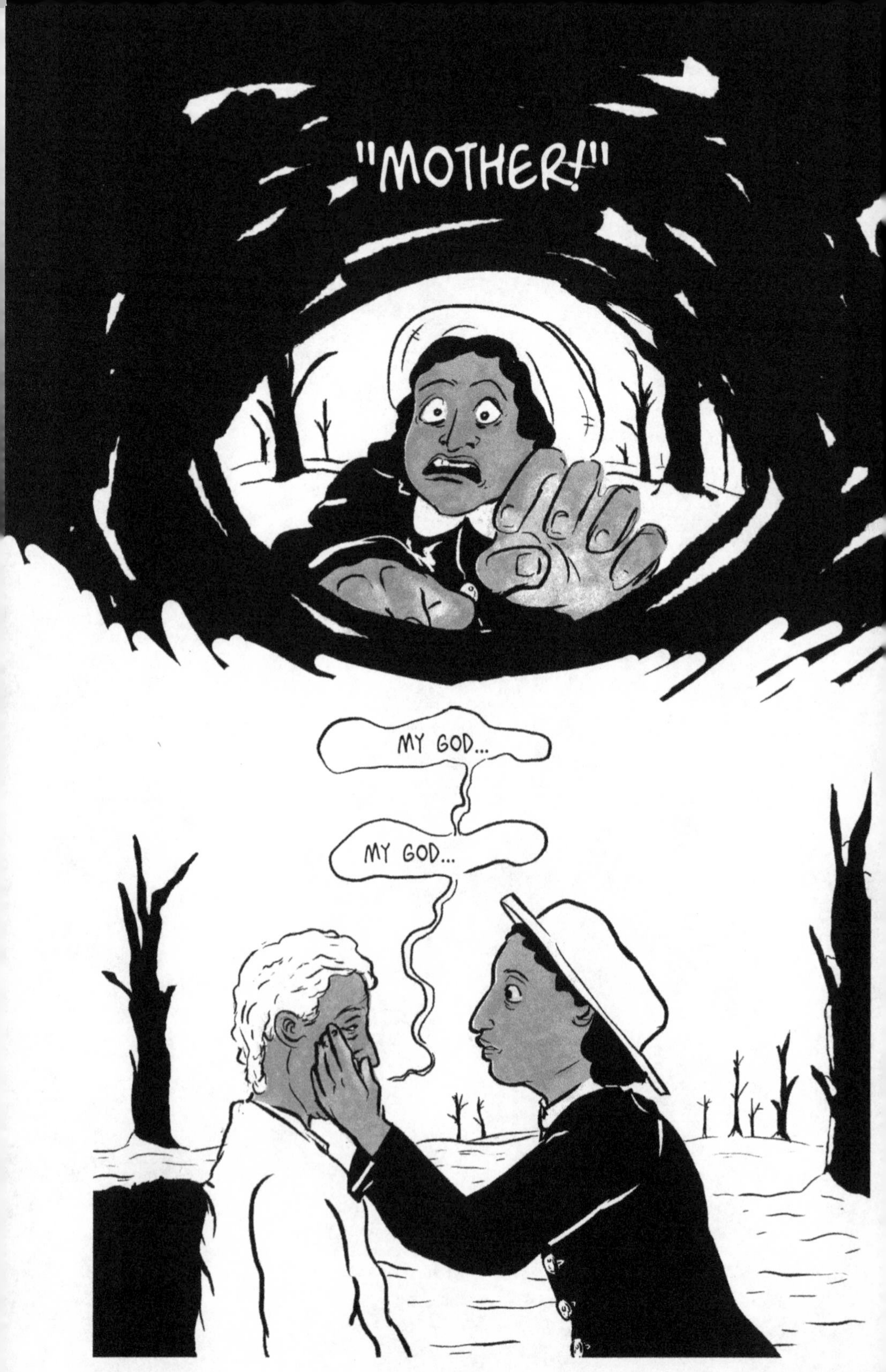
"MOTHER!"
MY GOD...
MY GOD...

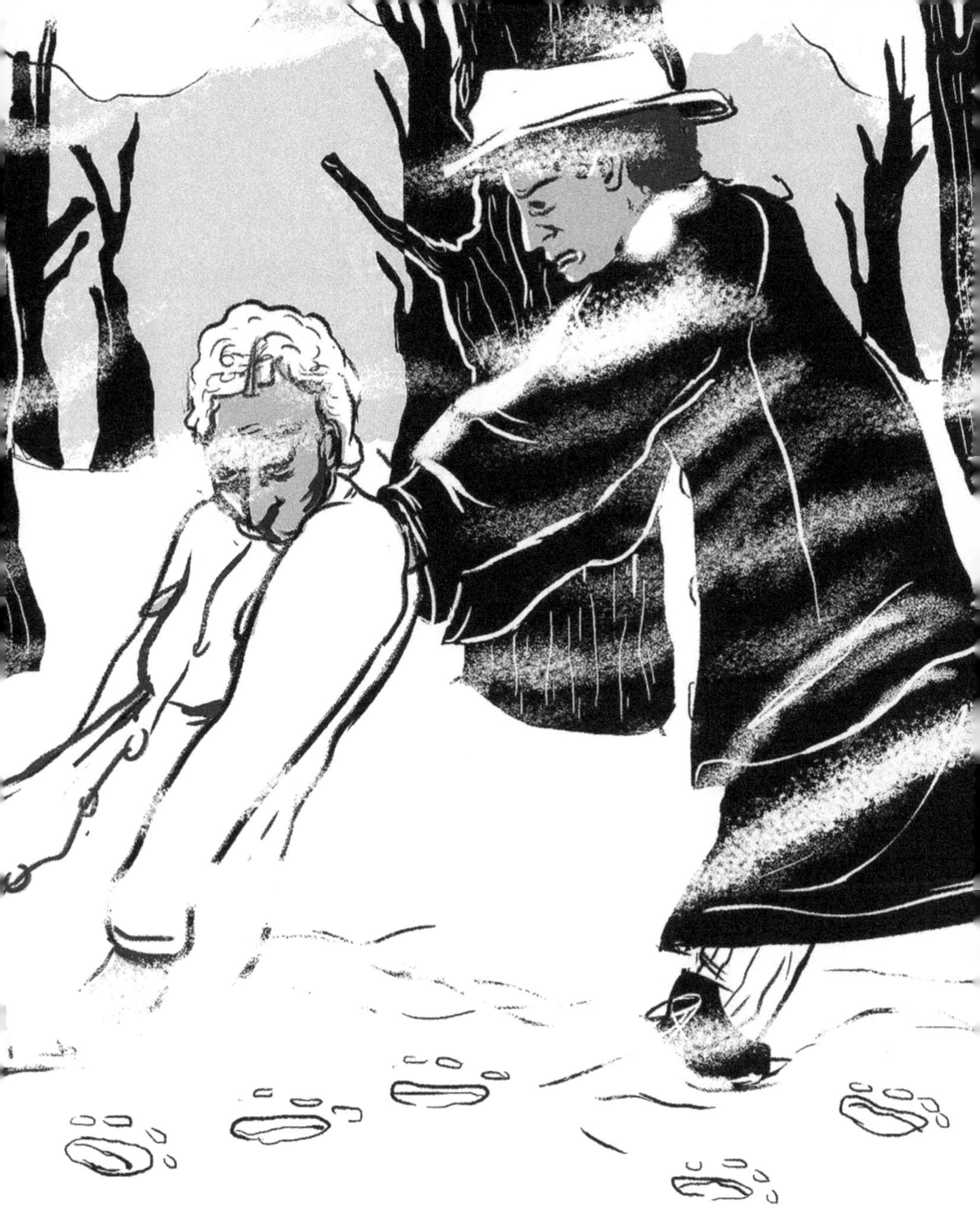

"I GRABBED HER IN MY ARMS...

SHE WAS COVERED IN ICE AND SNOW.

IT MUST'A TAKEN THREE QUARTERS OF AN HOUR
BUT I GOT HER BACK INTO THAT HOUSE."

"WE GOT HER TO THE KITCHEN FLOOR,
TORE HER CLOTHES RIGHT OFF HER.

GOT SOME BRANDY DOWN HER MOUTH
WITH A TEASPOON...

...AND FATHER JUST KEPT PRAYING."

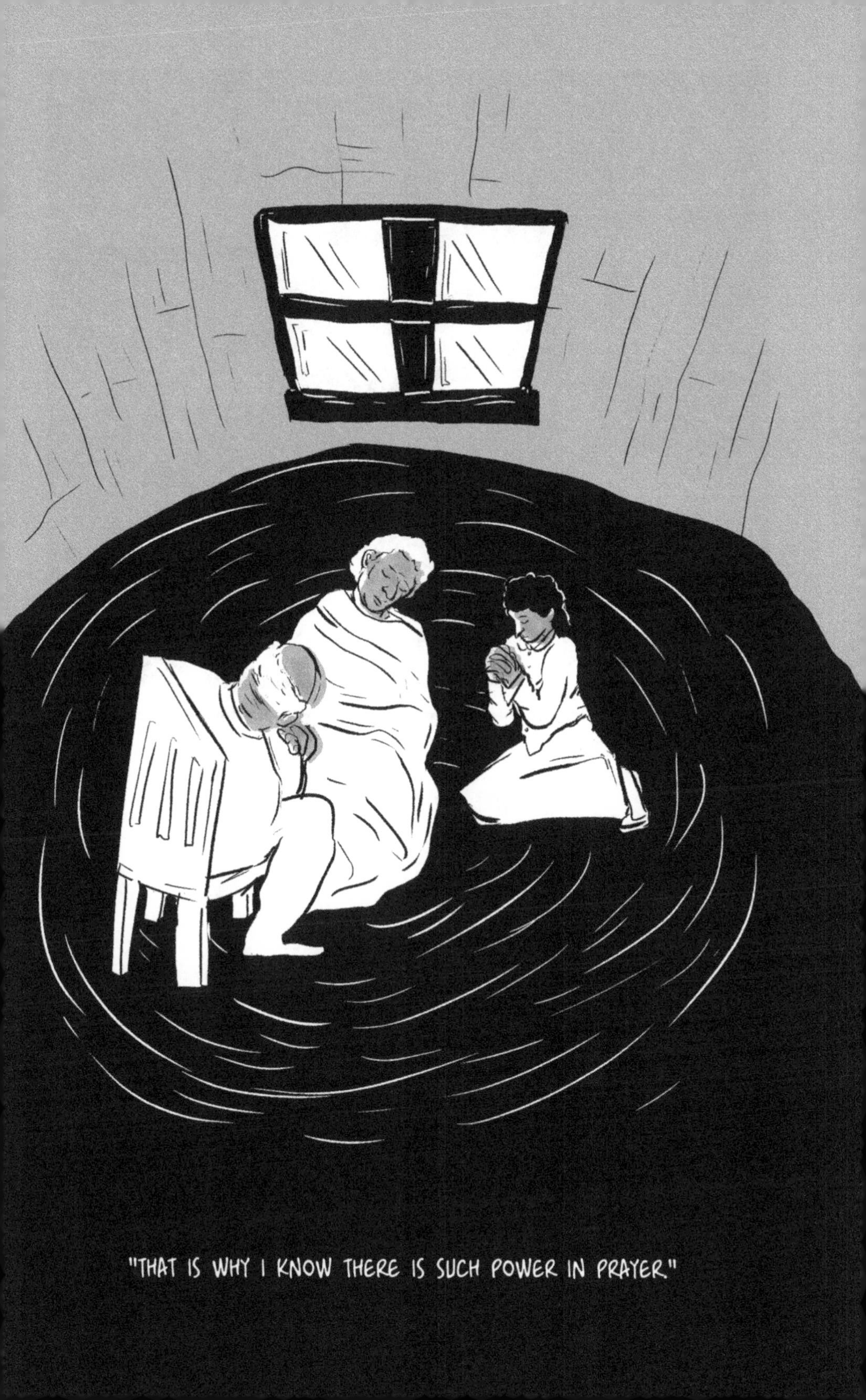
"THAT IS WHY I KNOW THERE IS SUCH POWER IN PRAYER."

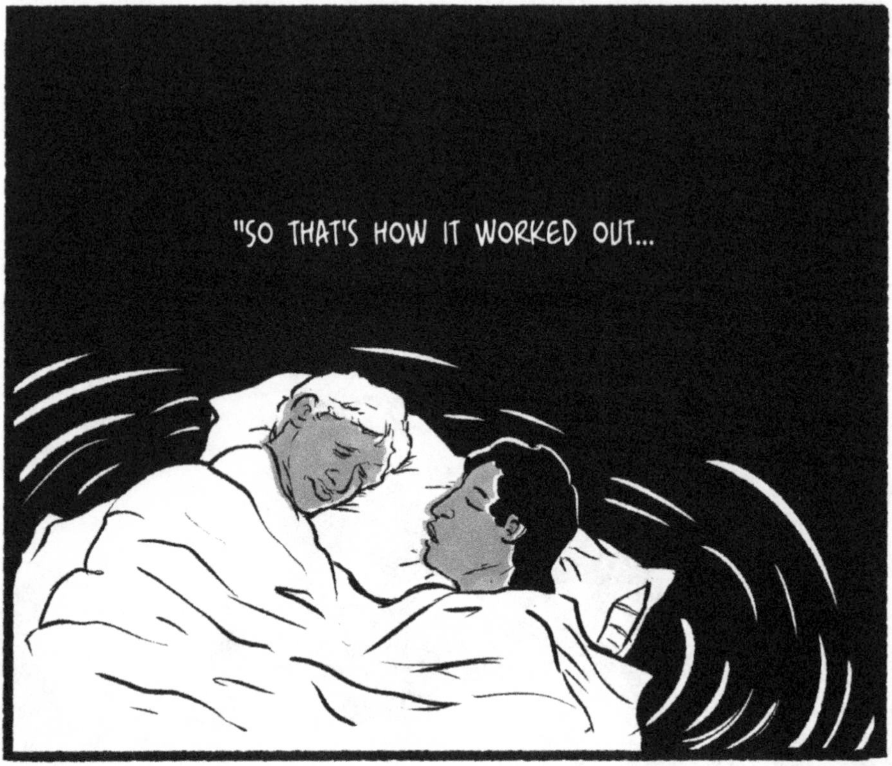
"SO THAT'S HOW IT WORKED OUT...

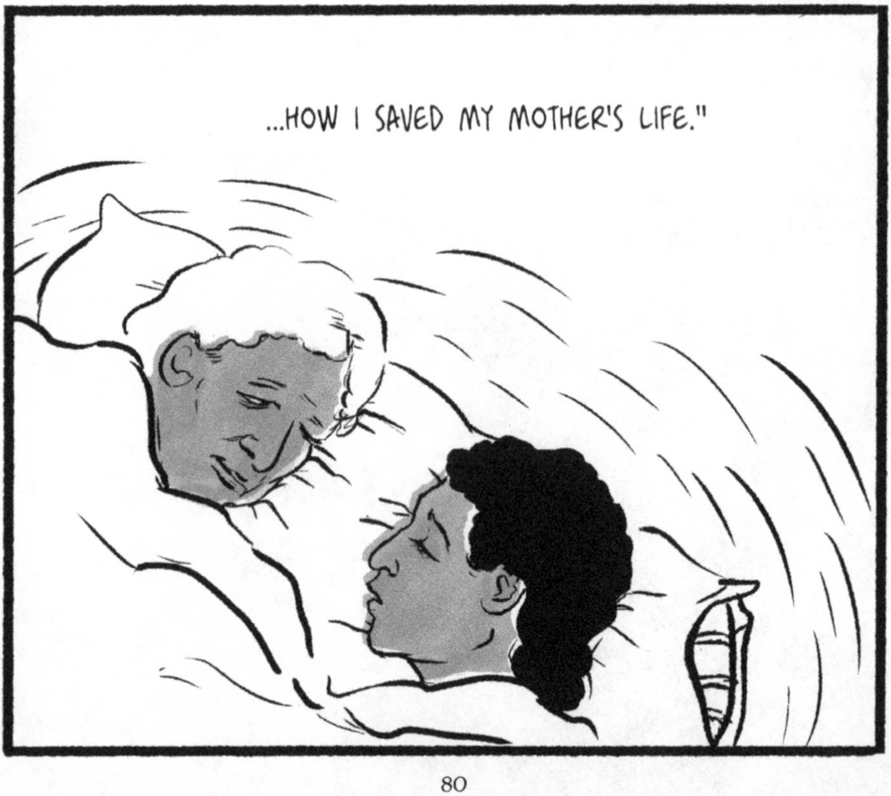
...HOW I SAVED MY MOTHER'S LIFE."

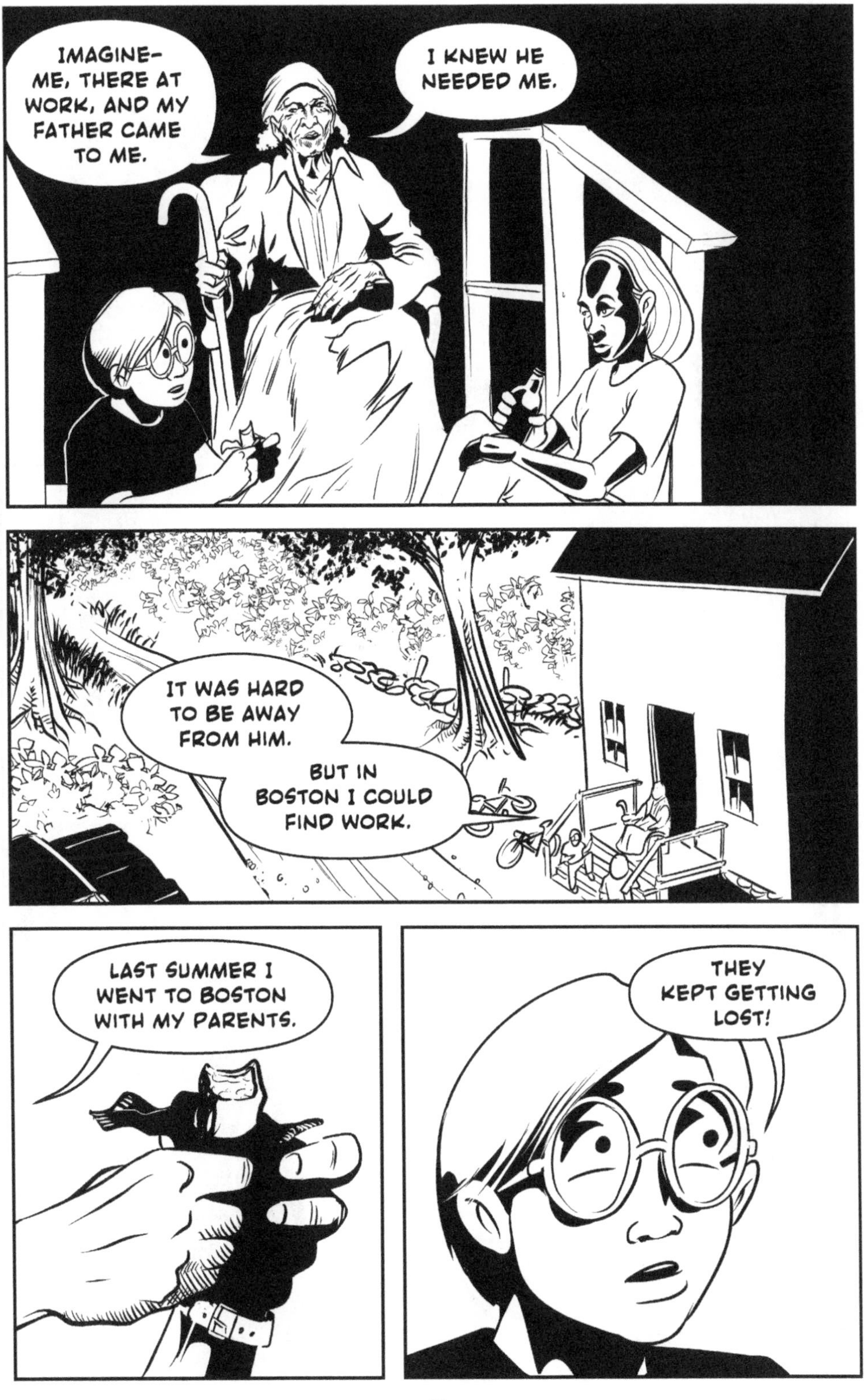
IMAGINE- ME, THERE AT WORK, AND MY FATHER CAME TO ME.
I KNEW HE NEEDED ME.
IT WAS HARD TO BE AWAY FROM HIM.
BUT IN BOSTON I COULD FIND WORK.
LAST SUMMER I WENT TO BOSTON WITH MY PARENTS.
THEY KEPT GETTING LOST!

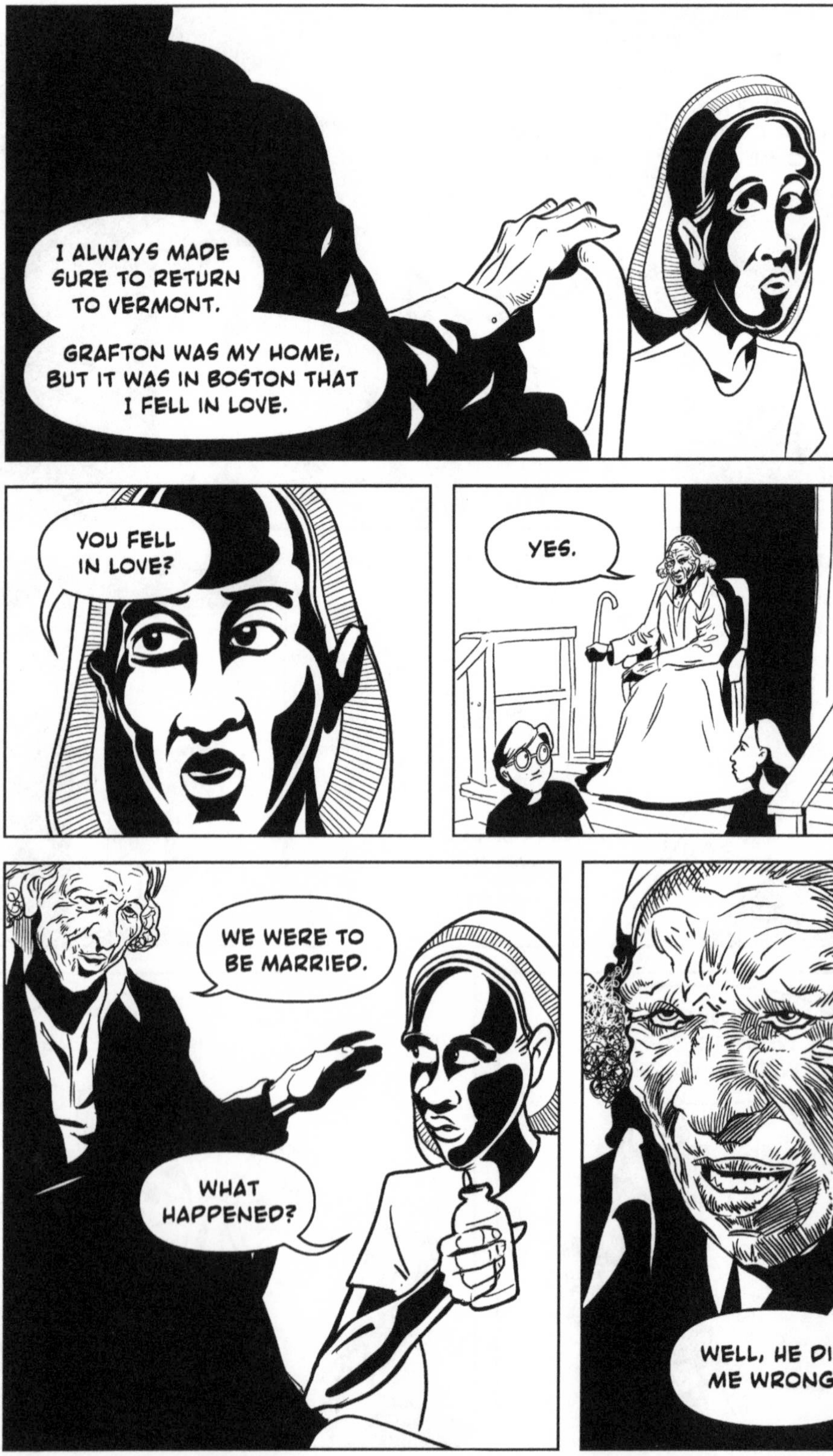
I ALWAYS MADE SURE TO RETURN TO VERMONT.
GRAFTON WAS MY HOME, BUT IT WAS IN BOSTON THAT I FELL IN LOVE.
YOU FELL IN LOVE?
YES.
WE WERE TO BE MARRIED.
WHAT HAPPENED?
WELL, HE DID ME WRONG.

I AM VINDICATED

By Francis Bordeleau

DAISY TURNER FIRST MET JOSEPH BOINAY, A WHITE LIVERY AND AUTOMOBILE DEALER FROM EAST LEXINGTON, MASSACHUSETTS, IN 1916 WHEN SHE WENT TO HIS STORE TO PURCHASE A HARNESS ON BEHALF OF HER FATHER.

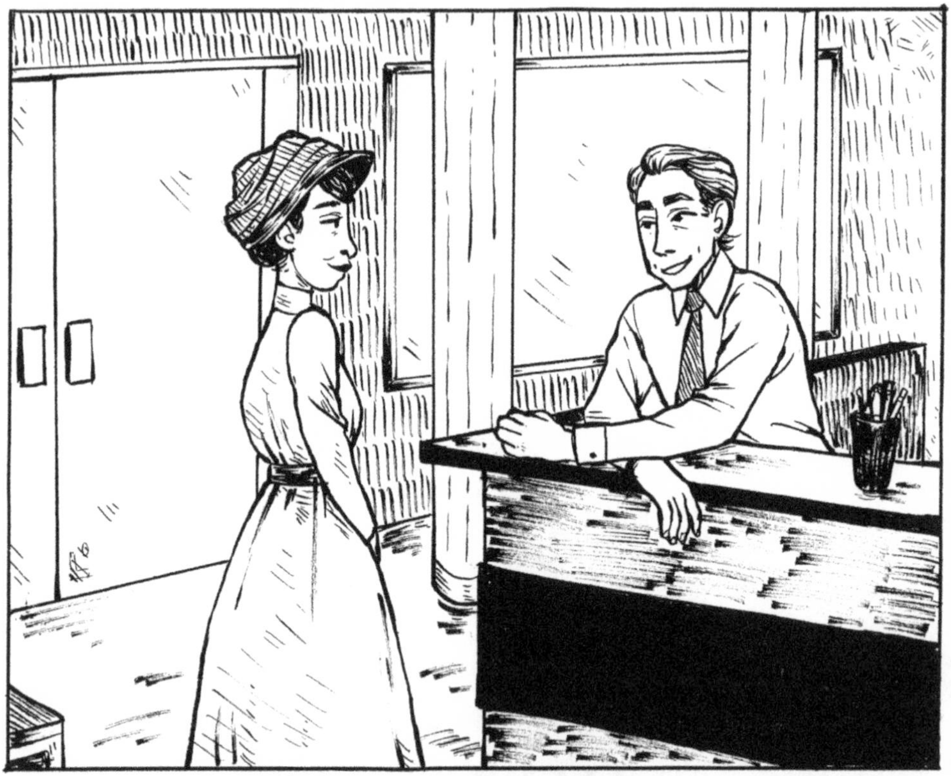

SHE FELL IN LOVE WITH HIM, BUT HE WAS ALREADY MARRIED. WITHIN A FEW YEARS THEY BEGAN AN AFFAIR.

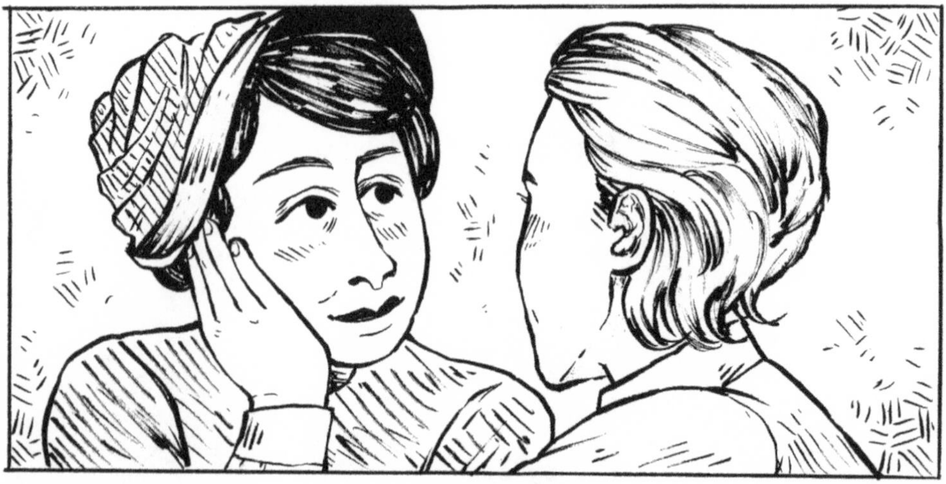

DAISY SPENT SUMMERS IN VERMONT WITH HER FAMILY.
BOINAY VISITED HER FREQUENTLY.

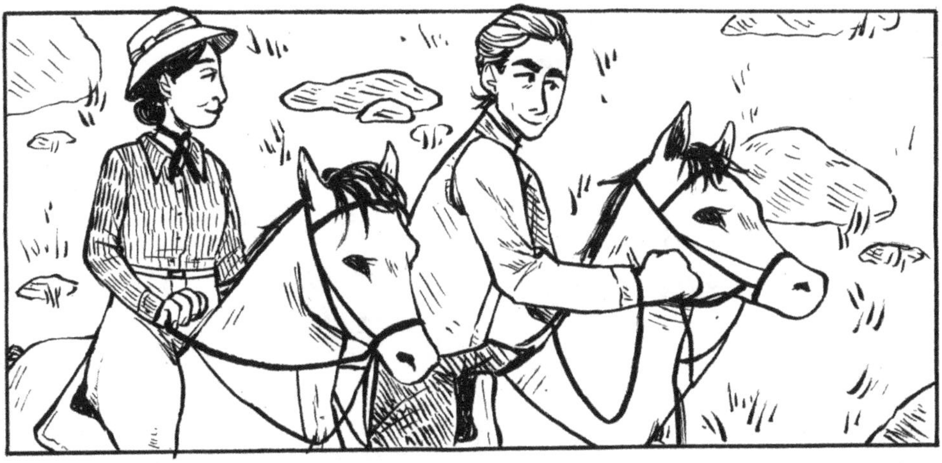

THE PAIR SPENT THEIR TIME TOGETHER OUT OF DOORS...

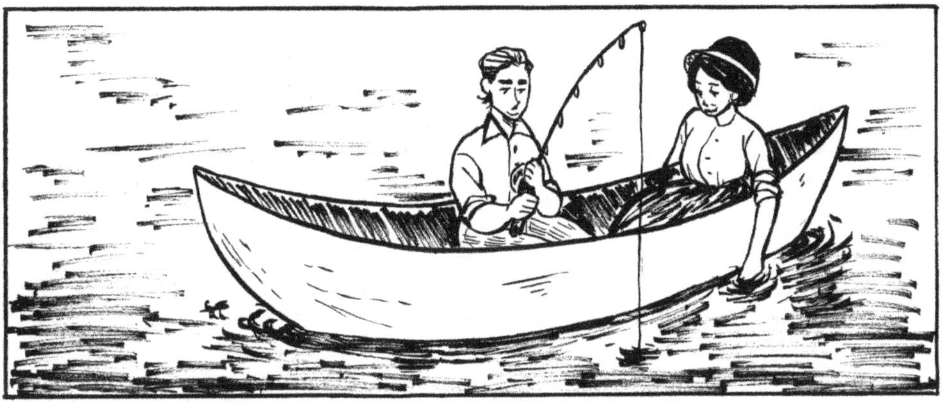

FISHING, HUNTING, AND COURTING.

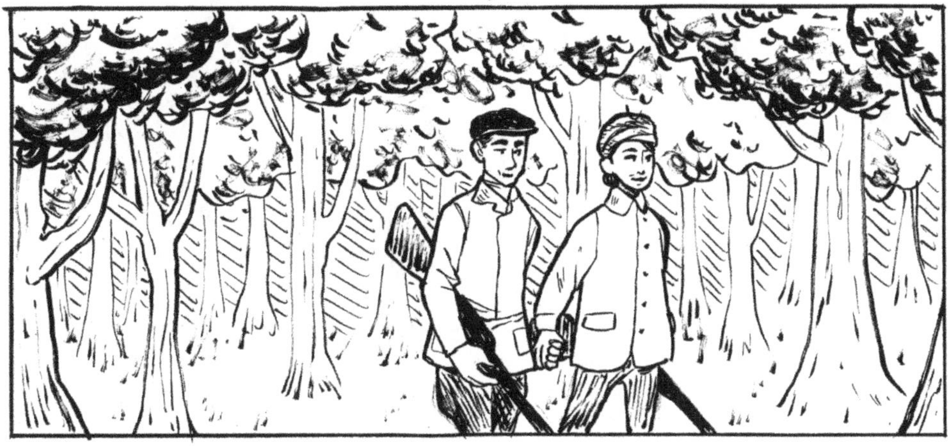

DAISY KNEW THE RELATIONSHIP WAS WRONG, BUT HER HEART CLOUDED HER JUDGEMENT.

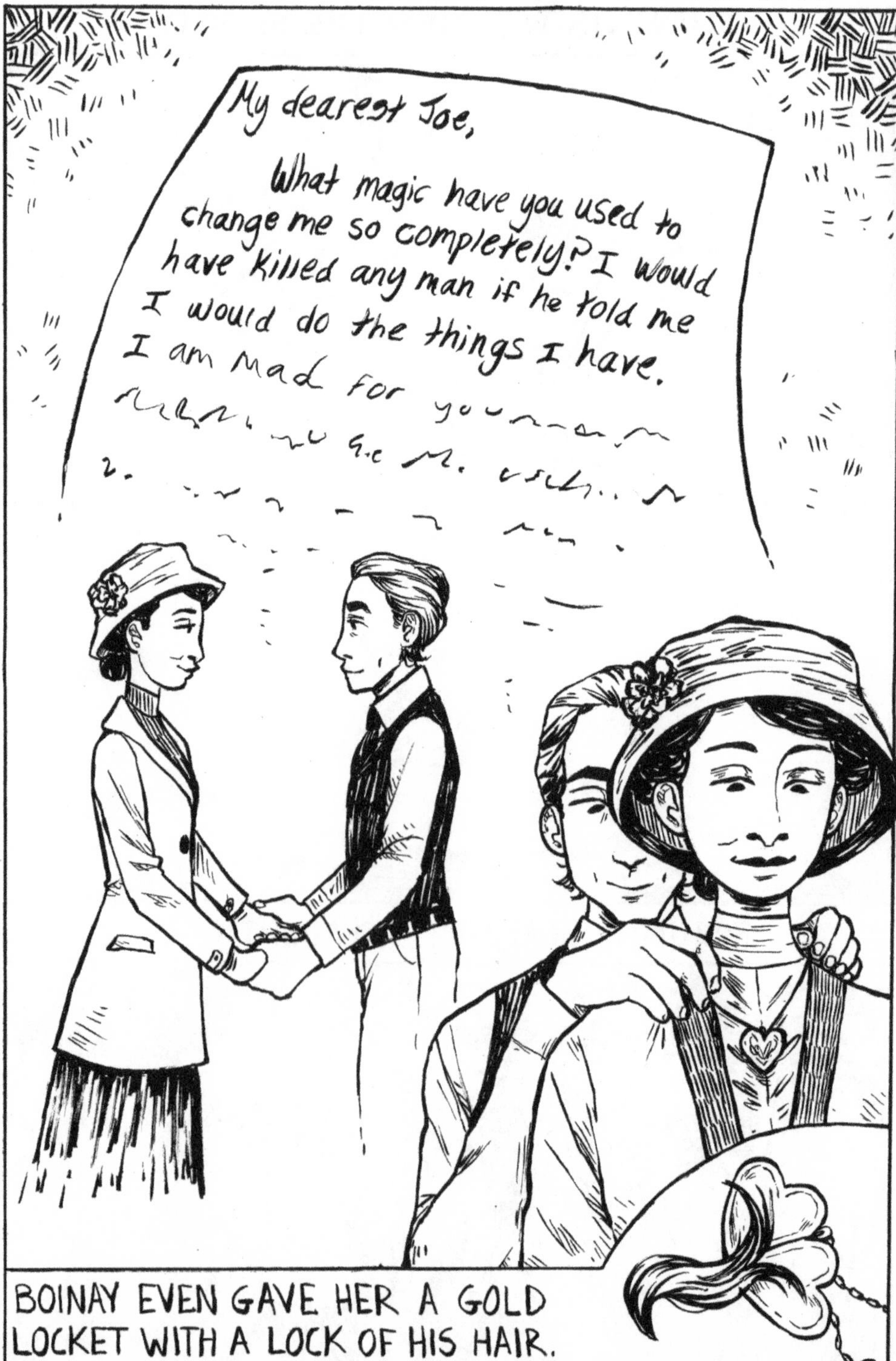
My dearest Joe,
What magic have you used to change me so completely? I would have killed any man if he told me I would do the things I have.
I am mad for you
BOINAY EVEN GAVE HER A GOLD LOCKET WITH A LOCK OF HIS HAIR.

SO THAT SHE COULD BE CLOSER TO HIM, BOINAY HIRED DAISY AS HIS MAID. IN THE SPRING OF 1923, HIS WIFE DIED.

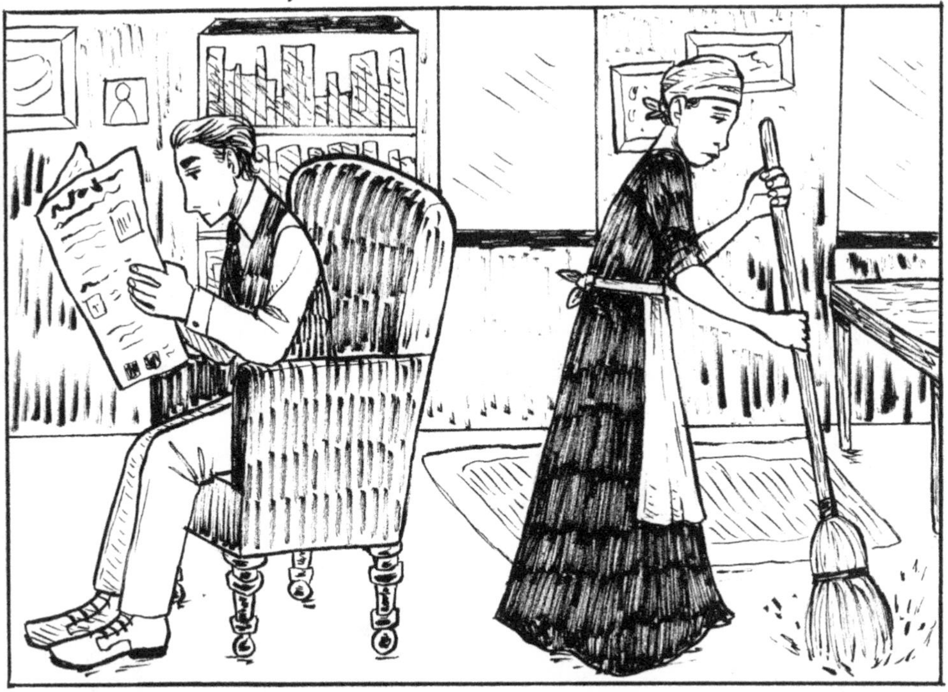

DAISY'S FATHER, ALEC TURNER, STRONGLY DISLIKED BOINAY AND DELIVERED HIM AN ULTIMATUM THROUGH HIS DAUGHTER ROSE.

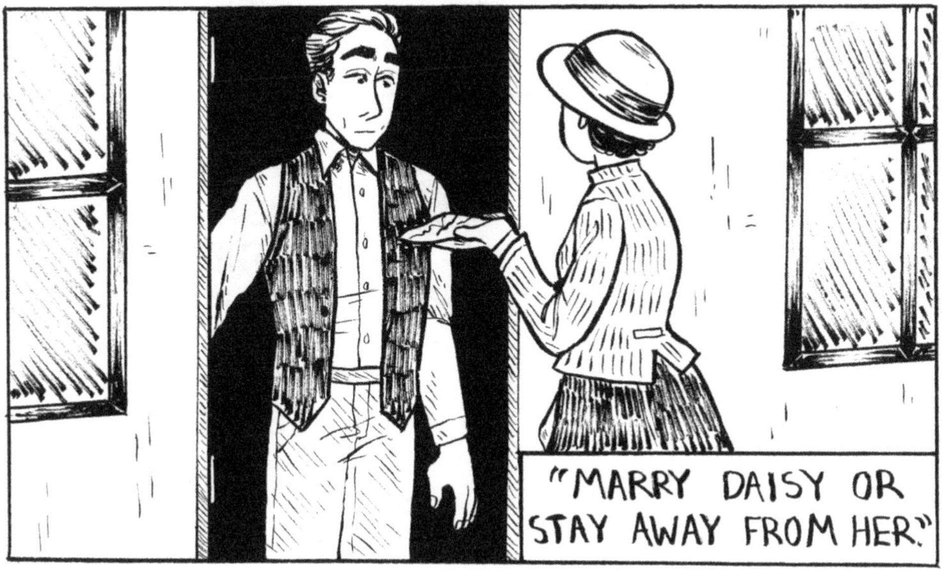
"MARRY DAISY OR STAY AWAY FROM HER."

THE TWO PLANNED TO BE MARRIED IN DECEMBER.

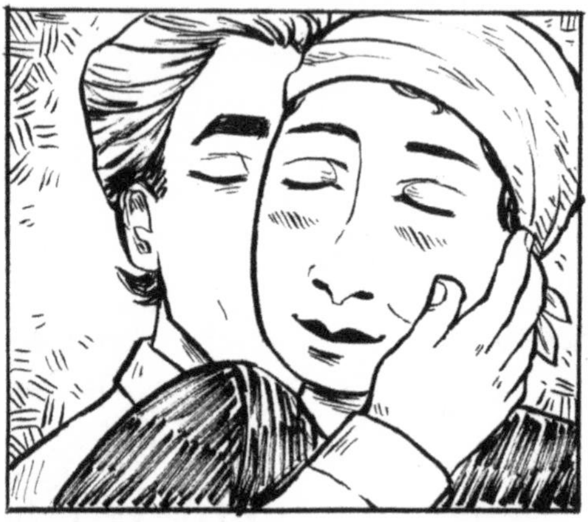

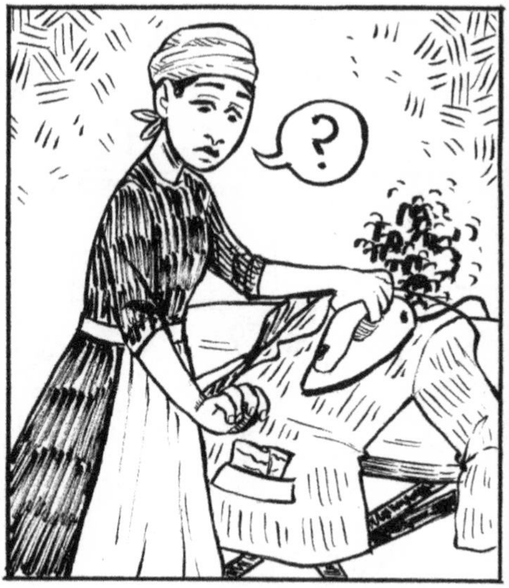
?

IN NOVEMBER, WHILE PRESSING BOINAY'S JACKET, DAISY FOUND TWO LOVE LETTERS FROM LURA LANDON, HIS BOOKKEEPER.

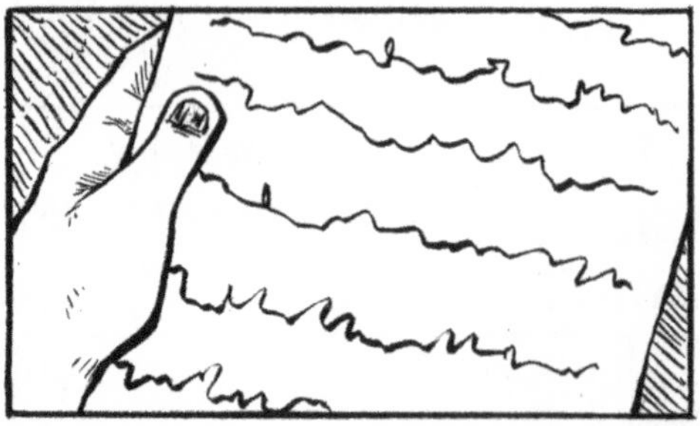

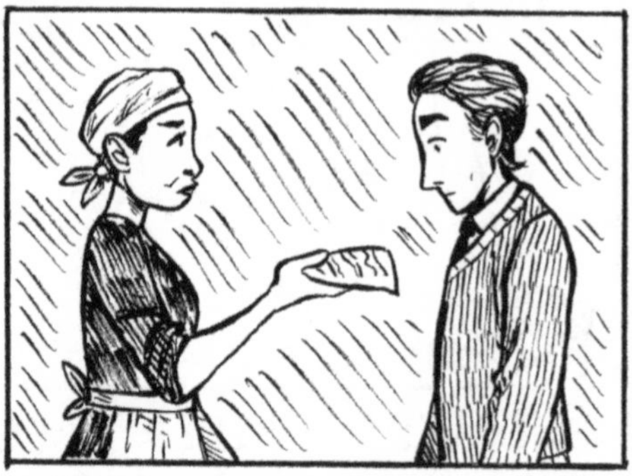

WHEN DAISY CONFRONTED BOINAY, HE TOLD HER NOT TO WORRY.

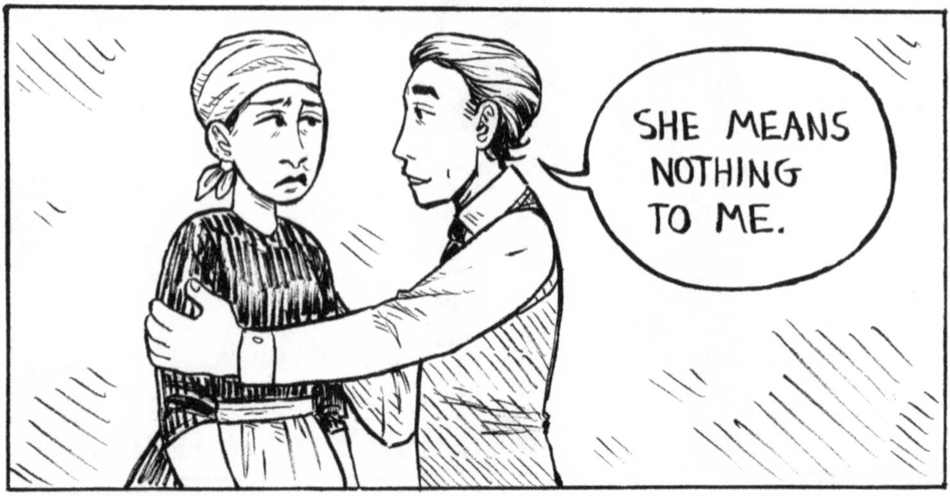
SHE MEANS NOTHING TO ME.

SOON AFTER, DAISY TRAVELED TO VERMONT TO BE WITH HER FATHER DURING HIS FINAL DAYS.

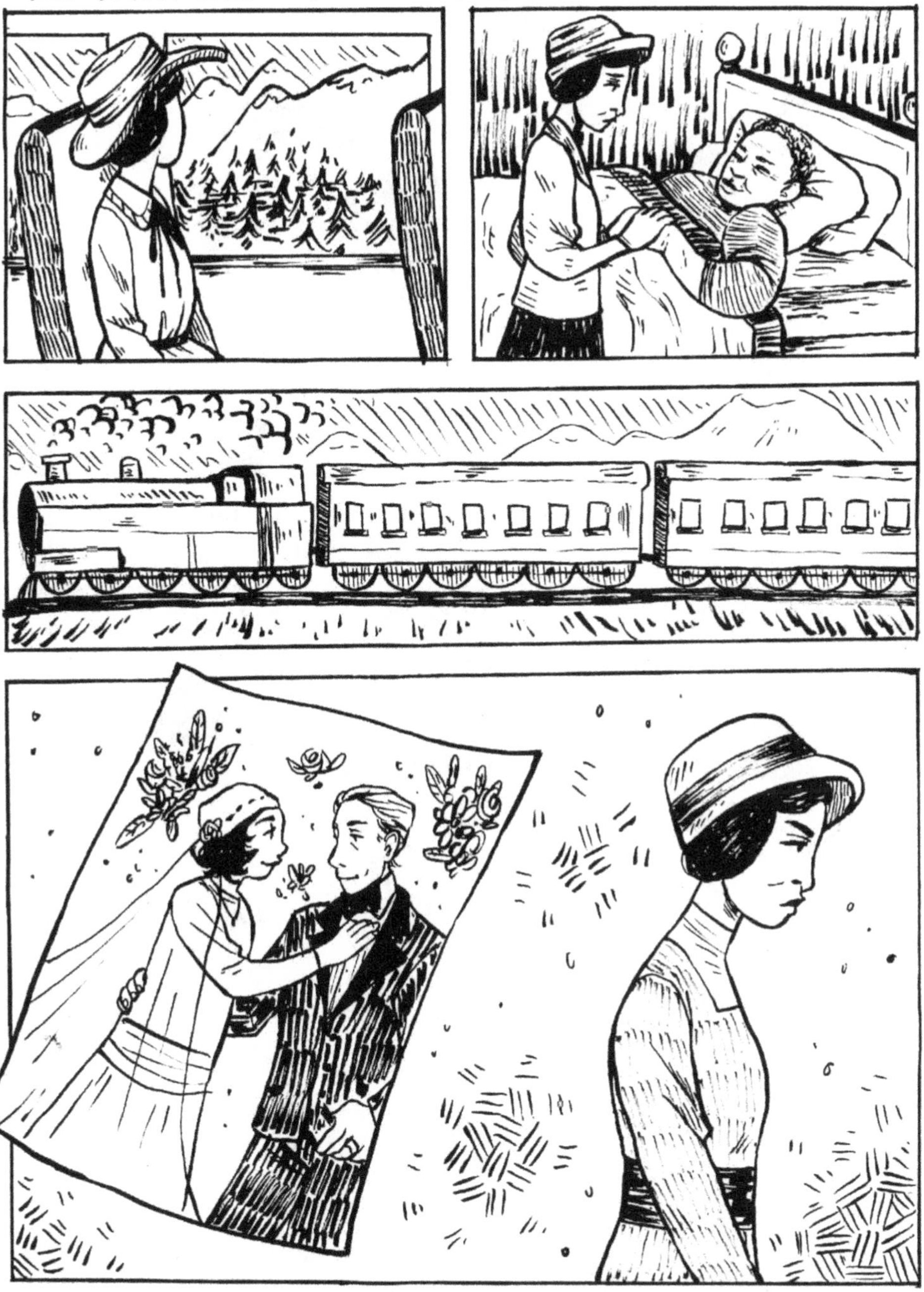

SHE RETURNED TO MASSACHUSETTS TO FIND HER WORST FEARS REALIZED. BOINAY WAS STILL SEEING LANDON. HE MARRIED HER A FEW MONTHS LATER.

BOINAY ATTEMPTED TO GET RID OF DAISY BY FIRING HER AND LEVELING FALSE CHARGES OF THEFT AGAINST HER.

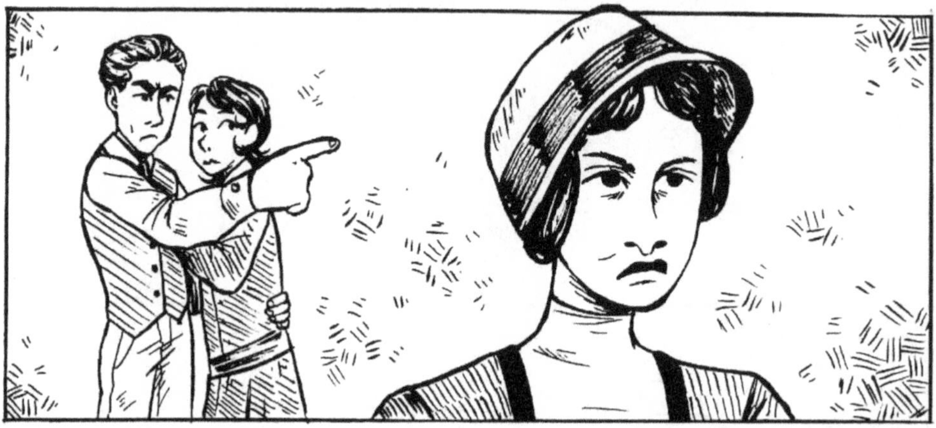

THE ACCUSATION DEVASTATED DAISY. IN NOVEMBER OF 1924, SHE BROUGHT THREE SUITS AGAINST HIM.

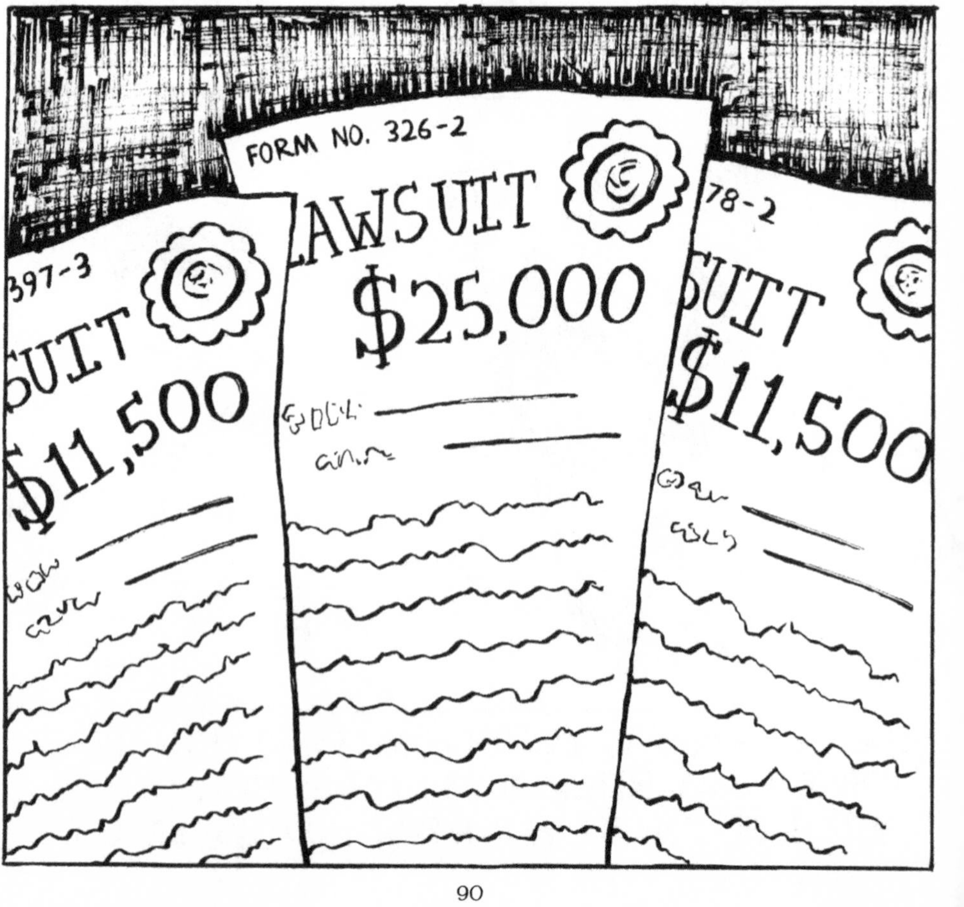

397-3
SUIT
$11,500
FORM NO. 326-2
LAWSUIT
$25,000
78-2
SUIT
$11,500

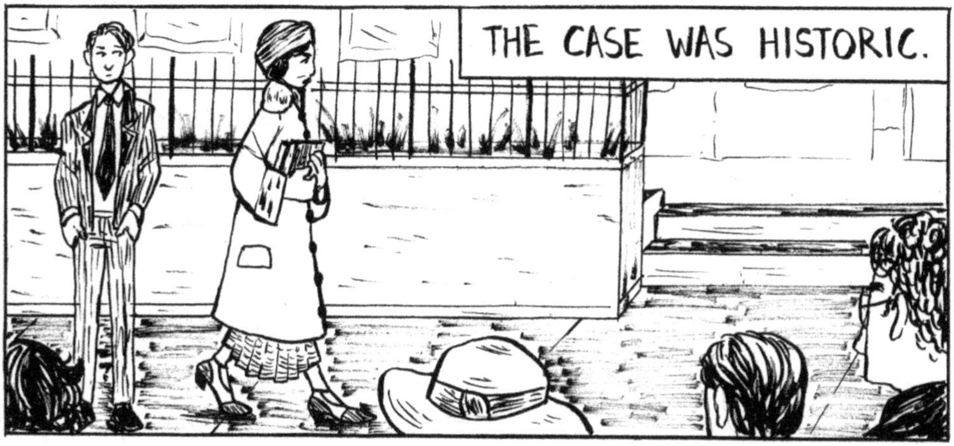
THE CASE WAS HISTORIC.

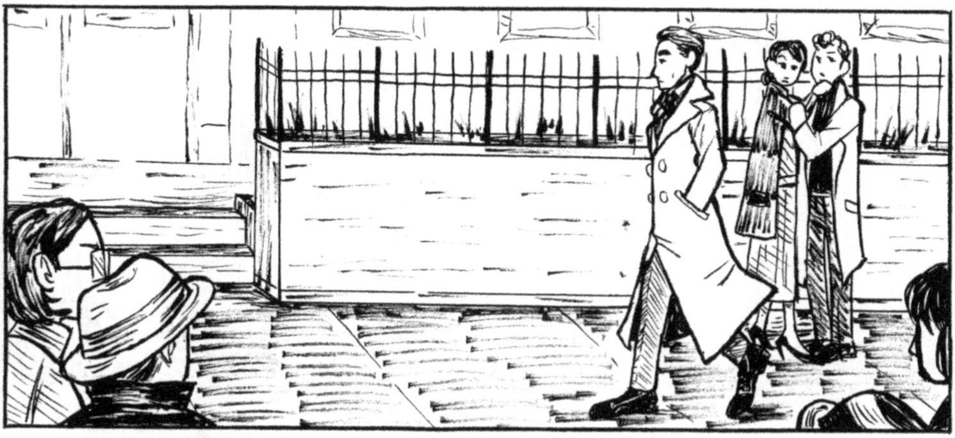

NEVER BEFORE IN A MASSACHUSETTS COURT "HAD A COLORED WOMAN FILED SUIT AGAINST A WHITE MAN FOR BREACH OF PROMISE."

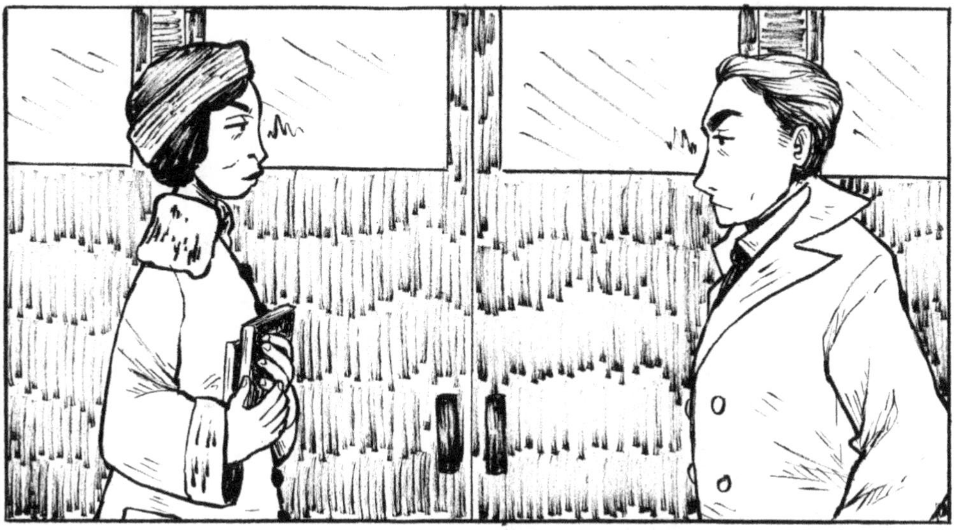

THE TRIAL BECAME A SENSATION.

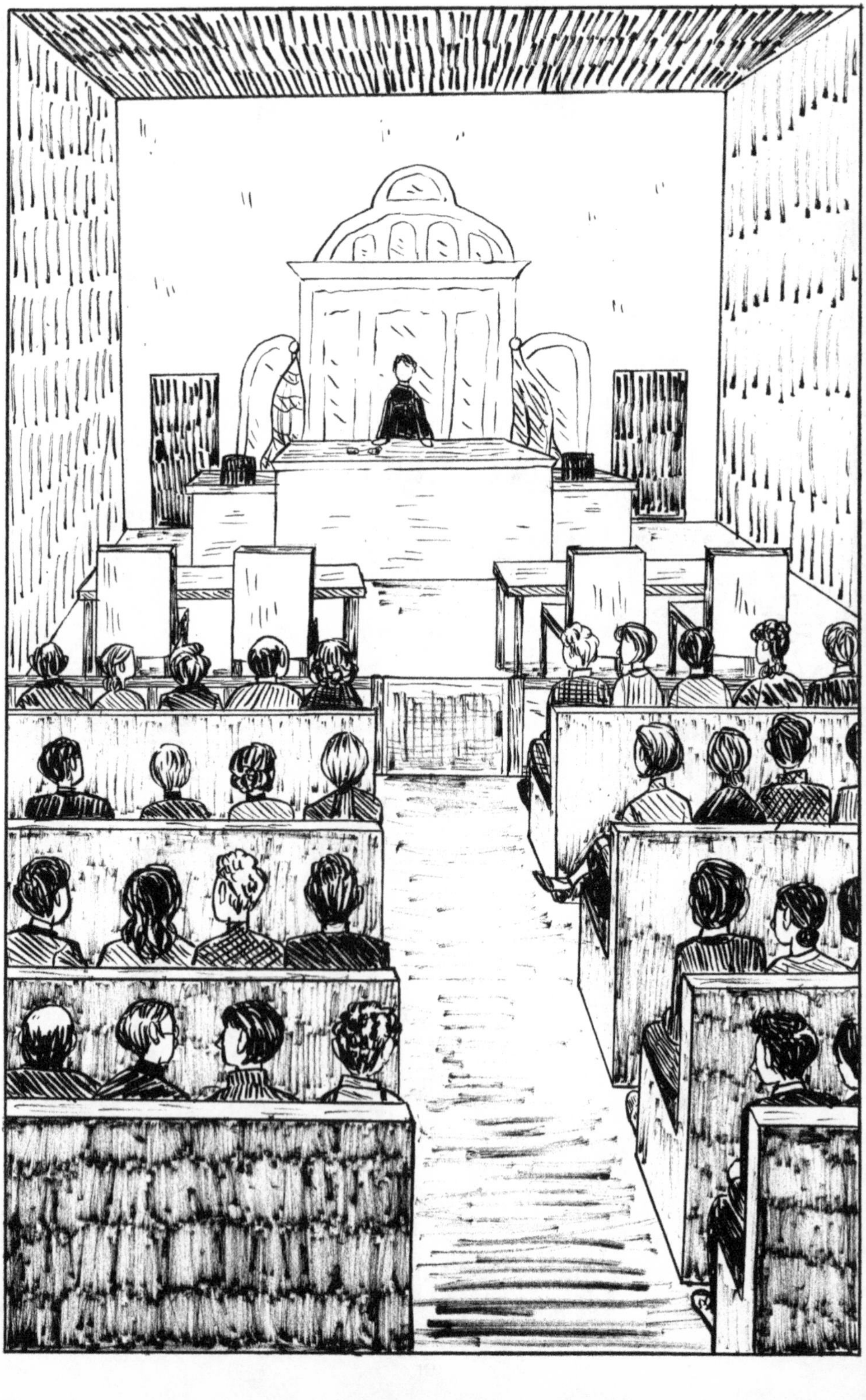

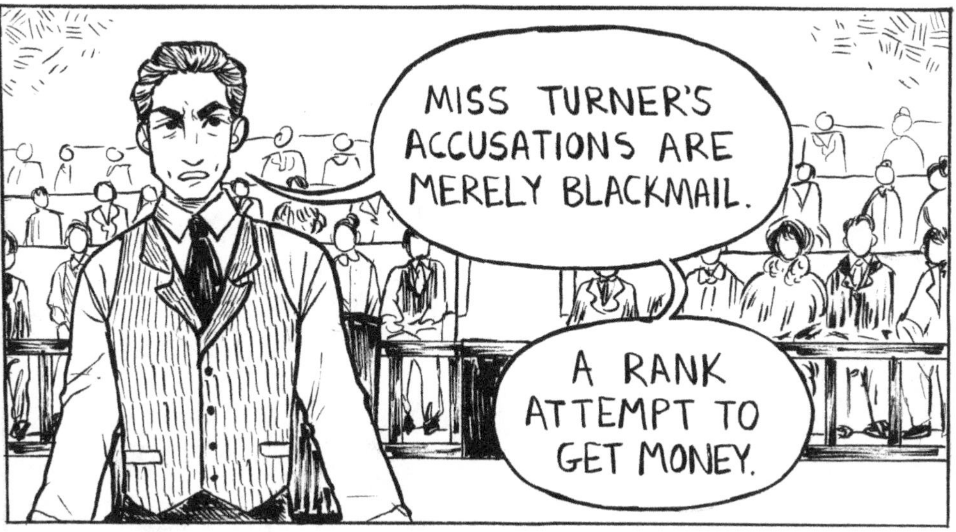
MISS TURNER'S ACCUSATIONS ARE MERELY BLACKMAIL.
A RANK ATTEMPT TO GET MONEY.

ALL THE BOSTON NEWSPAPERS COVERED IT.

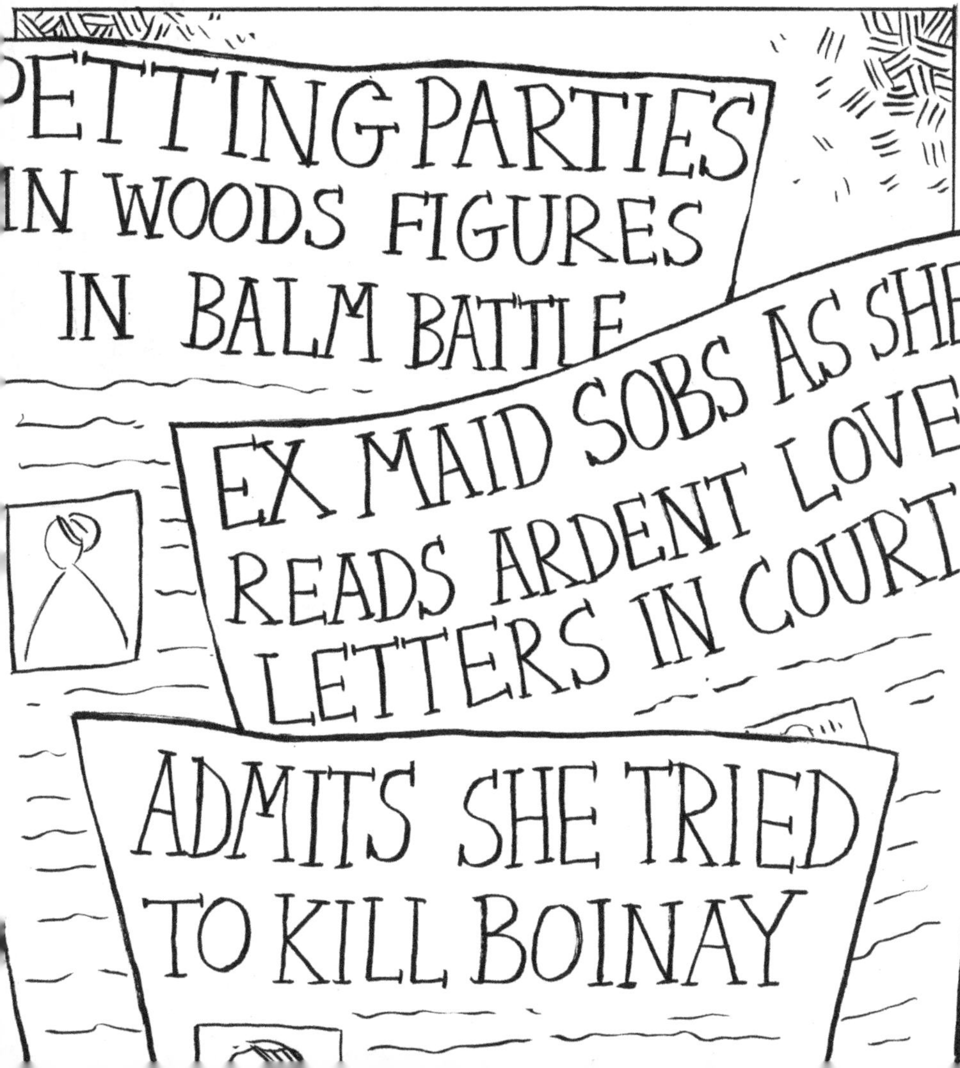
PETTING PARTIES IN WOODS FIGURES IN BALM BATTLE
EX MAID SOBS AS SHE READS ARDENT LOVE LETTERS IN COURT
ADMITS SHE TRIED TO KILL BOINAY

ONE EVENING WHILE WORKING AS A SERVER, DAISY OVERHEARD PARTY GUESTS DISCUSSING THE TRIAL.

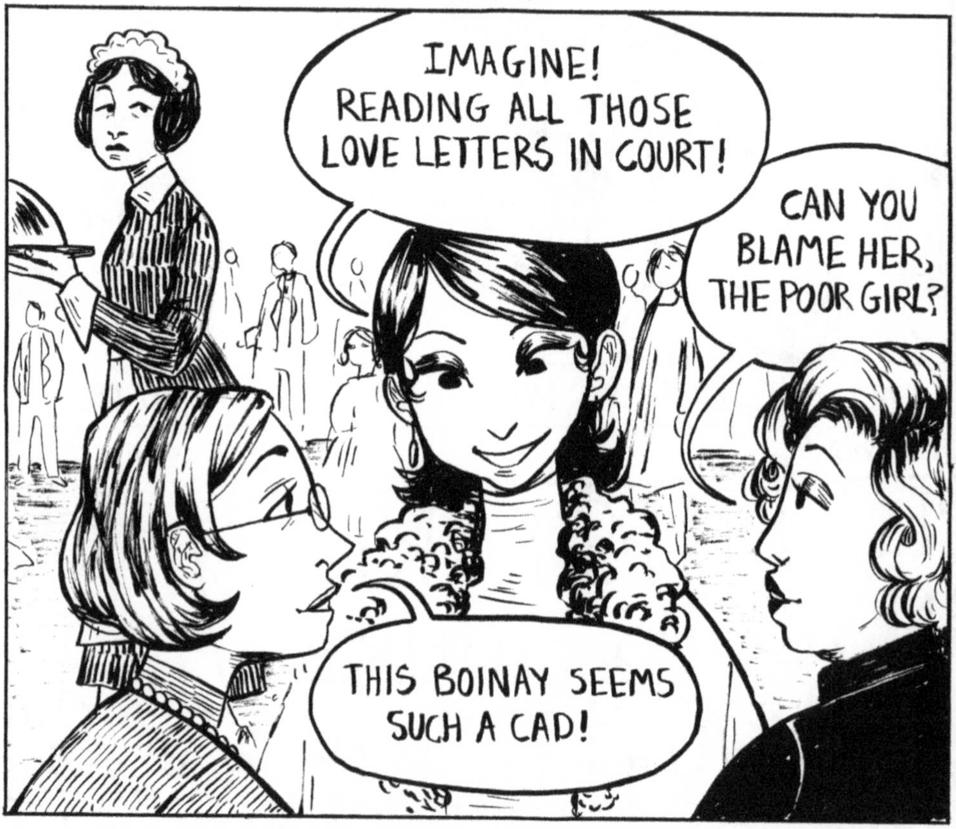
IMAGINE! READING ALL THOSE LOVE LETTERS IN COURT!
CAN YOU BLAME HER, THE POOR GIRL?
THIS BOINAY SEEMS SUCH A CAD!

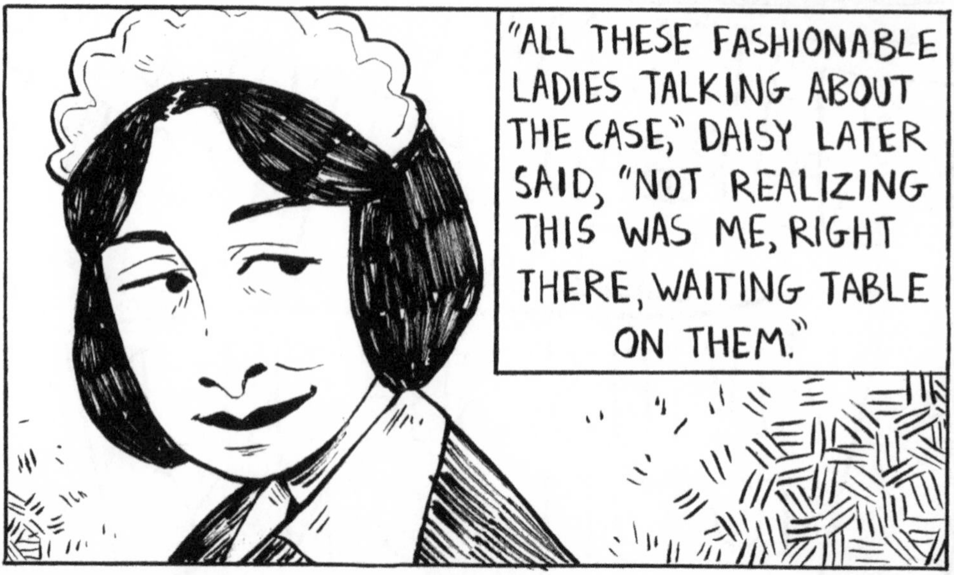
"ALL THESE FASHIONABLE LADIES TALKING ABOUT THE CASE," DAISY LATER SAID, "NOT REALIZING THIS WAS ME, RIGHT THERE, WAITING TABLE ON THEM."

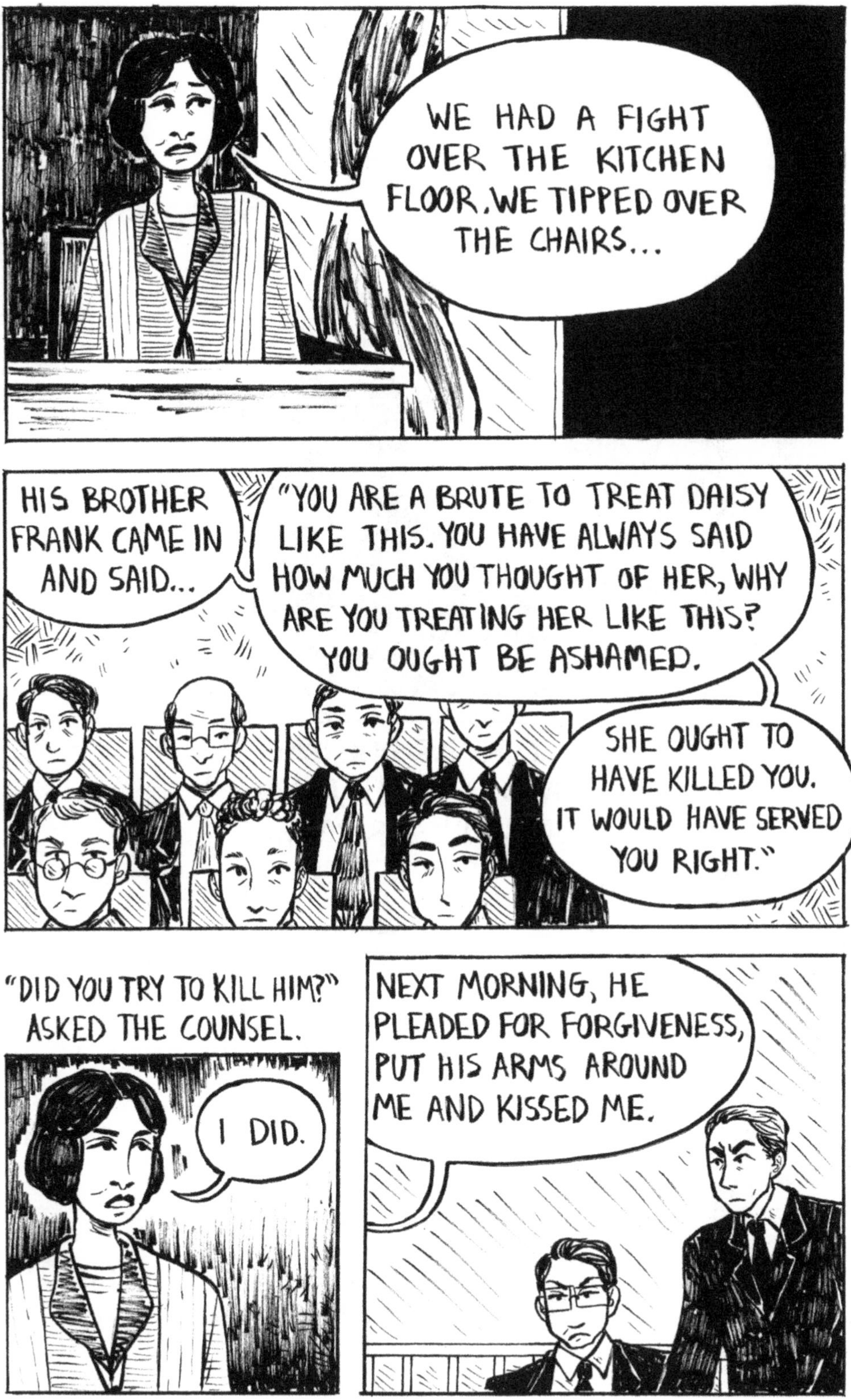
WE HAD A FIGHT OVER THE KITCHEN FLOOR. WE TIPPED OVER THE CHAIRS...
HIS BROTHER FRANK CAME IN AND SAID...
"YOU ARE A BRUTE TO TREAT DAISY LIKE THIS. YOU HAVE ALWAYS SAID HOW MUCH YOU THOUGHT OF HER, WHY ARE YOU TREATING HER LIKE THIS? YOU OUGHT BE ASHAMED.
SHE OUGHT TO HAVE KILLED YOU. IT WOULD HAVE SERVED YOU RIGHT."
"DID YOU TRY TO KILL HIM?" ASKED THE COUNSEL.
I DID.
NEXT MORNING, HE PLEADED FOR FORGIVENESS, PUT HIS ARMS AROUND ME AND KISSED ME.

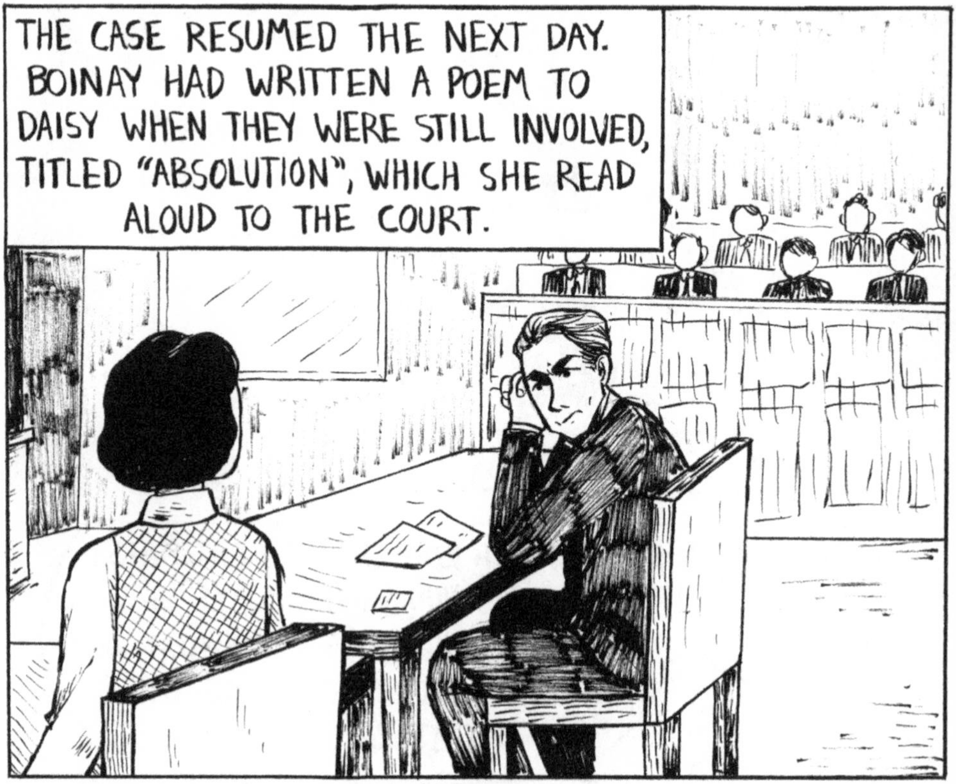
THE CASE RESUMED THE NEXT DAY. BOINAY HAD WRITTEN A POEM TO DAISY WHEN THEY WERE STILL INVOLVED, TITLED "ABSOLUTION", WHICH SHE READ ALOUD TO THE COURT.

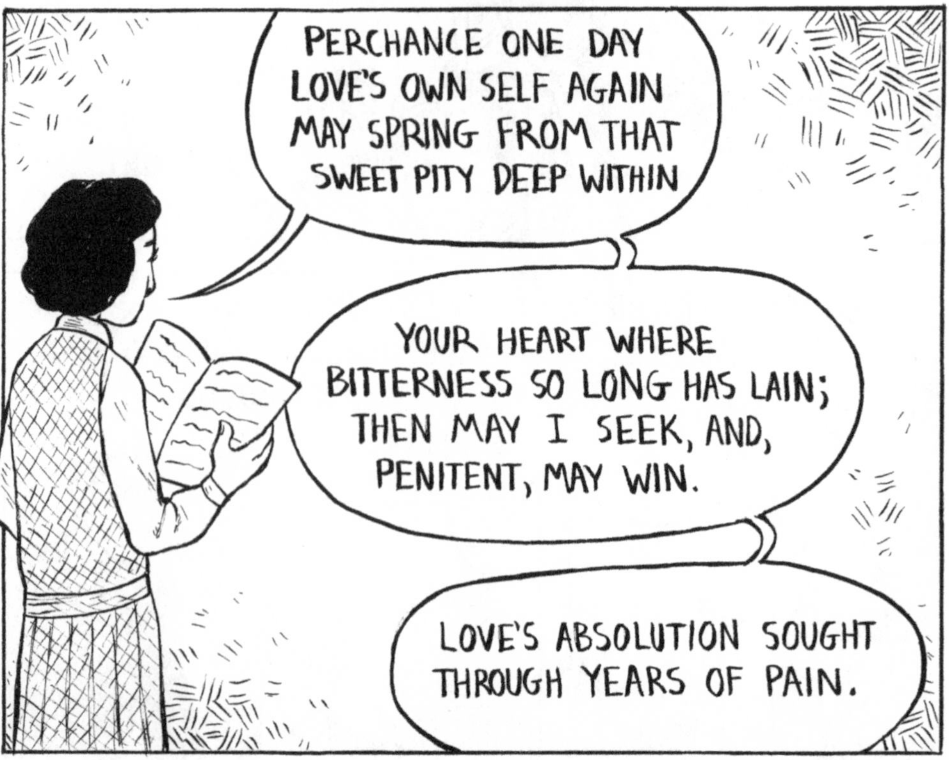
PERCHANCE ONE DAY LOVE'S OWN SELF AGAIN MAY SPRING FROM THAT SWEET PITY DEEP WITHIN
YOUR HEART WHERE BITTERNESS SO LONG HAS LAIN; THEN MAY I SEEK, AND, PENITENT, MAY WIN.
LOVE'S ABSOLUTION SOUGHT THROUGH YEARS OF PAIN.

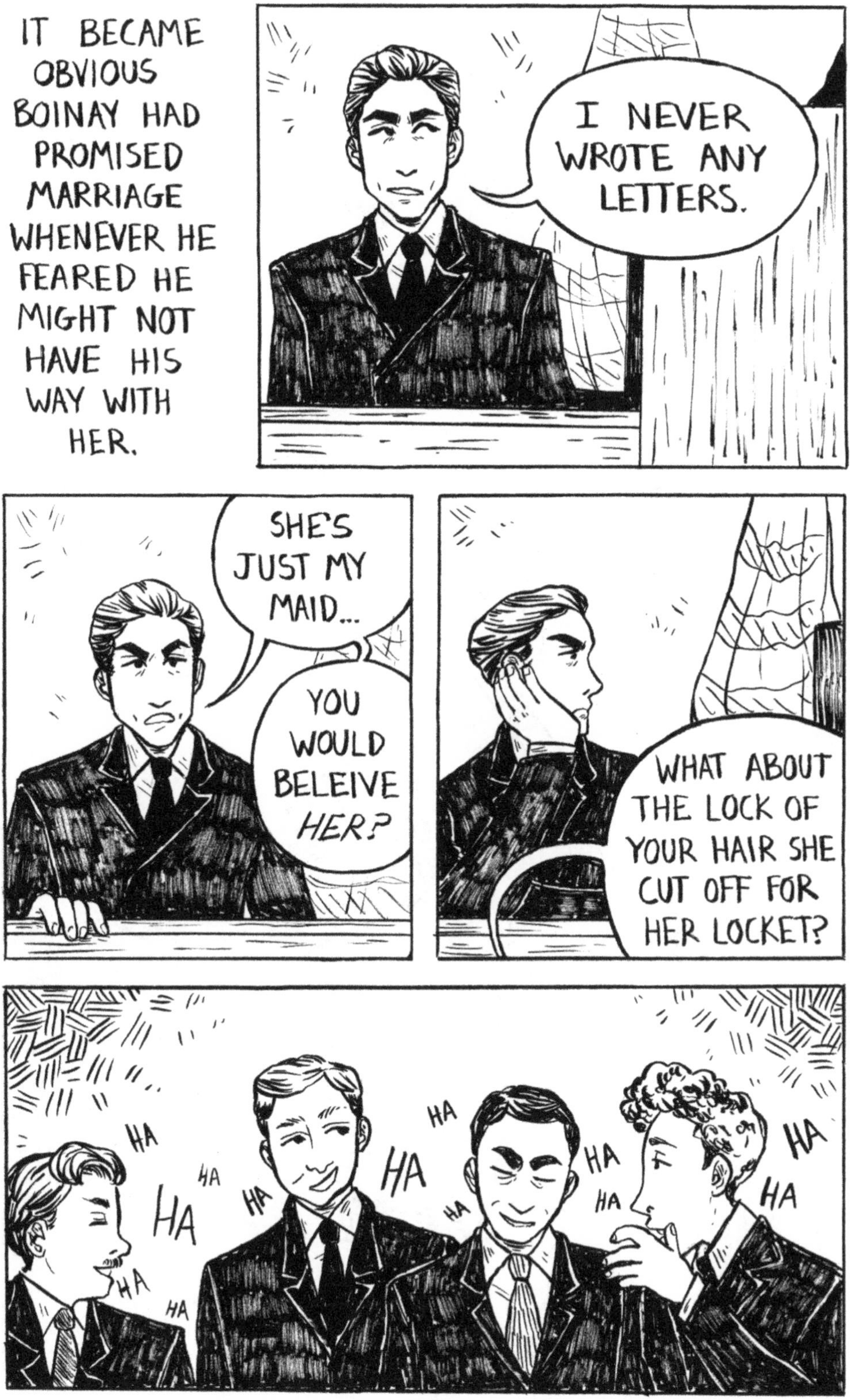
IT BECAME OBVIOUS BOINAY HAD PROMISED MARRIAGE WHENEVER HE FEARED HE MIGHT NOT HAVE HIS WAY WITH HER.
I NEVER WROTE ANY LETTERS.
SHE'S JUST MY MAID...
YOU WOULD BELEIVE *HER?*
WHAT ABOUT THE LOCK OF YOUR HAIR SHE CUT OFF FOR HER LOCKET?
HA
HA
HA
HA
HA
HA
HA
HA
HA
HA
HA
HA
HA
HA

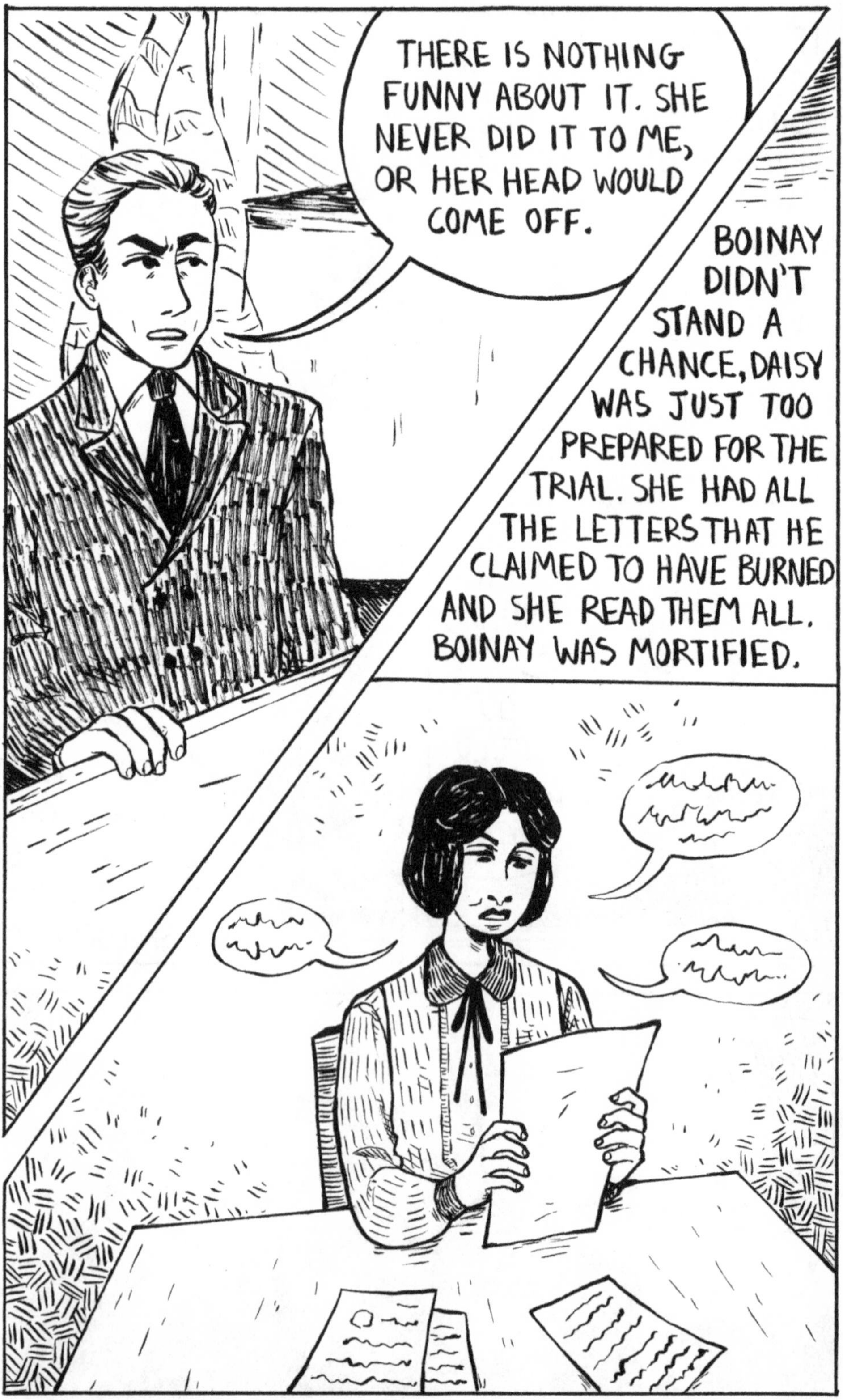
THERE IS NOTHING FUNNY ABOUT IT. SHE NEVER DID IT TO ME, OR HER HEAD WOULD COME OFF.
BOINAY DIDN'T STAND A CHANCE, DAISY WAS JUST TOO PREPARED FOR THE TRIAL. SHE HAD ALL THE LETTERS THAT HE CLAIMED TO HAVE BURNED AND SHE READ THEM ALL. BOINAY WAS MORTIFIED.

EVEN DAISY'S SISTERS TESTIFIED. ROSE TOLD OF HER FATHER'S ULTIMATUM TO BOINAY...

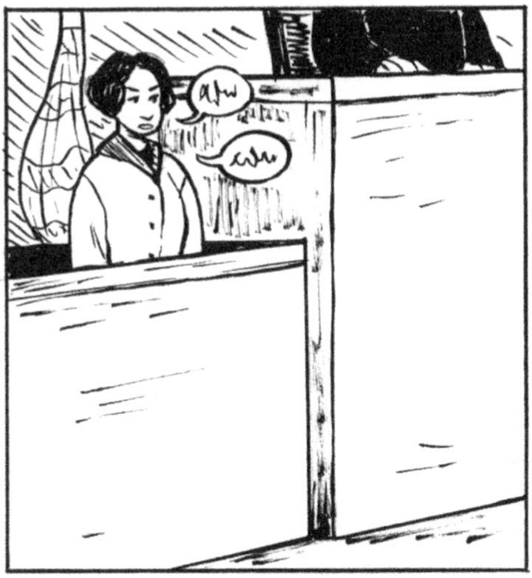

AND EVELYN TOLD OF HOW BOINAY PROCLAIMED HIS LOVE FOR DAISY WHILE HIS WIFE LAY DEAD IN THE NEXT ROOM.

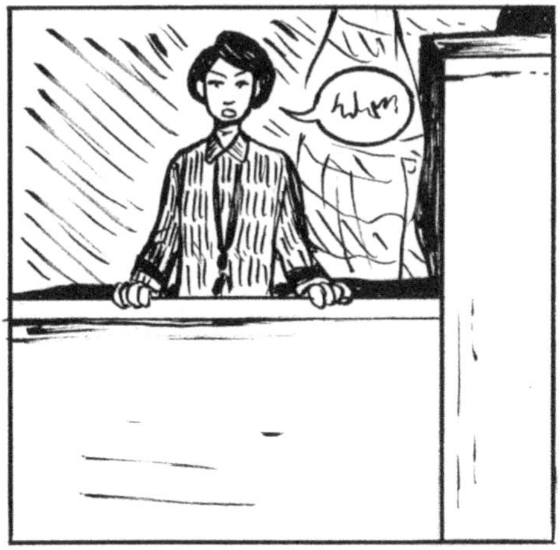

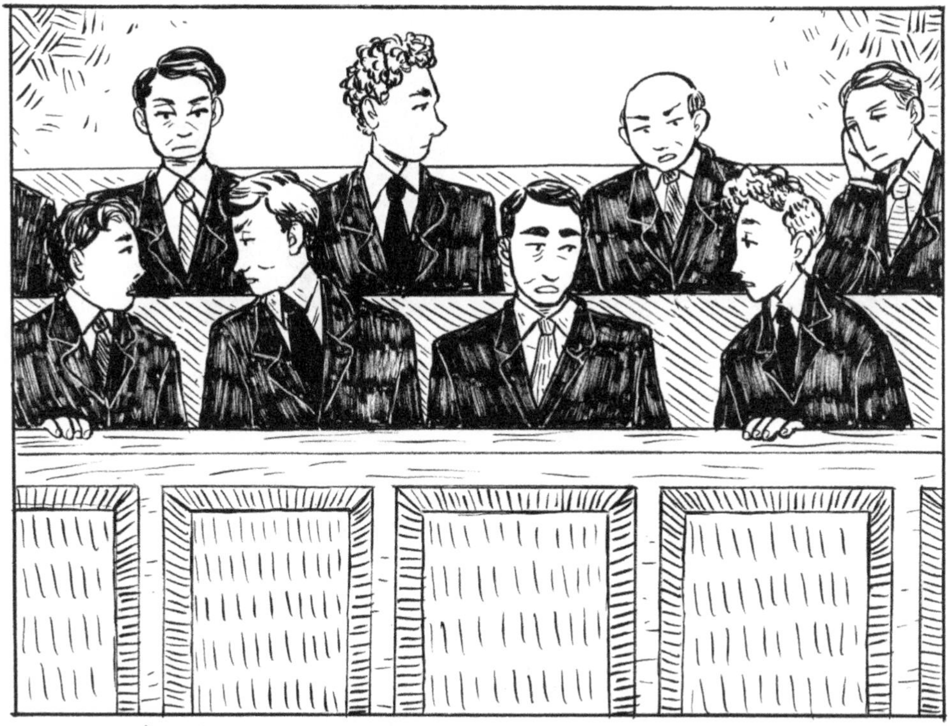

IT TOOK THE JURY EIGHTEEN HOURS TO DELIBERATE. BUT IN THE END...

'I Am Vindicated' Cries Maid After $3750 Love Award

Rich Lexington Auto Dealer, However, Wins on Two Charges

DAISY J. TURNER

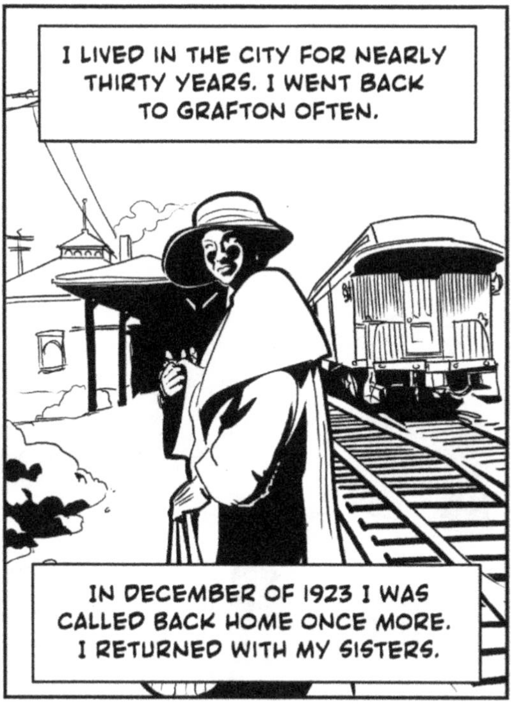
I LIVED IN THE CITY FOR NEARLY THIRTY YEARS. I WENT BACK TO GRAFTON OFTEN.
IN DECEMBER OF 1923 I WAS CALLED BACK HOME ONCE MORE. I RETURNED WITH MY SISTERS.

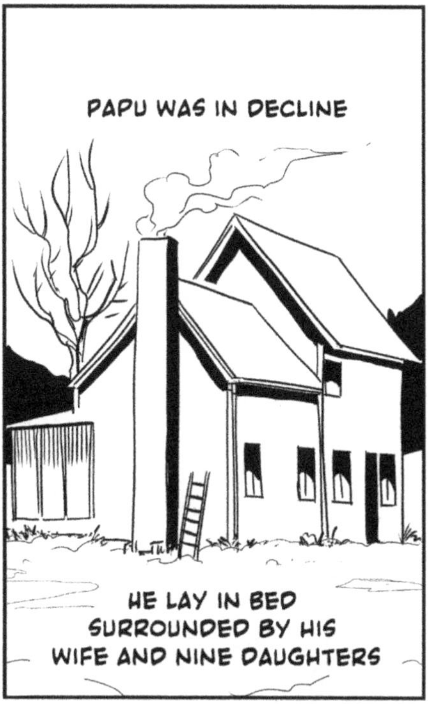
PAPU WAS IN DECLINE
HE LAY IN BED SURROUNDED BY HIS WIFE AND NINE DAUGHTERS

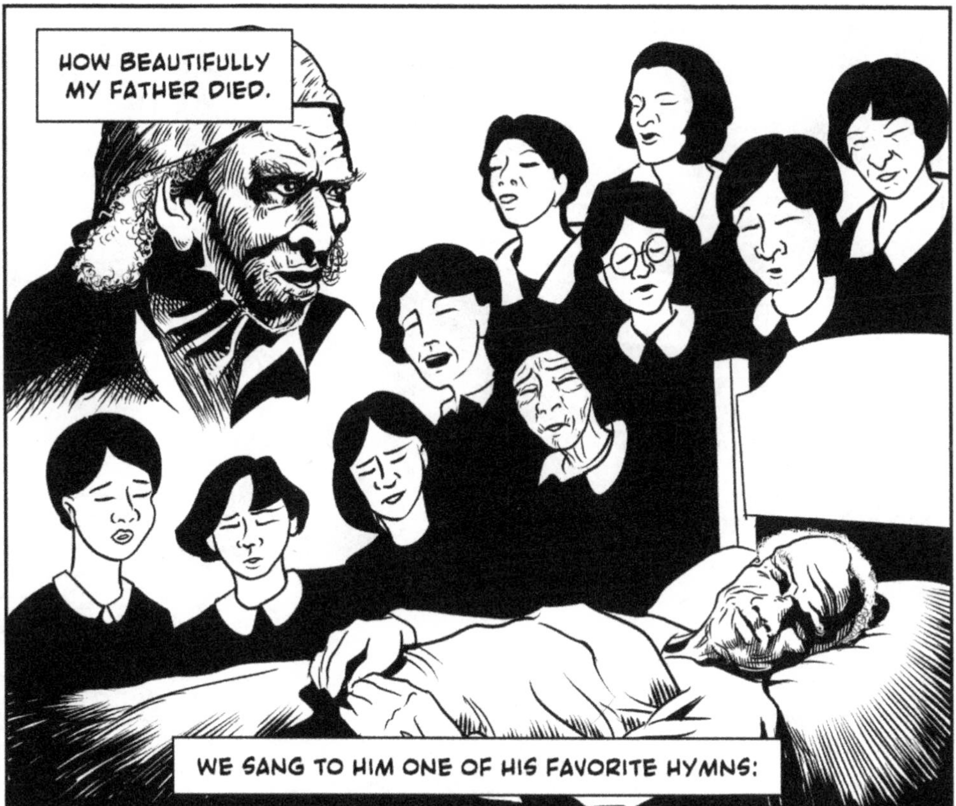
HOW BEAUTIFULLY MY FATHER DIED.
WE SANG TO HIM ONE OF HIS FAVORITE HYMNS:

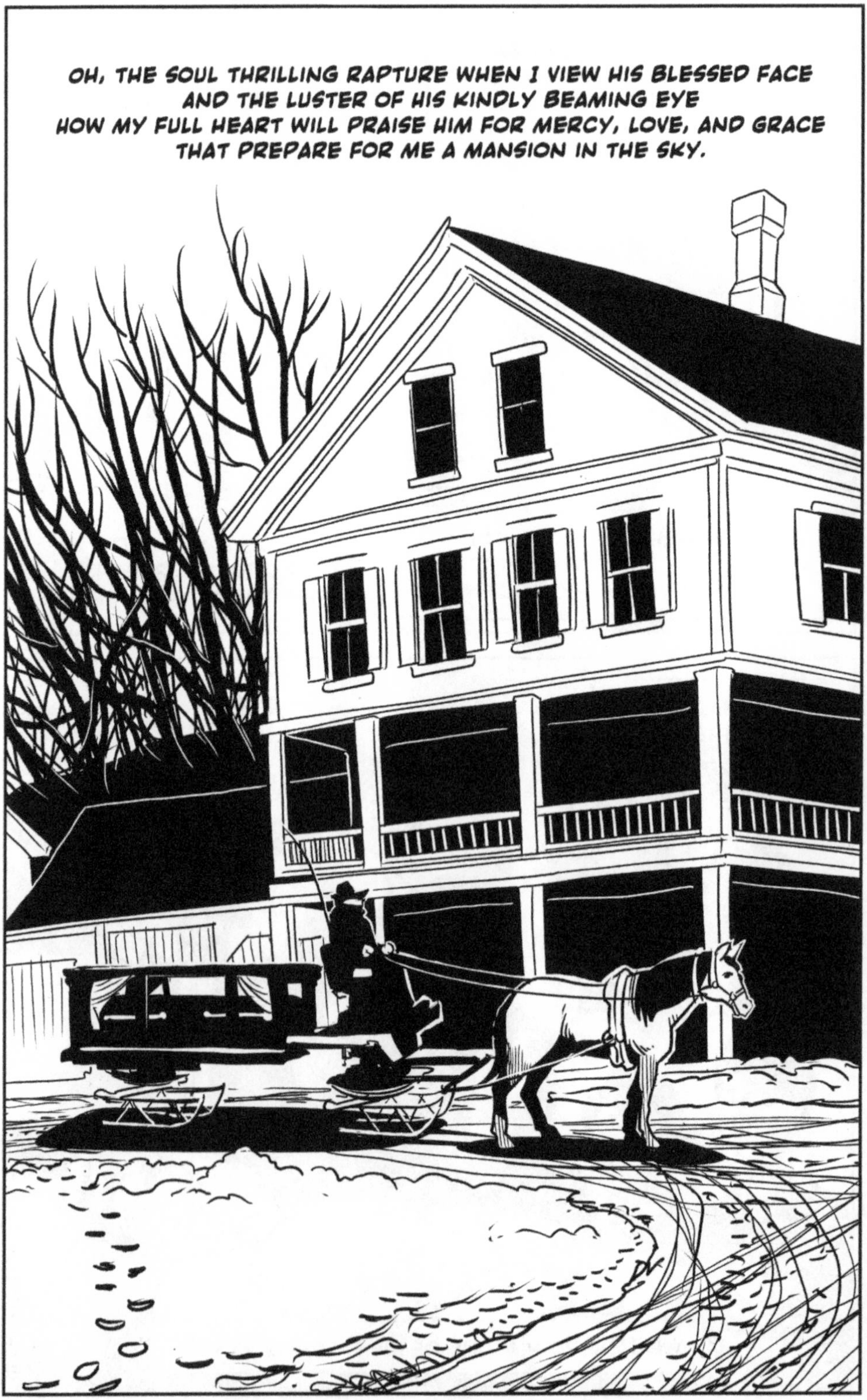
OH, THE SOUL THRILLING RAPTURE WHEN I VIEW HIS BLESSED FACE
AND THE LUSTER OF HIS KINDLY BEAMING EYE
HOW MY FULL HEART WILL PRAISE HIM FOR MERCY, LOVE, AND GRACE
THAT PREPARE FOR ME A MANSION IN THE SKY.

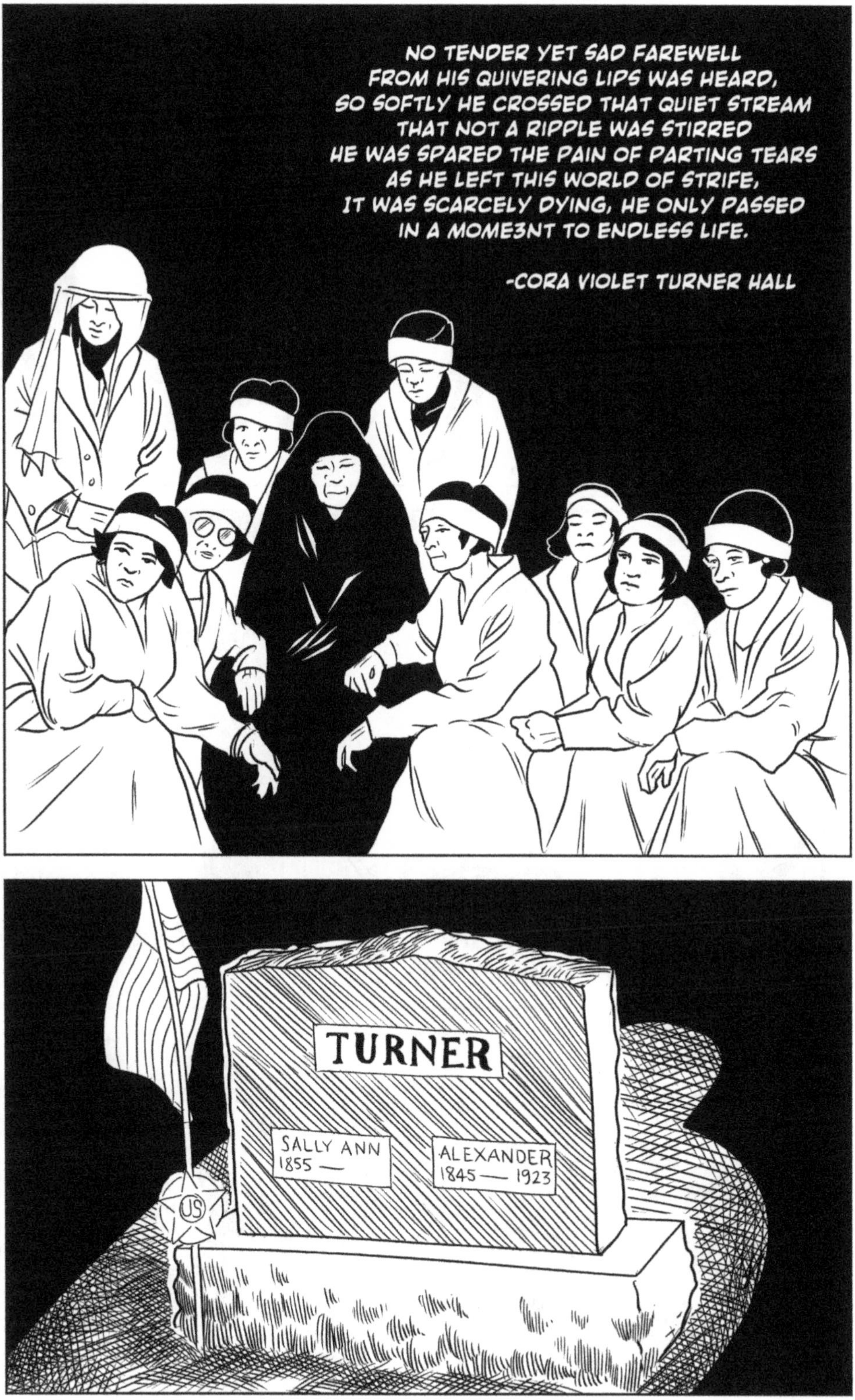
NO TENDER YET SAD FAREWELL
FROM HIS QUIVERING LIPS WAS HEARD,
SO SOFTLY HE CROSSED THAT QUIET STREAM
THAT NOT A RIPPLE WAS STIRRED
HE WAS SPARED THE PAIN OF PARTING TEARS
AS HE LEFT THIS WORLD OF STRIFE,
IT WAS SCARCELY DYING, HE ONLY PASSED
IN A MOME3NT TO ENDLESS LIFE.
-CORA VIOLET TURNER HALL
TURNER
SALLY ANN
1855 —
ALEXANDER
1845 — 1923
US

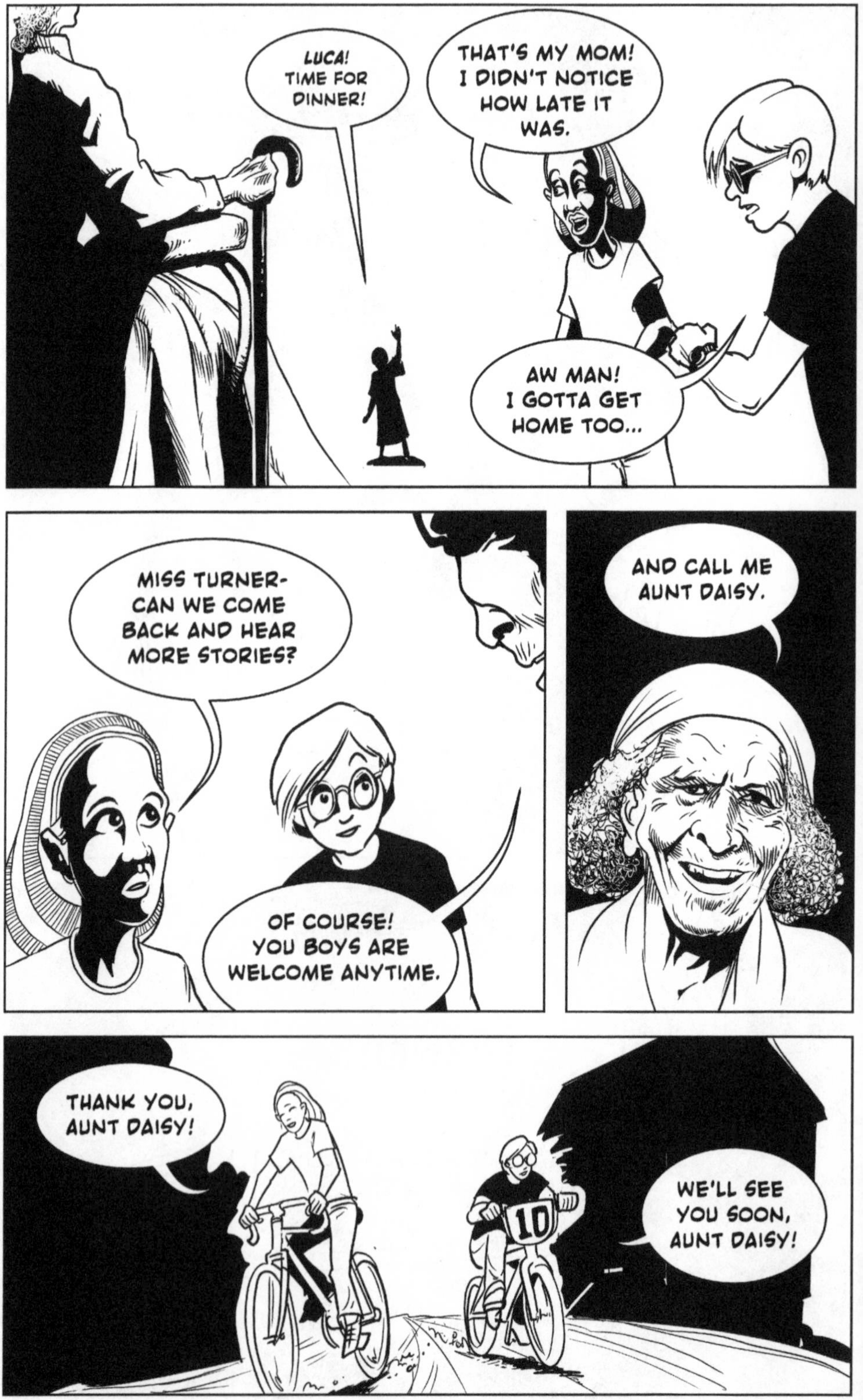
LUCA! TIME FOR DINNER!
THAT'S MY MOM! I DIDN'T NOTICE HOW LATE IT WAS.
AW MAN! I GOTTA GET HOME TOO...
MISS TURNER- CAN WE COME BACK AND HEAR MORE STORIES?
OF COURSE! YOU BOYS ARE WELCOME ANYTIME.
AND CALL ME AUNT DAISY.
THANK YOU, AUNT DAISY!
WE'LL SEE YOU SOON, AUNT DAISY!
10

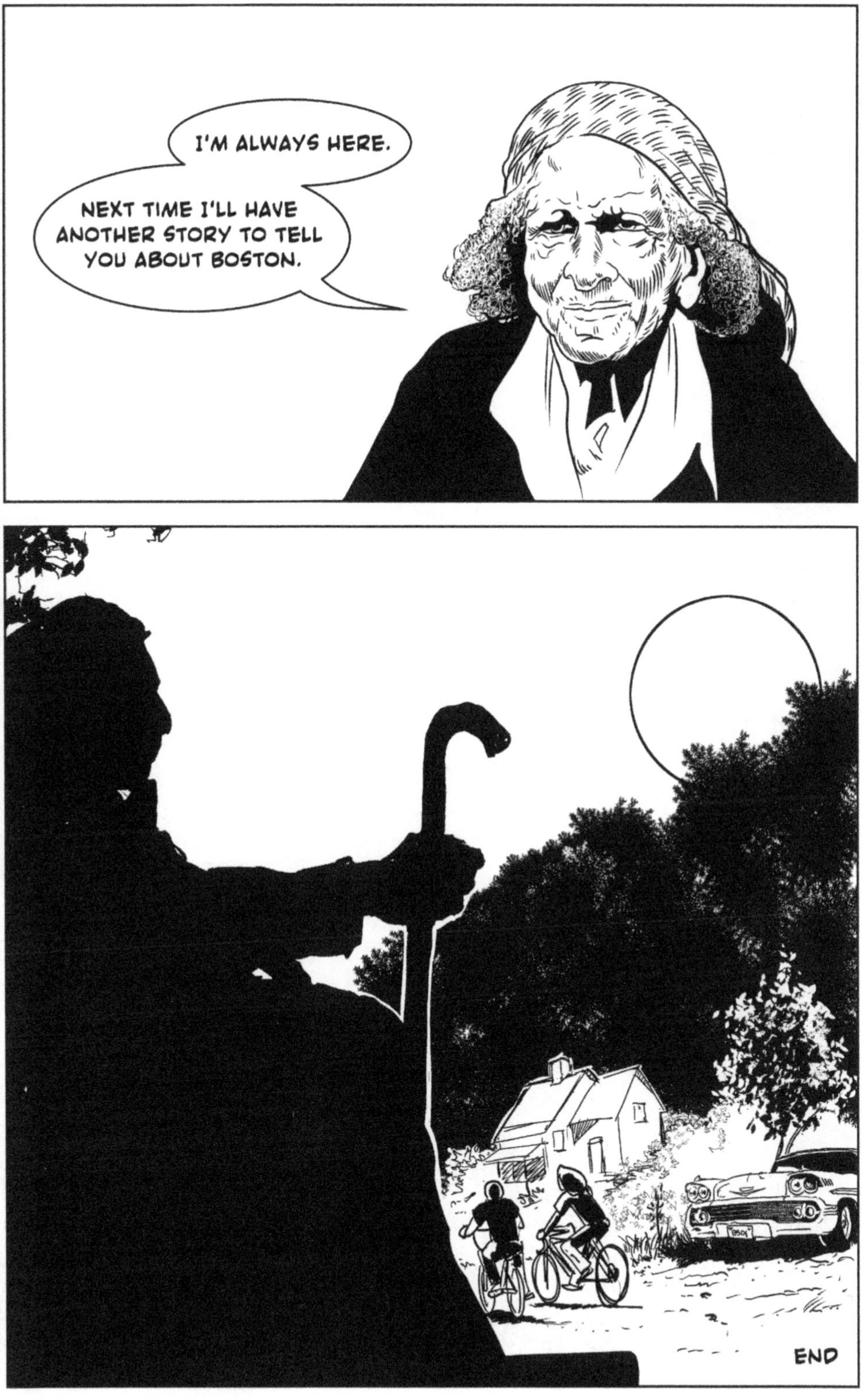
I'M ALWAYS HERE.
NEXT TIME I'LL HAVE ANOTHER STORY TO TELL YOU ABOUT BOSTON.
END

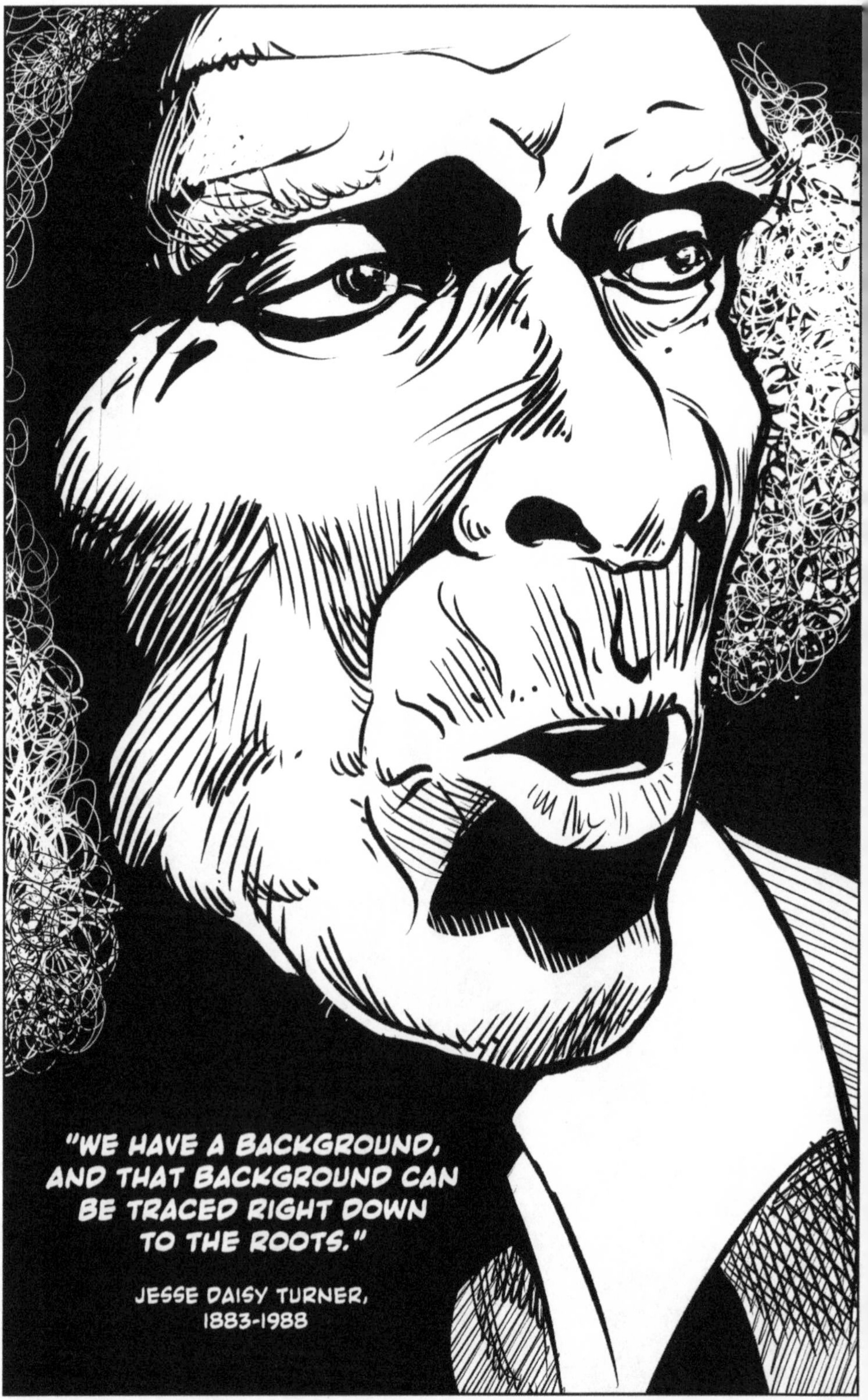
"WE HAVE A BACKGROUND, AND THAT BACKGROUND CAN BE TRACED RIGHT DOWN TO THE ROOTS."
JESSE DAISY TURNER, 1883-1988

LEARN MORE ABOUT THE TURNER FAMILY

Jesse Daisy Turner (1883-1985)

Daisy Turner, born in Grafton, VT in 1883, was the daughter of formerly enslaved Alec and Sally Turner, who settled there in the years following the Civil War. In 1983, the 100-year-old Grafton native sat down with Vermont Folklife Center founder and folklorist Jane Beck, and over a three-year period shared the epic narrative of her family.

Daisy Turner, 1984. Photo by Jane C. Beck. Vermont Folklife Center Archive.

Daisy spoke to Jane of her paternal grandfather Alessi, abducted on the West African coast and sold into slavery in the United States; her father Alec, born enslaved in Virginia, who escaped as the Civil War raged around him and joined up with the Union Army; her mother Sally, who met Alec in the wake of that war; and the trials they faced as they moved north, ultimately settling on the hilltop farm in Grafton, where they raised 13 children.

In addition to stories of her family, Daisy shared with Jane rich accounts of her own long life, from her childhood in Grafton, her adult years living and working in Boston, and her eventual return to Grafton after her mother's death in 1933. Beginning in her childhood, Daisy continually—and successfully—challenged the limits placed on her as a Black woman in New England during the late 19th and early 20th centuries, loudly asserting (even in court) her rights and the rights of her family members.

Alec and Sally Turner on the front porch of Journey's End circa 1920. Vermont Folklife Center Archive.

Daisy Turner circa 1920. Vermont Folklife Center Archive.

This volume features only a small selection of Daisy's stories. To learn more about Daisy and the Turner family, see these books, recordings and organizations that present and preserve the Turner legacy:

BOOK

Daisy Turner's Kin: An African American Family Saga by Jane C. Beck

(ISBN 978-0252080791)

PICTURE BOOKS

Alec's Primer (ISBN 978-0916718206)

Daisy and the Doll (ISBN 978-0916718237)

MULTIMEDIA

On My Own: The Traditions of Daisy Turner (Video Documentary)

Journey's End: The Memories and Traditions of Daisy Turner and her Family (Audio Documentary)

PLACES

Grafton Historical Society: graftonhistoricalsociety.com

Turner Hill Interpretive Center: turnerhillgrafton.org

Vermont Folklife Center: vtfolklife.org

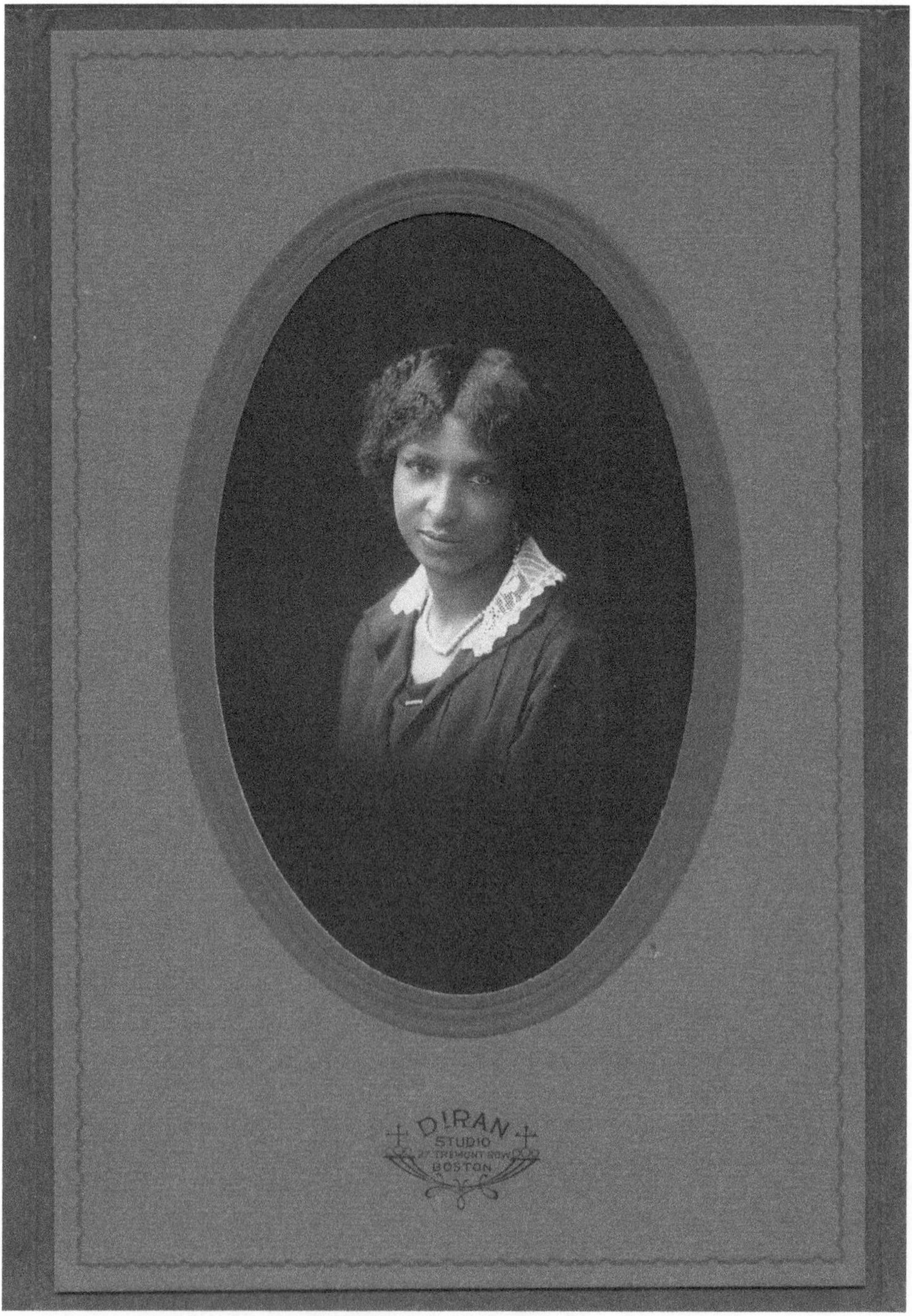
D!RAN
STUDIO
BOSTON

Daisy Turner circa 1930. Vermont Folklife Center Archive.

CARTOONIST BIOGRAPHIES

Marek Bennett

New Hampshire-based cartoonist, musician and educator Marek Bennett leads discovery-based Comics Workshops for all ages throughout New England and the world beyond! His comics work includes the graphic novel series, *The Civil War Diary of Freeman Colby*, as well as contributing to and co-editing *The Most Costly Journey* (2021) with the bilingual El Viaje Project. His crowd-funded cartoon travel memoirs include *Sharjah Sketchbook* (2020) and *SLOVAKIA: Fall in the Heart of Europe* (2013). Marek plays Civil War folk music with The Hardtacks and "hot gonzo primitive folk jive" with The Cold River Ranters. His website is: www.MarekBennett.com

Francis Bordeleau

Francis Bordeleau is a New England based cartoonist and illustrator. Born and raised in small town Southern New Hampshire, they received their Associate's degree in Studio Arts from Middlesex Community College in Lowell, Massachusetts. When they're not busy making art they enjoy listening to folk music, sewing, and watching bad TV.

Joel Christian Gill

Joel Christian Gill is a cartoonist and historian who speaks nationally on the importance of sharing stories. He is the author of the acclaimed memoir *Fights: One Boy's Triumph Over Violence*, cited as one of the best graphic novels of 2020 by The New York Times and for which he was awarded the 2021 Cartoonist Studio Prize. He wrote the words and drew the pictures for *Fast Enough: Bessie Stringfield's First Ride* and the award-winning graphic novel series *Strange Fruit: Uncelebrated Narratives from Black History*, as well as three volumes of *Tales of The Talented Tenth*, which tell the stories of Bass Reeves, Bessie Stringfield and Robert Smalls. He is currently at work on the graphic novel of Ibram Kendi's National Book Award-winning *Stamped From the Beginning: The Definitive History of Racist Ideas in America*, forthcoming from Ten Speed Press in 2023. Gill has dedicated his life to creating stories to build connections with readers through empathy, compassion and, ultimately, humanity. He received his MFA from Boston University and his BA from Roanoke College.

Lillie Harris

Lillie J. Harris is a cartoonist and illustrator from Clinton, Maryland. They are currently based in Vermont after graduating from The Center for Cartoon Studies in 2021. Lillie's work has been in both The New Yorker and Burlington City Arts Gallery, and the first volume of their debut graphic novel, *Wilderness* is being sold through Radiator Comics. Themes of tension and empathy play a large role in Lillie's work.

Robyn Smith

Robyn Smith is a Jamaican cartoonist known for her mini-comic *The Saddest Angriest Black Girl in Town*, illustrating DC Comics' *Nubia: Real One* (written by L.L. McKinney) and Black Josei Press' *Wash Day* (written by Jamila Rowser). She has an MFA from the Center for Cartoon Studies, and has also worked on comics for College Humor, Nike, and The Nib. She loves cake and her cat, Benson, and holds onto dreams of returning home to the ocean.

Ezra Veitch

New England cartoonist Ezra Veitch is the son of cartoonist Rick Veitch. Raised on a steady diet of comic books and graphic novels, Ezra patiently found his way to the comic book medium via a fine arts education and his own ventures into self publishing. He contributed to *The Most Costly Journey: Stories of Migrant Farmworkers in Vermont Drawn by New England Cartoonists* and published the fantasy-based series, *The Chronicles of Templar*, which is currently on hiatus. Ezra looks forward to making some new content for release in 2022, and going to some local conventions!

THANK YOU

Funding for the creation of *Turner Family Stories: From Enslavement in Virginia to Freedom in Vermont* provided by

NATIONAL ENDOWMENT for the ARTS
arts.gov

vermont arts council
working for a creative state

Vermont Humanities

WINDHAM FOUNDATION

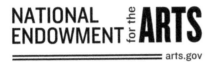

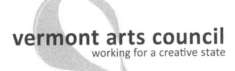

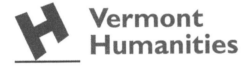

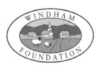

The Windham Foundation, Inc.
Promoting Vermont's Rural Communities

The editors would like to thank the Vermont Department of Libraries for distributing copies of Turner Family Stories to public libraries in the state and Thalia Rose Dickinson Kolovos for her insight and valuable suggestions.

Vermont Folklife Center

vtfolklife.org

CPSIA information can be obtained
at www.ICGtesting.com
Printed in the USA
LVHW111510280821
696353LV00019B/2314

9 780916 718015